Awaken

Awaken

The Path to Purpose, Inner Peace, and Healing

Raj Sisodia

WILEY

For general information on our other products and services or for technical support, please contact our Customer Care Department within the United States at (800) 762-2974, outside the United States at (317) 572-3993 or fax (317) 572-4002.

Wiley also publishes its books in a variety of electronic formats. Some content that appears in print may not be available in electronic formats. For more information about Wiley products, visit our web site at www.wiley.com.

Library of Congress Cataloging-in-Publication Data:

Names: Sisodia, Rajendra, author.
Title: Awaken : the path to purpose, inner peace, and healing / Rajendra
   Sisodia.
Description: Hoboken, New Jersey : Wiley, [2023] | Includes index.
Identifiers: LCCN 2022015278 (print) | LCCN 2022015279 (ebook) | ISBN
   9781119789192 (cloth) | ISBN 9781119789215 (adobe pdf) | ISBN
   9781119789208 (epub)
Subjects: LCSH: Peace of mind. | Self-consciousness (Awareness) | Social
   perception.
Classification: LCC BF637.P3 S54 2022 (print) | LCC BF637.P3 (ebook) |
   DDC 158.1—dc23/eng/20220407
LC record available at https://lccn.loc.gov/2022015278
LC ebook record available at https://lccn.loc.gov/2022015279

Cover Design and Image: Wiley

Author photo: Jesús Alejandro Salazar Villa

SKY10043126_022023

To Neha Sangwan

With love, gratitude, and admiration — for her courage and integrity, her selfless service to others, her idealism, and her authenticity. Neha is strong, wise, purposeful, unwavering, generous, compassionate, playful, and brilliant. She is a loving and healing teacher and coach who has altered the trajectories of countless lives for the better- including mine. She has helped me awaken to what really matters and to become more fully myself.

May her message spread and her impact multiply throughout the world to benefit the countless millions who are in pain.

Contents

Foreword

This is a remarkable book. Anyone who intends to exercise leadership in today's complex and volatile business and social environment needs to read it.

Here, Raj Sisodia describes the personal journey we must all take in order to step into our personal power; gain full agency; and participate in healing the fragmentation in America and the world. This is a book full of wisdom – wisdom that Raj acknowledges came through him and not from him – the most profound gift we can receive – the gift from universal consciousness – the gift of Grace.

The journey Raj describes is distinctly his own painful and ultimately successful journey toward accessing the wisdom to make instant and informed choices. At the same time, it is an archetype for the necessary developmental path we must all take with commitment and fortitude to trust and cross the threshold. Once we do, we encounter the inevitable "road of trials" that the philosopher Joseph Campbell describes as the Hero's Journey. In trusting ourselves, if we don't turn back, we will meet our guides who will help us through the most difficult of these trials.

Like Raj, we will ultimately reach our destination – that level of development when our life becomes the one that was intended for us: a life of service infused with gratitude, joy, and fulfillment. Most importantly, this is the point at which we regain our inborn innocence – like that of the peaceful warrior – immune, inviolable, and resilient. This is the Call of our Time: to develop this quality of leadership; for, as Raj points out, only the truly innocent can be trusted with the power required to heal today's world.

This book will guide you to reflect on your own Life's journey, making it more whole, as you understand your past in order to reshape your present and future. You will discover how to embrace both the masculine and feminine sides of your personality. You will learn how to stay tuned to Life's opportunities and synchronicities, reframing challenges as opportunities for growth and discovery. You will gain the capacity to challenge orthodoxies and break free of cultural norms that harm and constrain all of us. And finally, you will be guided to become a peaceful warrior, living by what Raj refers to as the LIST: manifesting Love, Innocence, Simplicity, and Truth in your very being and in all your actions.

This book illuminates the deeper dimensions of transformational change and leadership in general. As we have observed before, the most important inquiry today is not about the "what" and "how" – it's not about what leaders do and how they do it – but the "who": who we are and the inner place or source from which we operate, individually and collectively.

The lessons and principles contained in this book enabled Raj, among other high accomplishments, to cofound the Conscious Capitalism movement, one of the most compelling endeavors existing today, with the intention to transform free enterprise capitalism into a powerful system for social cooperation and human progress.

I am deeply privileged to have been invited to write this brief Foreword.

—Joseph Jaworski
January 14, 2022
Wimberley, Texas

Prologue

How did an idealistic, trusting, peace-loving, harmony-seeking scion of a ferociously feudal family in rural India come to cofound a global movement to bring love, compassion, and transcendent purpose to the rough-and-tumble world of business? How did a left-brained, hyper-analytical engineer from the warrior caste in India come to write books like *Firms of Endearment, Conscious Capitalism, Everybody Matters, Shakti Leadership,* and *The Healing Organization*? How did a self-loathing marketing professor (who almost wrote a book called *The Shame of Marketing*) channel timeless wisdom and alchemize his own suffering to help corporate leaders learn how to use business to serve, uplift, and heal?

"What is most personal is most universal." The truth of this phrase from Carl Rogers struck me in 2018, as I was working on *The Healing Organization: Awakening the Conscience of Business to Help Save the World*. I shared very little of my own life journey in the book, limiting it to a few reflections in the Prologue. In all my earlier books, I hadn't referred to my personal experiences at all. But I now realize that the books that had the most profound impact on me were those in which the author shared deeply from their own life journey. These included Viktor Frankl's *Man's Search for Meaning*, Joseph Jaworski's *Synchronicity*, and Lynne Twist's *The Soul of Money*, among many others. I also realized that two of my own books that have had the greatest impact were built in part around the stories of two individuals: *Conscious Capitalism* wove in the journey of Whole Foods founder John Mackey, and *Everybody Matters* was in part about Bob Chapman's life story and the personal awakenings that led him to become a "truly human" leader.

My book *Firms of Endearment* – my on-ramp to the world of more human-centered business – reflected my evolving personal consciousness and beliefs about life, business, and leadership. But I studiously avoided using the "I" pronoun even in that book. I am an academic, after all, and am supposed to not inject my biases into works that are meant to illuminate objective truths. I also thought of myself as an intensely private person and believed that my life experiences were mine and mine alone, to learn from and transcend if I could.

I now feel ready and called on to share my personal story. While I have worked to help heal the world of business, this book is my journey home to myself. I have written it for my children and others who may struggle to understand themselves and decipher what their life is really about.

My family history on my father's side is dark; the feudal system I grew up in was profoundly abusive. It has not been easy to write about. But I have learned that what we fear confronting the most is what needs the deepest healing. As the estimable "Mister" Fred Rogers taught us, "Anything that is human is mentionable, and anything that is mentionable can be more manageable."

I have led what many would consider an unusual and what some now call a "psychologically rich" life: a diverse blend of geographies, cultural milieus, political contexts, religious influences, and familial backgrounds. The hard-won wisdom and insights I've gained in life are not just for my benefit; I have learned lessons I believe it would be selfish *not* to share.

The year 2018 was my year of metamorphosis. I turned 60, coauthored *The Healing Organization*, and went through a variety of healing experiences at the insistent urging of wise friends. I was in a constant state of inquiry, seeking and gaining guidance from within as well as from the outside world. I experienced frequent awakenings and received wisdom so abundantly that I could barely keep up, filling up notebook after notebook. Unexpected teachers showed up in my life, and I was given many opportunities for further learning and growth.

Why did it take until I turned 60 for some basic truths to be revealed to me? I remained unconscious for so long because I was stuck in the past and was carrying many unhealed wounds. I did work that was meaningful in a joyless way. I was running on fumes, sourcing the fuel for my work from the praise and gratitude of strangers. I gave 70–80 talks a year, produced a new book every 18 months on average, and was away from home at least 60% of the time (I was scared to calculate exactly how much). I was always on the run. I had no idea what I was running away from, or toward.

In writing this book, I had the sobering realization that I had been unhappy for as long as I could remember. I had minimized or denied my wounds and traumas to myself. I did not have the courage or ability to face them; there was too much darkness there, and my sensitive soul just could not take it. All I aspired to was survival. If I could just make it through the next 15 to 20 years, I would be done with it. I found myself looking at obituaries, at how old people were when they died, wondering how much longer I had to endure. A line I read years ago from *The God of Small Things* kept resurfacing in my mind: "Not old. Not young. But a viable-diable age."

Remember the classic video game Pac-Man? Pac-Man is chased by ghosts, trying desperately to outrun them, until he eats a power pellet that temporarily changes the game. He then starts eating the ghosts and being fueled by them. For many of us, that seems to be the whole game: being chased by ghosts or being fueled by ghosts. Either way, the ghosts are running the game. Even when you're fueled by ghosts, using them as a catalyst for a different, more positive way of living/being, they're still running you! What we need to do is exit the game, get out of the maze we are trapped in, and free ourselves to navigate life without being chased or fueled by ghosts!

In 2019, I lost both my parents in quick succession. Through my grief, I saw that I had more work to do to heal myself than just writing *The Healing Organization*. I needed to continue to work on myself and share with the world the hard-won wisdom that I had gained from my life experiences.

I have written this book to understand my life journey in a deeper way so I can live more consciously while helping others do the same. It is about looking back, not with anger, resentment, or regret, but with awe, wonder, and curiosity. It is about making more explicit what has so far been implicit. It is about being the driver of my life rather than being driven by it. It is about alchemizing the pain and suffering I have experienced into wisdom of lasting value to myself and to others. It is about recognizing the preciousness and finiteness of life and learning how to live in a way that is aligned with my inner being and the needs of the world. It is about waking up and staying awake. Most of all, it is about striving to live a more meaningful, impactful, and joyful life.

I hope this book will inspire you to ask deeper questions about life for yourself and apply some of what I have learned to your own journey. To aid in that, I have added Reflections at the end of each chapter to give you additional opportunities for self-reflection.

1

Roots

In December 1960, my father, a brilliant iconoclast who had overcome every obstacle to attaining a higher education, scraped together the enormous sum of Rs 5,000 rupees (about $700 then) for a one-way passage from New Delhi to Winnipeg, Canada – leaving behind his fledgling family. Narayan Sisodia was 24. I was two, and my mother, Usha, was 23 and pregnant with my sister, Manjula.

Life Without Papa

Rising from a tiny village in central India, Narayan had flown across the seven seas to Canada, like a bird that miraculously migrates thousands of miles to better climes. He would be gone for four long years getting a doctorate in cytogenetics, or plant breeding, at the University of Manitoba. As the months and years passed, he slowly morphed into a mythical figure.

After he left, my mother, in Indian tradition, retreated to her parents' house for the birth of my sister. A few months later, she returned to my father's village, Kesur, where she was embedded in a deeply conservative joint family, surrounded by her husband's parents, his brothers and sisters, her sister-in-law, and their young children. It was an unhappy and lonely time for her. The women did little to comfort her. Instead, there was much malicious talk of how most men failed to return after leaving for America (which was indistinguishable from Canada in their minds). My aunt would say, "He's not coming back. He's going to find and marry a *Mem* there [white women were called *Memsahibs* in colonial days]." Every photograph sent by my father, every line in every letter he wrote was scrutinized for evidence to support this theory. My mother cried herself to sleep many nights – a young bride forced to live like a widow.

As time passed, my memory of my father faded. I came to know him only from photographs, as a glamorous figure dressed in dark suits, knit T-shirts, turtlenecks, dashing Aviator sunglasses, occasionally sporting a beard. He seemed like a character from a movie, not my flesh-and-blood father.

When I turned five, my mother sent me to Ratlam, a small city 50 miles from Kesur, to acquire a proper education at St. Joseph's, an English-language convent school run by missionaries. This led to snide commentary from my aunts in Kesur, who had been perfectly content to send *their* children to the Hindi-language village school. My grandfather joined in the taunts. He routinely mocked Usha: "With this aristocrat's spoiled daughter living with us, we will all be bankrupt and begging in the streets soon."

My mother's five half-siblings were all enrolled in the same school. Her father had rented a large house for the brood in Retired Colony, where railway pensioners lived. I lived there for two years with my eight-year-old aunt and four young uncles, with a live-in house-keeper to feed and hover over us.

Periodically, my mother came to visit and complained to the housekeeper that I had gotten thinner and darker. The housekeeper grumbled about my raids on the sugar tin. Fortunately, my report cards reassured my mother that I was reasonably happy and doing all right.

I spent summers and other vacations back in Kesur. My cousin Gajendra (18 months older) and I were inseparable. We ate every meal out of the same plate, insisting on feeding each other instead of our-selves. We were passengers on every trip taken by the tractors, return-ing muddy and disheveled, to our mothers' exasperation. Mimicking the adults, we gathered up *beedi* butts (thin Indian mini-cigars) and attempted to smoke them. If that didn't work, we tried to smoke reeds of straw. We were carefree little desperadoes.

From Kesur to Canada

Reports of my father's academic achievements in the doctoral pro-gram were met with little surprise, as most people had come to define him almost solely in terms of his relentless success in education. Narayan had defied great odds in coming this far.

Kesur was a large village, by Indian standards, with about 3,000 people. Situated in the middle of India, it was unusual in that it had a roughly equal blend of Hindus and Muslims. Our house resembled a small fort complete with ramparts and turrets, and was called the Rowla ("the landlord's house"). It separated the saffron-flagged Hindu homes of the village on our right from the green-flagged Muslim homes to our left. Like most Rowlas, it was situated at the highest point in the village. Across from the house and down a steep incline flowed a river.

Our family were of the warrior (or Kshatriya) caste, just below Brahmins in social standing in India's rigid caste system. Within that, we were part of the Rajput subculture (see sidebar), descended from rulers who held dominion over much of northern India for many centuries.

As a child, Narayan was often sternly reminded that his first responsibility was to his assigned duties on the farm; school was not to interfere with the serious business of working. At peak times such as planting and harvesting, my grandfather deployed all the Rowla boys to various tasks. The older sons drove the tractors and supervised the workers, while the younger ones patrolled the fields with slingshots, waving and shouting to shoo the swarms of bright green parrots from the crops. My grandfather sent a messenger to the school informing the teachers that the Rowla children would not be coming in until the crop was in storage or the seed was in the ground.

Narayan's early education at the village middle school was mediocre, but that did not hold him back. His father – Thakur Girwar Singh, a hard-driving, self-made man with a fourth-grade education – dismissed Narayan's educational ambitions. In his view, too much education simply created impractical *lakir ke fakir*, a popular expression among the wise old nodding heads of the village that meant "worshipper of words." Education beyond the basics of reading, writing, and simple addition and subtraction was for those unfortunates who were forced to take salaried jobs – not for someone with the abundance of property and prestige that Girwar had worked maniacally all his life to accumulate for himself and his four sons.

My father was brilliant and had vast energy. Unlike his siblings, he was determined not to let the circumstances of his birth determine the course of his life. For virtually everyone around him, the blueprints of their lives were handed to them at birth. Rather than chafe at his father's strictures, Narayan simply worked harder than anyone else to please his father as well as himself. He did his schoolwork late into the night under the light of a sooty kerosene lamp (it would be decades before electricity came to the village) and completed many of his chores before sunrise.

My grandfather said to his kids, "Eighth grade is more than enough. You know how to read and write; now get to work on the farm." But Narayan insisted on continuing his education beyond that. He moved to Dhar, 12 miles away, to get his high school diploma. His grandfather, the unusually mild-mannered Thakur Hari Singh, moved there to look after him in a rented house.

Upon graduating from high school, Narayan dreamed about becoming a doctor and secretly went to Indore (a large city about 30 miles from Kesur) to take the highly competitive PMT (Pre-Medical Test), which he aced. When my grandfather found out, he wouldn't hear of it. After a great deal of arguing and pleading, he agreed that Narayan could go to college, but only if he got a degree in agriculture science, which would at least have some practical value back on the farm. In 1955, 19-year-old Narayan set off to Gwalior, a city about 300 miles away. There, he enjoyed a stellar academic career, becoming president of the student body and earning a gold medal for topping his class academically. He came home to Kesur for every break, however brief, and threw himself into farm work.

Rumor has it that Narayan had fallen in love with a girl while he was at college – a blasphemous offense in his hidebound feudal culture. Compounding his folly, the girl was not from a Rajput family. Narayan was not free to choose his own bride; that duty and privilege were irrevocably his father's. As soon as Girwar found out, he set the gears in motion to arrange Narayan's marriage. Narayan quickly gave in; he understood the culture he was part of. He knew that a Rajput father's love was completely conditional; anyone who strayed from the fold and refused to obey paternal dictates would be summarily expelled from the family. I would learn that harsh lesson.

This was the second time Narayan had given in to his father's wishes; he had abandoned his dream of becoming a doctor, and he now submitted to his father on the question of a life partner. It would not be the last time. These and future capitulations would eventually calcify into deep resentments as Narayan struggled to shape a life between the competing poles of self-determination and duty to family.

The Rajputs

The word *Rajput* derives from the Sanskrit *Raja Petra*, or son of Kings. Rajputs are a prominent branch of the Kshatriya caste, who were warriors traditionally charged with maintaining law and order and defending against attacks from outside forces.

Rajputs emerged in the ninth and tenth centuries in the northwestern part of India. They were the rulers of many fiercely independent kingdoms that frequently warred with each other until they faced a common threat from Muslim invaders. Rajputs resisted the conquerors until finally acceding to Mughal control in the sixteenth century. The last of the holdouts was Maharana Pratap (to whom we Sisodias trace our ancestry).

Rajputs are socially conservative and fiercely protective of their many customs. Traditionally, they were celebrated for being brave and self-sacrificing. They had a strict code of honor. Many had shown genuine nobility and extraordinary courage in the face of insurmountable odds.

The strict code of honor extended to women and children, who were expected and often coerced to commit mass self-immolation in a ritual called *jauhar* to avoid humiliation and abuse at the hands of conquerors. This tradition derived from the practice of *sati*, in which widows were pushed onto funeral pyres. The men would subsequently head off to their certain death – a practice known as *saka*. The practice of *sati* is venerated and celebrated by Rajputs to this day, though no longer legal.

Over time, many Rajputs came to be defined by their indulgent, often decadent lifestyles: rich food, alcohol, opium, hunting, concubines. They developed a reputation for being cruel and violent to peasant farmers. Many still live in mini-palaces and fortress-like homes surrounded by walls with rifle sights.

The Rajput culture remains harshly patriarchal and misogynistic. Until recently, women couldn't own land or make decisions about financial matters. Working outside the home was almost unthinkable, even in educated families. Most women keep their faces covered in the company of older men. To this day, most Rajput women do not call their husbands by their given name. As one told the *New York Times*, "For a wife, your husband is God. And you don't call God by his first name."

Both my grandfathers were Thakurs, a privileged landowning category of Rajputs just below the kings. They each had about 500 acres, a vast holding by Indian standards (most farmers have less than five acres). Many Thakurs controlled their little fiefdoms with an iron hand, while some were more paternalistic. Old Bollywood movies often depicted Thakurs as villains: hard-drinking, murderous rapists with colorful turbans and ostentatious moustaches.

Narayan's hopes for a college-educated wife proved impossible to fulfill. Rajput girls were not highly educated in those days; most did not complete high school. My grandfather found a good match for my father: the oldest daughter of Thakur Jaswant Singh Pawar of Berchha, an educated man of refined, Westernized tastes and leisurely ways. Usha had studied up to eighth grade, and from all accounts had the makings of a suitable bride.

Figure 1.1   My parents in their twenties

The families of the bride and bridegroom were quite different, and there was no way for anybody to judge the compatibility between Narayan and Usha. However, their astrological charts suggested an excellent match. After the fathers had agreed to the marriage, Narayan sneaked a peek at a tiny black-and-white photograph of a beautiful and demure Usha. Usha did not even see a picture of my father; she was told that she was to get a highly educated man for her husband and to trust in fate for the rest.

On May 20, 1957, when Usha had just turned 20 and Narayan was a few weeks shy of 21, the wedding party (comprising 60 men and one female servant who would attend to the new bride on the return journey) left Kesur for the dusty, bouncy six-hour bus ride to Berchha, a tiny hamlet of a few hundred people. Five days later, the bus returned, bearing the wedding party and a flower-bedecked Narayan and Usha, cordoned off with an improvised curtain near the front. She was resplendent in a red Rajasthani saree and glittering gold jewelry, her face completely covered by the *pallu* of her saree. The bus was weighed down with her dowry − wooden furniture, trunks of clothing, a Singer sewing machine, new pots and pans, and stainless-steel glasses, and round steel trays that her family had given her to help set up her household. That was in addition to the money her father had paid to Girwar as part of her dowry.

Narayan soon headed back to Gwalior for his senior year of college. Usha set up her lonely marital home in a single room with mud-covered walls inside the sprawling Rowla. Three months later, Narayan returned to Kesur on school break, and soon after, Usha left once again for Berchha, this time to be looked after by her stepmother through her newly discovered pregnancy.

When Narayan graduated in 1958, there was a repeat of the scene with his father from three years earlier. The prestigious Indian Agriculture Research Institute in New Delhi had offered Narayan a full scholarship to its master's program. My grandfather eventually relented, this time without conditions, realizing that Narayan was not to be deterred.

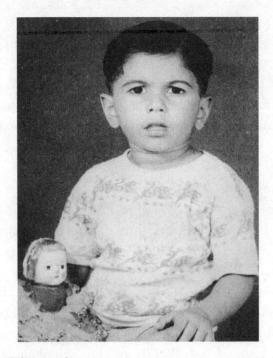

Figure 1.2 The author at age one

I was born on June 28, 1958, in Ratlam, which was midway between my parents' villages. My mom had a name picked out. I would be Rajendra, which means "lord of kings" or the "king of the Gods"; she had high hopes for this chubby, scowling baby. It also was the name of Usha's favorite movie star, the impossibly handsome Rajendra Kumar. To ease the pressure, she gave me the nickname *Pappu*, which connotes gentleness and innocence – qualities she herself embodied like no other. My father spent a few days with us and then headed to his new life in New Delhi.

The next two years were a repeat of Usha's first year of marriage – struggling to maintain her sense of self in a suffocating joint family in which she had no freedom or power, but plenty of responsibility – interspersed with brief, hectic visits from Narayan.

Usha's sister-in-law wanted her to do most of the kitchen work. Because Usha now had a baby that demanded her time, my aunt slipped a kernel of opium in my mouth every time I woke up and started fussing, knocking me out for hours and freeing my mom to keep working.

Usha was anguished about it but felt powerless to object. Under normal circumstances, her husband would have stood up for her. But he was not around. In desperation, she wrote a tear-stained letter to her father. As soon as he read it, Jaswant Singh boarded the next bus to Kesur. Upon arrival, he didn't mince words. With a rare flash of anger, he demanded, "What the hell are you doing to my grandson? Stop this nonsense at once."

In 1960, Narayan returned from New Delhi with his master's degree and another gold medal. He had just turned 24, and his education had gone as far as it could in India. His master's degree had elevated his academic status, but also sparked in him a desire to help transform Indian agriculture. Many of his professors in Delhi had been educated in the United States and Canada; they had infected him with the palpable sense of excitement that came from working at the frontiers of science. They thought highly of him and begged him not to leave the field. The Indian "Green Revolution" in agriculture was just beginning, kindling hope that India could become self-sufficient in food, and make its frequent famines a thing of the past.

Filled with idealism, Narayan wanted more than anything to contribute to advancing scientific agriculture by creating new hybrid species. The genetics of plant breeding could deliver miraculous benefits to people everywhere. However, those research opportunities were open only to those with a doctorate.

He felt trapped in tiny, remote, still unelectrified Kesur, burdened with a young wife and infant son. His gold medals and diplomas provided no solace. He had no intellectual stimulation or companionship. His father had expected him to come home and miraculously elevate productivity on the farm. He tried to explain to people in the village that his interest in agriculture was on another plane. He certainly did not possess any magic formulas for turning the farm around. Besides, the farm was doing well enough; his father was knowledgeable about crop rotation, irrigation, fertilizing, and disease prevention. Soon, the inevitable cynicism set in; Narayan had wasted everybody's time, including his own. What could one expect of a *lakir ke fakir?*

Finding no understanding or pride from his father, Narayan now turned to his former professors in New Delhi. Among them was the legendary M. S. Swaminathan, considered the father of India's Green Revolution, who enthusiastically recommended Narayan to several PhD programs in the United States and Canada. Of these, the University of Manitoba in the frozen flatlands of Winnipeg boasted an outstanding faculty and offered him financial support – enough for him to live on, but not enough to bring and support a family.

In the summer of 1960, Narayan asked his father-in-law to help raise the princely sum of 5,000 rupees for his ticket. That was over six times the annual per capita income in India then. His own father had refused to have anything to do with this latest in a seemingly never-ending series of foolhardy notions; he had stopped speaking with him entirely. In December, Narayan left New Delhi bound for Winnipeg and a doctorate in cytogenetics. He left behind a worried, newly pregnant wife and an uncomprehending son; he carried with him the weight of enormous expectations and hopes.

Papa Returns

Confounding the doomsday predictors, my father returned to India in early 1965. He was met with a tumultuous, almost euphoric welcome. He had gone to the furthest reaches of the world and triumphantly returned, back to his family, his people, and his roots. My grandfather, who had strongly opposed his leaving, had orchestrated a series of welcoming parties along the 50-mile single-lane road between Ratlam and Kesur.

My first glimpse of my father was an intimidating one; he cut a resplendent figure in his brown knit polo shirt, his gold-rimmed RayBan sunglasses, his big shiny golden watch, his neck festooned with marigold garlands. I was filled with awe – and shame. Suddenly, I became acutely conscious of my own sloppy appearance and frayed clothes. I thought, "Oh God, how could I be *his* son?"

A lengthy motorcade wound its way toward Kesur. At several small towns and villages along the way, local Thakurs had set up elaborate welcoming arches over the main squares, emblazoned with "Welcome Back, Dr. Sisodia" (in Hindi). At each stop, as the motorcade discharged its passengers, the town elders came forward to greet and embrace my father, and a local band jauntily struck up a suitable melody, such as *Ghar aaya mera pardesi* ("my wanderer has returned home"). I snuck into the edges of a few of the hundreds of photos taken of the occasion, a disheveled figure on the margins of all this pomp and ceremony, ignored in the excitement.

We reached Kesur as dusk approached. The 50-mile journey had taken over seven hours. The entire village had turned out. Thousands of people lined the narrow main street, thrusting garlands toward my father. Others showered rose petals from balconies. Bands blared from every direction. Fireworks lit up the evening sky.

My father's *Masterjis* (teachers) were all there, dressed in their whitest *kurtas* and *dhotis*. Narayan, in the traditional gesture of a student toward his teachers, bent down to touch their feet, at which show of humility and grace the teachers sprang back, barely able to contain their pleasure and awe. The village's contingent of *seths* (traders and shopkeepers) had put on their ill-fitting Nehru jackets and sweat-stained conical Congress caps to greet him, palms joined at heart level in the traditional *namaste* greeting.

Like the Wizard of Oz, my grandfather had choreographed all of this, but befitting his status as the patriarch, had remained in the Rowla. When the procession finally made its way up the steep incline leading to the house, my father went up to my waiting grandfather and touched both his feet. My grandfather wore a long gray coat and a bright red *saffa* (turban). He blessed my father by putting both hands on Narayan's bowed head, saying *jeete raho* (live long). They then embraced and walked through the large main gate to the Rowla's expansive main courtyard.

Several hundred people gathered at the Rowla that night, and the celebration lasted until dawn broke. My favorite picture of the day is one in which my mother sat next to my father, gazing at him as he animatedly spoke to someone else. After four long years of being brave, strong, and alone, she was finally a married woman again. All the doubts and insecurities, the slights and the cutting remarks, all her suffering had melted into the past. She looked carefree, suddenly seeming even younger than her 27 years.

Meanwhile, my sister (then four) was entirely unimpressed. It took several days before she allowed my father to hold her and much longer before she deigned to call him Papa.

At seven years old, I was neither confident nor self-assured. Around this otherworldly Papa, I felt like a stumbling, mumbling fool. My appearance, while better than that of a street urchin, certainly reflected my rough surroundings. I was missing a couple of front teeth, my hair looked like a porcupine's, and my meager wardrobe consisted mostly of thin shirts with loud geometric prints and baggy shorts. My father looked like a young Indian John F. Kennedy. He seemed as unimpressed with me as I was awed by him. I am sure he sensed my discomfort, but did nothing to make me feel at ease. We were virtual strangers to each other. As he wasn't physically affectionate, little could penetrate the invisible wall that separated us. That would become a lifelong condition; I would spend decades trying to earn his approval and affection.

Three months later, Papa broke the news to my grandfather: once again, he would be leaving home. He had interviewed with a firm in London on his way back from Canada and had accepted a job as chief scientist for the British West Indies Sugar Corporation in Barbados to do research on sugarcane. This bombshell led to an extended, expletive-filled blowup with my grandfather, who had taken it for granted that my father was back for good and would now settle down in Kesur or nearby. Once again, my father was "dead" to his father. Narayan made plans for my mother, my sister, and me to leave India and be a part of his next adventure.

For Mummy and me, it would soon be a case of "Innocents Abroad."

Reflections

I grew up in the shadow of generations of patriarchs, embedded in the customs and traditions of a land I would not fully understand for decades. Those early years were a foreshadowing of the struggles that would come later in my life: the differences between my grandfather and my father would parallel the gulf between me and my father.

Every memory that stands out is there for a reason: it has something important to teach you. What are the memories that stand out to you from your early years? Reexamine them with curiosity. Why do you think they are significant in your life?

More than half a century later, I can see how the experiences of my early life impacted the trajectory of the rest of my life. The most significant is that I didn't know my father until I was seven. His absence allowed me to be rooted in my mother's unconditional love, but he and I never became close.

Were both of your parents present in your early years? How did their presence or absence affect you?

My true nature was evident when I was very young. My mother named me *Pappu*, the innocent one. I was trusting, idealistic, and peace-loving. That was my essence; it was what defined me as. However, I had been planted in soil that was not hospitable to those qualities.

Your true nature combined with the environment in which you were nurtured either allows you to become more of yourself or causes you to develop masks and shields in order to survive. What kind of "seed" were you as a young child? What were your essential qualities? What kind of environment, what kind of soil, did you find yourself in for your early years? How well did that environment nurture you? What coping strategies did you have to develop to survive in your environment? If it was not the "right" environment, were you eventually able to find or create an environment that was more hospitable to your nature? Do you understand what kind of environment you thrive in?

2

Changing of the Guard

A Whole New World

Proud, somewhat stunned owners of brand-new passports, my mother, my sister, and I packed up our belongings to leave India in the summer of 1965. I had just turned seven. We made our way to Palam International Airport in New Delhi for our flight to Aden and then to London. We were beside ourselves with excitement as we boarded the plane. We gripped the armrests tightly as the plane rumbled down the runway and ascended into the dark night.

In those days, international flights were luxurious experiences. My parents dressed formally, and Mummy had cleaned us kids up as much as she could. Soon, the glamorous flight attendants arrived with an array of exotic drinks and foods. Everything I put into my mouth was a brand-new sensation.

It was cold and rainy when we landed in London, so our first stop was at Harrods department store. I emerged transformed, in a stylish trench coat, baggy trousers, and shiny black shoes. We then went to see one of the iconic sights of London: the changing of the guard at Buckingham Palace. This was an apt metaphor for what was happening in my family: a new regime, my father replacing my mother as the dominant influence in my life.

Bewildered in Barbados

After a few magical days in London, we boarded a flight to Bridgetown, Barbados. We spent the first couple of weeks at the Hilton Hotel on the beach – the first time I saw the ocean. My mother and I sat on chaise lounges on the sand, being served drinks with little umbrellas in them and fried flying fish, a uniquely Barbadian delicacy.

Barbados is a tiny speck of an island in the South Caribbean, just 21 miles north to south and 11 miles east to west. With just over 235,000 people, it was a far cry from colorful, chaotic, crowded India.

We moved into a big colonial-style house, acquired a black Labrador we named Bello, and slowly adjusted to our drastically different new lives. Mummy and I were "innocents abroad" in this unfamiliar environment. We had always been extremely close, but now we were joined in this adventure together. Manju was too young to experience much culture shock, and my father was deeply engrossed in his work. I helped my mother cook, and we figured things out together as best we could.

One day, an old man stopped by the house and offered to transform our garden for a small amount of money. The trusting souls we were, my mother and I hired him. He took our money, and we never saw him again. When we sheepishly confessed to my father, he shook his head. "You two are the same – too *bhola*" (meaning innocent or gullible).

My school was called Holy Family, and I found it utterly delightful. I had never been in a school with girls. I soon had a crush on a little girl with curly blonde hair. This was a Catholic school and Bible study was required. I won a prize for being the best student in Bible class, having virtually memorized the children's version we were using! My glowing report card was filled with As and included the comment "Raj is an ambitious young student." I wonder what the teacher saw in me at age eight to come to that conclusion.

I thought my father would be proud, but he seemed unimpressed by my grades and the teacher's comment. He remained a distant,

intimidating figure to me. It did not help that soon after arriving in
Barbados, he grew a beard. It came in thick and bushy, making him
appear even more formidable than he already did.

Papa had been diagnosed with asthma some years earlier and used
an inhaler to treat it when an attack came on. One Sunday afternoon,
he and I were in our large living room at opposite ends. An asthma
attack came on, and he needed his inhaler, which was lying on a table
close to where I was playing. Struggling to breathe, he gestured to me
to bring him the inhaler. Not understanding what he wanted, I picked
up the inhaler and started mimicking the way he used it. To get my
attention, my father took off his slipper and threw it across the room.
I was not looking his way, and the slipper hit me squarely on the side
of my head. I was stunned. Being struck by a shoe is considered a
grave insult in our culture. I already didn't feel worthy of being his
son. Now the thought arose in me, "Oh God, he hates me."

That framing of the episode stayed with me for decades. Eventually, I understood that this was just a story I had made up, since I was
so afraid and unsure around this man. I realized that desperate people
do desperate things. I asked him about the episode decades later; he
couldn't recollect it. What stood out as a defining moment in my
childhood was a nonevent for him.

But it certainly affected me. I felt I needed to reinvent myself.
That meant rejecting Pappu, the nickname my mother had lovingly
given me. I needed to become Raj, the person my second-grade
teacher described as ambitious. Perhaps then I could eventually win
my father's approval.

Meanwhile, my parents were learning to live with each other. My
mother started wearing Western clothes for the first time in her life.
She experienced her greatest freedom and joy in the water, venturing
far out into the ocean until she was a tiny speck to us. But mostly she
remained sweet, simple, unsophisticated Usha – a wonderful home-
maker unequipped to manage more sophisticated household affairs.

Determined to make her a woman of the world, Papa decided to
teach her how to drive our little British Hillman Imp. We drove to an
open field. Manju and I sat on the grass and watched the lesson.

A sloping ridge ran along one edge of the field; my mother steered parallel to it but then drifted toward it. Soon both right wheels were on the steep incline. Suddenly, the car flipped onto its left side, its wheels slowly spinning. Somehow, our parents clambered out of the car. A few passersby helped tip the car back onto its wheels. Neither of my parents was hurt, and the car was fine too. But it left Usha deeply shaken and effectively ended her driving aspirations.

My father started to express something about her that would become a frequent refrain for the next 53 years of their lives together: "Why are you so helpless? I can't count on you for anything." He was trying to mold her into something she wasn't. She developed a deep sense of insecurity and inferiority. Since I identified so closely with her, every one of his criticisms of her stung deeply and felt like a rebuke of me as well.

Serene in Salinas

Nearly two years after we arrived in Barbados, my father came home with a glossy brochure of a place in California called Salinas. It had a picture of a man and a dog sitting on a hill overlooking a city surrounded by lush green agricultural fields. He told us that he had just accepted a job there to work on wheat research with a company called World Seeds, Inc.

Narayan always valued the journey as much as the destination. He loved creating new and interesting experiences for himself and the family. As it would take a couple of months for us to receive our green cards for the United States, we flew first to Winnipeg, Canada, to meet my father's friends from his doctoral days. A few weeks later, we flew to Montréal, which was hosting a six-month-long World's Fair called Expo 67. We spent a month there, staying with a warm French-Canadian family and soaking in the culture of that beautiful city. We enjoyed the many attractions of the fair, which featured pavilions from 62 countries. We then flew to New York City for a few days. We climbed the Empire State Building and toured the United Nations before finally boarding a plane for San Francisco.

A city of 50,000 people, Salinas was the center of an incredibly fertile valley known as the "lettuce bowl" of America. John Steinbeck was born there and had made the little city famous through his writings. It was 50 miles from San Jose and about 100 miles from San Francisco. We were the only Indians in Salinas and considered quite exotic.

We settled into an apartment on a cul-de-sac next to a golf course, just a couple of blocks from Los Padres Elementary School, my home away from home for the next two years. This is where I truly blossomed. School was sheer delight for me. I was successful and popular, and my confidence grew rapidly. I brought home report cards filled with straight A-plusses. Though I was never particularly athletic, I excelled at a schoolyard game called Four Square. Instead of just throwing the ball straight on, I applied all kinds of spin to it so that it took off in unexpected ways after it bounced. The kids marveled at my mysterious Eastern wizardry. My teachers, Mr. Walton and Mr. Roman, put me in charge of the classroom when they had to step away. The atmosphere was lighthearted and fun. At the end of the school day, we learned square dancing in the playground, getting to touch actual girls. How good could life get?

My best friend was Jay Peterson, a pint-sized freckled kid with curly red hair who lived in the same complex. We were at each other's homes or on the phone every evening, as I helped him with his homework. Jay and I were free-range kids, exploring every corner of the little city on our banana-seat Sting-ray bicycles with high handlebars. We sneaked into convenience stores and nervously flipped through the *Playboy* magazines they kept in the back. Because my father had not adopted the American practice of giving kids an allowance, I had no money at all. So Jay and I rode around with a bag, picked up empty bottles and returned them to stores for the deposit money. With that, we bought ice cream cones for 10 cents, and *Archie* and *Superman* comics for a quarter. We marveled at the ads in the back of the comics for X-ray glasses and magical seahorses.

On Halloween, my parents took advantage of the fact that we were the only Indians in town and dressed me up as a maharaja. I put on my mother's blue silk Japanese kimono and her pearl necklace. My father tied a turban on my head and attached a fake mustache on my upper lip. Jay and I took our pillowcases and headed out. My costume was a big hit. Neighbors prostrated themselves on the ground seeking the maharaja's blessings and doled out generous quantities of candy into my pillowcase.

I woke up every morning savoring what was to come, whether it was a school day or the weekend. We spent Saturday mornings sprawled on the tan carpet in front of the TV, watching cartoons for four hours straight: *Superman, Batman, Scooby Doo, Archie, Tom and Jerry, Looney Tunes*. It was a nonstop garden of delights, topped off with a breakfast of pancakes. One magical day, a color television was delivered to the apartment. My joy knew no bounds. On Sunday morning, we had pages and pages of cartoons in the newspaper to revel in. On Sunday afternoons, my father lay down on the carpet, and my sister and I took turns walking on his back. Later, we plucked white hairs from his head. He paid us one cent for each hair – my only steady source of income other than the bottles. His vanity was a gold mine for us; even though he was only 32 years old, he already had plenty of white hairs for us to harvest.

This was the one time in my life when I had a relatively easygoing relationship with my father. Perhaps it was because I had become more confident and we were outside the cultural expectations and pressures of Indian life. We were all freer to be ourselves. Unfortunately, it wouldn't last.

The late 1960s were a time of great social upheaval in the United States. When we arrived in 1967, I was nine years old, just becoming conscious of the larger world. I learned that there was a war raging in Vietnam and a large peace movement, much of it centered around San Francisco. The hippie culture was booming. Timothy Leary was urging young people to take psychedelics like LSD and "tune in, turn on, and drop out." The soaring oratory of Martin Luther King Jr. and presidential candidate Robert F. Kennedy inspired and moved me. They dreamed of creating a better world and gave hope to millions.

When MLK was gunned down on April 4, 1968, it caused a volcanic eruption of grief and rage around the country. Bobby Kennedy, then campaigning in Indianapolis, gave a moving, heartfelt speech pleading with all Americans, especially African Americans, to stay true to MLK's gospel of nonviolence and keep the faith that better days would come.

Then came the California primary on June 6. As we watched the results come in, it soon became clear that Robert Kennedy had won. We were euphoric as he delivered a rousing victory speech. He was now the clear front-runner to become the Democratic nominee and likely next president of the United States. Hope was alive that the United States would soon exit the war in Vietnam. RFK concluded his speech and started to exit the hotel through the kitchen when Sirhan B. Sirhan stepped in front of him and shot him – live on national TV. We sat in our living room in stunned silence.

I was in my usual spot on the carpet. I turned around to look at my father in his easy chair. His eyes were bloodshot, and tears streamed down his face. It stunned me that this man could cry. That instantly multiplied the gravity of the moment tenfold for me. Something truly earth-shattering had just happened. I was 10 years old; I wouldn't see my father cry again for the next 40 years. His mother died, his father died, his nephew and his brother died, his beloved brother-in-law died. None of it cracked his hard exterior.

With Robert Kennedy removed from the race, Vice President Hubert Humphrey won the Democratic nomination. The entire country was roiled with grief and torn apart by political discord. There were riots at the Democratic National Convention in Chicago. Richard Nixon won the election, and American history unfolded very differently than it might have had MLK lived and RFK governed.

The country was entering a new chapter, and so was our family. My brother Sanjay was born in Salinas General Hospital on February 28, 1969. My father had recently embroiled into a bitter dispute with his boss at World Seeds. He had discovered wrongdoing in the company and confronted the CEO. When the CEO refused to come clean, my father resigned.

Not having any other options, my father called his professors at the University of Manitoba in Winnipeg. They immediately offered him a professorship. In short order, we made plans to move to Canada. My father turned what could have been a tedious trip into a memorable adventure. On March 9, 1969, my mother's 32nd birthday, we hitched a U-Haul to our gold 1967 Chevy Impala coupe and embarked on a month-long journey to Winnipeg. My brother was nine days old.

Confused in Canada

Shyam Joshi had been a PhD student with my father at the University of Manitoba. They were close friends. Shyam and his wife, Sushma, had just moved into a new house. Their baby was a few months older than Sanjay. We moved in with them. A couple of days later, I started at Van Belleghem Elementary School a few blocks away. All our moves had made me quite adaptable. I made friends right away.

Uncle Shyam soon became my first substitute father figure. He started every sentence to me with "Son." He noticed that I always dressed rather conservatively, in turtlenecks, button-down shirts, and dress pants. Strangely, I did not own a single pair of jeans. For my 11th birthday, he took me to a Winnipeg Blue Bombers football game. He talked to me about life and about girls. I loved the attention. When we came home, he gave me my birthday presents: bell-bottomed blue jeans, a bright pink shirt, and a gold chain belt. There was no way I was going to wear any of that!

By far the most momentous event of that summer was the Apollo 11 moon landing, which we watched live on a Sunday afternoon. I got goosebumps as Neil Armstrong's immortal words fluttered through the static: "That's one small step for man, one giant leap for mankind." It seemed like the pinnacle of human achievement.

Not to be outdone in miraculous feats, the New York Mets that year rampaged through the National League. A team that had never placed better than ninth in a 10-team league won the World Series over the Baltimore Orioles.

That was the year I realized that anything was possible!

I enjoyed an idyllic summer, unaware that my father was plotting yet another dramatic change in our lives in just a few months. The gravitational pull from his father was proving to be too much to resist. In his typical way, Girwar had stopped communicating with my father after they had a spat in 1968. My grandmother had died, and my father had gone to India for the funeral. It is a Rajput tradition for sons of the deceased to get their heads shaved as a mark of mourning. My father refused, which my grandfather took as a sign of disrespect. Girwar had resumed his letter writing, and all but commanded my father to return and do his duty to the family. His older brother incapacitated by mental illness, Narayan was in effect the oldest son. He could no longer "selfishly" pursue his career so far away and ignore his responsibility to his family.

My parents had become increasingly distressed that my sister and I had forgotten almost everything about India. Even though we went with them to see subtitled Hindi movies at the university every month and enjoyed them, we could not converse with our parents in Hindi. We had lost connection to our culture in just about every way; we had no memory of our grandparents, uncles, aunts, or cousins.

After five years abroad, still not able to speak much English, my mother was lonely and missed her family in India. It broke her heart that she couldn't be present for weddings and childbirths and other family milestones that mattered so much to her. My father's sister had gotten married while we had been abroad. My mother had written to her father-in-law, pleading with him to delay the wedding until we returned. He ignored her pleas.

My father accepted a job with the Jawaharlal Nehru Agriculture University in a small city in India. Our parents told us we would return to India "for good." No strangers to moving, we looked forward to this new experience with some anticipation.

The plan my father dreamed up for our trip home was a doozy even by his lofty standards. Instead of flying to India, we would drive 2,500 miles to San Francisco and take an ocean liner to Hamburg,

Germany. From there, we would embark on a mind-boggling, 8,000-mile road odyssey through Western Europe, Eastern Europe, Eurasia, Afghanistan, and Pakistan to India. The trip would take about three months. We would traverse many poorly developed communist countries along the way – with three young children, including a nine-month-old baby. My father put an ad in the paper to sell our Chevy Impala, and purchased, sight unseen, a brand-new dark blue Mercedes-Benz diesel sedan directly from the company in Germany.

How does one even imagine such a plan? My father had a "larger than life" quality to him. He wanted to experience life on a grander scale, and took his family along for the ride.

Alas, the trip was not to be. My father received a letter from the Indian government with grim news. The country's deeply protectionist, socialist-minded government had just passed a law that no one could import a foreign car into the country unless it was at least a year old. Our Mercedes would be only a few months old by the time we reached India. There was no way around it. He had to sell the car back to the company. Because the car was right-hand drive and a new model year had already come out, he lost a considerable amount of money on the transaction. We would now fly back to India and ship our impractical gas-guzzling Impala there.

We boarded a flight to Tokyo, where we spent three days. From there we flew to Hong Kong, where we bought gifts for everybody in our extended family. This included an air gun for me, part of my father's plan to initiate me into the warrior ways of our Rajput culture.

On Christmas Day, 1969, we boarded an Air India flight from Hong Kong to New Delhi. Air India's famed Maharaja class service was then considered the best in the world. They had specially printed menus and festive food for Christmas day. We landed in the smoky, foggy night air of Delhi in the early morning hours of December 26.

The wanderers were back home. The "innocents abroad" were returning to India wiser and worldlier, but I was ill-prepared for what awaited me.

Reflections

When my father threw the slipper at me, it was traumatic to me. My experience reflects one of the three common types of traumas that most of us experience in our childhood – "I am not enough" – when we first experience our parents' disappointment in some aspect of our being. Another universal childhood trauma is "I do not belong," experienced the first time your friends reject you. The third is "I am alone," when you believe that you are all alone in a big, scary world.

What are your memories of events from your childhood, especially with your parents, that left a scar on your psyche? Have you discussed these incidents with the people involved?

After my mother failed her driving lesson, the tension between my parents grew exponentially. I found myself torn between the poles my parents represented. I identified with my mother, but I wanted to be like my father.

When you were a young child, did you experience the energies emanating from your parents as being in harmony with each other or in disharmony.? Did you feel you needed to choose sides?

Living in North America in the late 1960s made a permanent impression on my being. I saw the heights and depths of what humans are capable of. It horrified me to see two inspirational leaders gunned down in their prime, and I watched in wonder as a man frolicked on the moon.

What significant world events took place during your formative years? How do you remember those experiences? Do they evoke cynicism or a sense of hope and possibility?

3 | Return of the Native

I returned to India on the cusp of adolescence and was soon plunged into the mystery, romance, excesses, subtleties, and brutality of that world. We left the dynamic, materialistic, hedonistic *Peyton Place*, *Mad Men* zeitgeist of the United States in the late 1960s and arrived in an India that had one foot in the eighteenth century and the other in the twentieth. Just 22 years removed from its independence from the British Empire and struggling to shed the deep-seated vestiges of colonialism, India was a place of dizzying contrasts. An intensely patriarchal, misogynistic society that worshipped goddesses and was led by a woman (Indira Gandhi, whom my grandfather routinely referred to as "that *raand*," meaning slut or whore). A chaotic centrally planned economy. An ancient civilization that was an infant democracy. A place of high ideals and daily indignities. A country that taught the world the power of nonviolence but where unspeakable atrocities were commonplace. A place where cows were worshipped but countless humans were deemed untouchable. A culture that manifested the depths of spirituality and the heights of superficiality.

★★★

We landed in New Delhi in the middle of night; the crowded airport was chilly and dimly lit with flickering fluorescent tubes. India can feel like a multitiered assault on the senses for even the well-seasoned traveler. For an 11-and-a-half-year-old child, the contrast between the bright modern interiors and sparsely peopled geometric streets of Salinas and Winnipeg and the airport in New Delhi was almost surreal. Suddenly, I was surrounded by people who were shorter, browner, and more numerous than I was accustomed to. I was told that these were "my" people – they looked like me, I supposed, yet I had never felt so different, so conspicuous in all my life.

A large contingent of relatives had made the train journey to New Delhi to receive us. They spoke to me in a language I barely understood, called me "Pappu" (a nickname I had shed and now disliked intensely), ruffled my hair, and pinched my cheeks. My 13-year-old cousin Gajendra eagerly took the toy Apollo 11 rocket we had bought in Hong Kong. My sister and I complained, "Mummy, that boy just grabbed our toy!" evoking laughter all around; in fact, we had bought the rocket for him. It would be his pride and joy for decades to come (he kept it in its original packaging and brought it out only on special occasions).

It was difficult not to get caught up in the evident euphoria of the moment. We had suddenly become celebrities. Everything we said struck these people as funny; they found our accents incongruous, unintelligible, and thus quite comic. I was uncomfortable with the overbearing attention. My father, of course, took it in stride.

The Ratlam "Suar" System

After a few sleepless hours in a spartan hotel near the airport, we made our way to the train station for the 12-hour journey to Ratlam. My mother's family greeted us at the house that I had lived in from the age of five to seven with my four uncles and aunt. The memories came flooding back. That afternoon, we walked down the street to a small tailoring shop, where I was effusively welcomed by the diminutive tailor who used to stitch my school uniforms. Between the house and a field across the street ran an open, two-foot-deep cement gutter. I flashed back to how my uncles and I made paper boats and floated them in the rushing brown water during the monsoon season.

The house had a dank, dimly lit room for taking baths. There was no running water; the water was stored in a tall metal drum with a brass faucet. To bathe, you filled a bucket and used a copper mug to pour the water over yourself as you sat shivering on a low wooden stool. It was winter, so a servant heated a pot of water on a kerosene stove and added it to the freezing water in the bucket to make it bearable. Not exactly the hot steamy showers we took for granted in California and Canada!

But where was the toilet?

It was at the end of the narrow pathway outside the left side of the house: two side-by-side structures, similar to porta potties. We were told to carry water with us in a small brass container called a *louta*. Each toilet had inch-high foot-shaped ridged risers, with a gaping hole between them. There was, of course, no toilet paper. You had to squat down and somehow move your underwear and pants out of the way. After you were done, you were supposed to pour the water with your right hand and wash your bottom with your left hand. Yikes!

As I settled down to do my business, I heard grunting and squealing sounds emanating from below. I looked down and saw two pigs with long, reddish snouts and thick, dark-gray bristles jostling to position themselves under the hole. They were there to eat whatever came through and were literally inches away from my body. I was horrified and nauseated, but helpless to move.

The Caste System

India has given many gifts to human civilization, but the 3,000-year-old caste system – the world's oldest surviving form of social stratification – is certainly not one of them.

Brahmins are at the top of the hierarchy; they are said to have come from Brahma's head and were traditionally teachers and intellectuals. Brahma (the Creator) is the first god in the Hindu trinity, along with Vishnu (the Preserver) and Shiva (the Destroyer).

(continued)

(*continued*)

On the second rung are the Kshatriyas, traditionally warriors and rulers, said to have sprung from Brahma's arms. At the third level are the Vaishyas, traditionally farmers, traders, and merchants. They supposedly emanated from Brahma's thighs. At the bottom of the hierarchy are the Shudras, confined to menial jobs; they were believed to have come from Brahma's feet. Within these broad categories, there are an astonishing 3,000 castes and as many as 25,000 subcastes based on specific occupations (such as weavers, leather workers, potters, launderers, and so on).[1]

Below these are the unfortunate group known as the *achhoots*, meaning "Untouchables," considered to be contaminated from birth and outside the four main castes because of their actions in previous births. They do dirty, demeaning work, such as dealing with dead bodies, human waste, and animal waste. Mahatma Gandhi rejected the cruel label and referred to them as *Harijans* (meaning "children of God"). Leaders of the group later chose to self-identify as the *Dalits*, which means "oppressed" or "broken."

The caste system originally was supposed to match people with occupations based upon their inherent nature and skills. But predictably, caste identity over time became hereditary and hardwired into Hindu society. The caste system came to dictate most aspects of Hindu religious and social life. Most stringently, one could only marry within the caste of one's birth. Upper and lower castes lived apart from each other and did not share water wells. Brahmins refused to accept food or drink that Shudras or Dalits had touched. Many upper caste members performed elaborate purification rituals if a Dalit touched them; some did so even if a Dalit's shadow fell upon them.

Despite the Indian government's efforts to establish quotas favoring "lower" castes, their social conditions remain severely

---

[1]https://www.bbc.com/news/world-asia-india-35650616

disadvantaged. Education and urbanization have moderated the impact of caste only slightly. Intercaste marriages remain a rarity; in rural areas, such affronts to caste orthodoxy still routinely get people killed. The caste system remains the darkest aspect of Indian society.

I thought to myself, "How is my dainty little 8 and-a-half-year-old sister going to face this ordeal?" On cue, I heard her humming a Christmas tune – I think it was "Jingle Bells" – as she approached the toilet next to me. I braced myself. A minute later, she let out a piercing scream, slammed the door and ran back toward the house crying, "Mummy, there's a monster in the toilet! There's a monster!"

I learned later that these hogs were owned by the poor "Untouchables" who lived in a separate walled-in "colony" behind the house (see sidebar). It was their job to clean toilets and deal with human waste. These hogs are called *suars* in Hindi, so our joke afterwards became that this had been our introduction to the "Ratlam Suar System."

Objects of Curiosity

From Ratlam we headed to Kesur. It was as though we had entered a time machine or were just waking up from a dream; suddenly, we were back in the nineteenth-century rhythms and mores of my forefathers' village. There was a strict hierarchy. We were told to touch the feet of our elders when we first saw them every day. I was told to append the word *hokum* ("my Lord") to the end of every sentence when I addressed my grandfather as a mark of deep respect bordering on subservience. We learned that Rajputs do not say "*Namaste*" like most Hindi-speaking Indians; we say "*Khama Ghani*" (meaning "many greetings" or "many blessings").

Our relatives found our casual American manners sorely lacking. In Indian culture, when somebody offers you something to eat or drink, you are supposed to say no. Once you accept it, you are supposed to offer it to any elders in the room before you take it yourself.

As part of the ruling land-owning family of the village, we had a lot of unearned status. Our clothes and accents made us objects of curiosity to those around us. Staring is not a taboo in Indian culture, and we were the prolonged focus of many eyes. All this may have gone to my head a little bit. Mimicking my elders, I uncharacteristically spoke arrogantly to someone in the village bazaar the first time we went there. My father muttered to someone, "*Apne mohalle mein billi bhi sher hoti hai*," a colloquialism that translates to "In its own neighborhood, even a pussycat becomes a tiger." I pretended I hadn't heard or understood. But his words stung and stayed with me: they were a window into what he really thought of me. It hadn't been like this when we lived in the United States and Canada.

After a few weeks in Kesur, we went to visit Berchha, my mother's village. As we walked from the Rowla toward one of our orchards, we encountered several stray dogs at the edge of the village. We were carrying the brand-new guns that we had brought with us from the United States: a double-barreled 12-bore shotgun, a Remington 22-caliber semiautomatic rifle, and a Beretta 45-caliber pistol. I was carrying my new pump-action air gun. Just for target practice, my father turned the rifle toward the dogs and shot three of them in quick succession. They lay on the ground quivering and bleeding out as we nonchalantly continued on our way. When they heard the shots, several stunned villagers came running and surrounded the dogs, wondering what had just happened and why. None dared say a word or even look directly at us.

This was the casual cruelty of our privileged patriarchy on display. It was an experience I would soon get used to: sudden unprovoked acts of violence with no justification, consequences, or remorse.

Hard Landing

Two months after returning to India, having visited all our close relatives, we made our way to Jabalpur, the city that would be our first home in India. As we exited the train station for the taxi ride to the university guesthouse, my heart sank. This was a singularly ugly, dirty, and smelly city. The roads were narrow, crooked, and full of potholes. The buildings were shabby and misshapen, many seemingly on the verge of collapse. On both sides of the road were open gutters filled with foul-smelling black liquid. Stray dogs and snorting hogs (the same kind we had seen in Ratlam) roamed the streets. Cows and buffalo sauntered down the middle of the road as the traffic weaved around them. Every driver had his hand permanently on the horn, contributing to the cacophony. We crossed two enormous concrete canals filled with smelly sewage water. Vultures circled above and enormous rats scurried amidst the piles of trash on either side of the open sewer.

We were not in California anymore.

As our house was not yet available, we took up residence in the university guesthouse, all five of us crammed into a single room. The campus was its own self-contained space, better ordered than the rest of the city. It comprised classroom buildings, student dorms, and fields for agricultural experiments. The rest of it was the "Agriculture Colony," numerous tan-colored, rain-stained concrete houses of varying sizes for the faculty and staff. In one corner of the campus stood four beautiful, large American-style houses with manicured lawns and rose gardens; these were for visiting professors from the United States. No such luck for returning professors from Canada; we were assigned a dingy two-bedroom duplex with a scraggly lawn and a small rooftop terrace.

My father was an associate professor at Jawaharlal Nehru Agriculture University. His salary in California was $1,500 a month; here it was Rs 800 rupees a month, or $106 at the official exchange rate, much less at the illegal market "black" rate. Narayan had never held a job in India before. The harsh economic reality of his new life hit him like a slap in the face, but he was too proud to admit it or ask his father for help. He had little left of his savings, having splurged on gifts for everyone, including his grandest gesture: a brand-new Massey Ferguson tractor that he had shipped directly from England to Kesur. To help pay the bills, he soon started selling many of the things we had brought with us (like a TV and refrigerator).

Within months, my father grew disillusioned and frustrated. How could he support his family on his meager salary? How could he do meaningful research given the lack of resources and the petty politics that prevailed in the university? He desperately searched for a way to get back to the United States, but we had surrendered our green cards upon leaving the country. There was no returning; we were well and truly stuck here.

My father invited the head of the University to our home for dinner and told him how unhappy he was with the research environment. In response, the Vice-Chancellor all but threatened to fire him. He said, "Remember, Narayan, no one is irreplaceable – not even you."

My mother was happy to be back in India amid her own people, and my baby brother was oblivious. But my father, sister, and I were each fighting our own lonely battles, struggling to cope with the harsh realities of our new lives.

School of Horrors

Perhaps school would be a respite from the general grimness that now enveloped me. In my fifth-grade class in Salinas, we affectionately called our balding teacher "Wally" or "Walnut" (his name was Mr. Walton). School was a pleasant, idyllic affair. There was laughter, play, flirting with girls at square dancing classes. I was popular, happy, and at the top of my class.

At the Christ Church Boys' Higher Secondary School, the headmaster, judging my educational preparedness purely by my ability to speak English, said, "He is a smart boy," and placed me in the eighth grade. Mind you, I had completed just three months of *sixth* grade in Canada. Making it worse, I joined the school in March, two months into the academic year.

The school resembled a medium-security prison. The uniform was starched khaki shirts and shorts, a blue striped nylon clip-on tie, wide canvas belt, and heavy black shoes. The classrooms were in a series of small, squat, shabby buildings, akin to barracks. They were barren of furnishings except for worn-out chalkboards, severely scratched-up tables, and uncomfortable, wobbly wooden chairs. It was oppressively stuffy; a grimy ceiling fan slowly churned the hot air, scattering the drowsy flies but doing nothing to cool us.

In my first class on my first day, the teacher finally noticed me after 10 minutes. He pointed at me with his chalk and said sharply, "New boy, introduce yourself!" In my California way, I replied from my chair, telling him my name and urged him and all the students to feel free to call me "Raj" instead of the more formal "Rajendra." This was met with shocked silence – except for a few barely suppressed sniggers. "Bloody fool!" the teacher thundered. "In India, we show respect to our teachers! STAND UP WHEN YOU TALK TO ME!" I stammered an apology and slowly rose to my feet, smoothing my billowing shorts.

"Where have you come from?"

"We just moved here from Canada."

"Do they not teach manners in Canada? SAY *SIR* WHEN YOU TALK TO ME!"

"Yes, Sir. I mean, no, Sir."

Glowering, and clearly pleased at his ability to subdue me, Sir turned around and proceeded to silently fill the blackboard with unintelligible math equations.

Several eternities later, the bell sounded. I ventured out into the blinding sun to eat the lunch of parathas and spiced potatoes my mother had packed for me. I sat alone under the shade of a scrawny tree, surrounded by hostile boys laughing and talking about me in Hindi.

At the end of the school day, I left the compound blinking back tears. I walked across the street to meet my sister, who had been sentenced to the female version of this penitentiary across the street. She was standing alone at the bus stop, quietly sobbing. I consoled her as best I could during the bleak 40-minute bus ride back home. We both cried the whole evening. It was our mother's birthday, one year to the day after we had left Salinas for Winnipeg in the Impala towing the U-Haul. That seemed like a surreal dream now. We sang "Happy

Birthday" to her between sobs, convinced that we ourselves would never again be happy. "We hate this horrible country," we wailed. "Please, please, can we go back to Canada?"

My father was due to return to Canada two weeks later for three months as a visiting professor (he had a contract with the University of Manitoba to do so for the first three years we were back in India). I pleaded with him to take me along, since there was no way I could continue to live in India. Desperate to be rescued from this nightmare, I composed a 17-page letter to Uncle Shyam. "Please, please let me come back and live with you. I'll mow the lawn, I'll paint the fence, I'll wear jeans, I'll look after Shaun, I'll help Auntie cook. I'll do whatever you need."

The next morning, my father took me to school on his Vespa scooter. He and the headmaster decided to demote me to the seventh grade. (I learned later that Indian school curricula were far more rigorous at each grade level than American or Canadian schools.) That day, I was able to decipher about 20% of what was going on. But at least I now knew exactly how to comport myself and escaped major humiliations. I think I called everyone "Sir," including the bus driver and some of the larger kids.

As the days and weeks wore on, I waged a lonely struggle with the Hindi alphabet, working with a tutor at home for two hours every evening. By the end of the school term in late April, I had mastered 14 of the 44 characters in the alphabet – quite an accomplishment, I thought.

When I got the midyear Hindi test, I could not read it. I wrote a little essay to the teacher (in English), explaining my predicament; she had never asked about my situation or offered any sympathy or help. I filled the rest of the exam book with line after neat line of those 14 characters I knew so well. I came home and reported that I had done well on my Hindi test. Imagine my surprise when I received a score of exactly zero out of 50 for my labors. Surely, there must have been some mistake. The same sad story was repeated in Sanskrit (the ancient language that is the Indian equivalent of Latin).

In my algebra exam, the first problem was to solve a set of three simultaneous equations in three unknowns. Since I had only recently learned the meaning of the word "algebra," I had no idea how to extract this information. I tested several hunches and found to my delight and relief that a solution of $x = 1$, $y - 2$, and $z - 3$ fit the three equations perfectly. Eureka! Quite pleased with myself, I wrote in my answer book, "Obviously and evidently, the answer is $x = 1$, $y = 2$, and $z = 3$." Imagine my chagrin when I got the exam back and found that the conspiracy to make my life miserable continued. The teacher had written, in big red characters, "Obviously and evidently, you get a zero for this answer." (I suspect he graded me harshly on the rest of the exam as well, as punishment for my insolence.)

My saving grace was English – or so I thought. The exam called for us to use pairs of similar-sounding words in sentences to show their different meanings. This seemed too obvious to me; I thought they meant that I was to use each word *twice* in the same sentence, but with a different meaning for each of the two uses. I constructed 10 sentences like "The Principal of the school promptly paid back the entire loan, including the principle and the accrued interest." Once again, I found myself misunderstood and unappreciated.

I was beginning to feel helpless and desperate. I had made no friends among the brownshirts and was failing multiple subjects; just one failure would condemn me to repeat the grade. At this rate, I would be lucky to escape that school in 20 years. After years of constructing an identity based primarily on excelling at school, this was a wrenching blow to my self-confidence.

Fortunately, my luck was about to change. At the end of that summer, we decided that since nothing could be worse than Christ Church, I should switch schools. There happened to be a more humane institution across town, which proved to be as nurturing an environment as the other had been predatory. St. Aloysius had a kind principal who said I would not have to pass Hindi or Sanskrit for a couple of years, and a sweet young English teacher named Miss Lobo who exclaimed, "What a lovely accent!" upon first hearing me speak. I could have kissed her (good thing I didn't).

At St. Aloysius, the teachers were reasonable individuals, and I soon felt more at ease – except in Sanskrit class. Mr. Shastri (the name means "scholar") was a quirky collage of tight, shiny Western suits, shaven head, a thin braided pigtail, and an elaborate horizontal *tilak* (a colored mark worn as a religious symbol by some Hindus) across the expanse of his forehead. The diminutive but fierce Mr. Shastri brooked no excuses for not memorizing the assigned Sanskrit *shlokas* (couplets), which were a complete mystery to me. Failure to do so meant standing on the desk and proffering your hands to him, which he swiftly swatted with his ever-present thin bamboo cane. While not particularly painful, the experience threatened to make me erupt into helpless laughter, as the five-foot-nothing Mr. Shastri sprung into the air on each swing to generate momentum and get a better angle on the palms of the taller boys.

The greatest joy of moving to St. Aloysius was making my first friend in India. Jitendra Malik's father worked at the same university, so he lived in my neighborhood. I was immediately drawn to this smart, sensitive, smiling, soft-spoken kid. Jitendra excelled at math and science, but also wrote beautiful stories, which he read to me as we rode the bus together every day. I stopped noticing the foul stenches and ugly sights outside the bus window. Jitendra introduced me to the British writers that most young convent-educated Indian kids were obsessed with: Enid Blyton and P. G. Wodehouse. Wodehouse was a revelation to me – to this day, I consider him the finest prose stylist and most delightful humorist I have ever read. Over the next decade, I devoured over 80 of his books.

Innocence Lost

As I walked to Jitendra's house one evening, a rough-looking kid accosted me. He demanded that I hand him my money; since I had none, he tried to take my prized American Timex watch. When I refused to give it to him, he started screaming obscenities, ending

with the Hindi equivalent of the MF word. I was immediately infuri-
ated and shouted, "How dare you insult my mother?" Blind with
rage, I pushed him hard in the chest. In an instant, I was flat on my
back on the gravel road. I caught a glint of metal and then felt the
knife's cold point pressing into my throat. He growled, "I could kill
you right now."

It was traumatic, but at least it was something I could tell my parents about and get some sympathy. What was happening at home was
worse. An uncle had moved in with us and started sexually abusing
me within weeks of our moving into that house. He was 18; I was not
yet 12. I became confused about what was right and what was wrong
and was too stricken with shame to tell anybody.

Those three traumas within a nine-month period in Jabalpur –
the torment of Christ Church, the near-death experience on the
street, and the sexual abuse at home – were assaults on my innocence,
making me fearful and hypervigilant.

Home Base Indore

I slowly adjusted to the harsh realities of our life in India. Within a
year, we were on the move again, this time to Indore, only 30 miles
from our village. My father's university had a branch campus there.
Compared to Jabalpur, Indore was a gracious and spacious city. We
settled into a rented home while we waited for my father to be allotted an official residence.

Though we had domestic help, we all had lots of chores. In those
days in India, you could not simply walk into a store and buy, for
example, flour. We got flour by first bringing wheat in large burlap
sacks from the village. My mother painstakingly went through the
wheat to remove stones and dirt and then washed and dried it in the
sun. She then poured 20 kilograms of the cleansed wheat into a square
tin. I attached it to my bicycle rack with an elastic band and took it
to a little flour mill about half a mile away. Likewise, when our cooking gas cylinder emptied, I strapped it sideways to the back of my bike
and wobbled over to the gas agency for a refill.

I was soon riding my bicycle to the various markets in the city to buy whatever was needed: fruits, vegetables, seeds, farm chemicals, tractor parts. Six days a week, through several kilometers of busy streets, I carefully ferried my little three-year-old brother, Sanjay, to his preschool before I headed to my school; he perched precariously on the bar that stretched from the seat to the handlebars. I did this through the brutally hot summers and the bone-chilling winters. I even did this wearing a raincoat and floppy hat during the months-long monsoon.

One day, I went to the government hospital to get my eyes tested. I parked my precious bike in the stand outside the hospital and locked it. The doctor put drops in my eyes to dilate them. When I came out into the bright sunlight, I could barely see anything. I went to the bike stand and looked for my bike. It was nowhere to be seen. Increasingly desperate, I kept searching. It was gone.

How could I have been so irresponsible? I knew that a new bike would cost Rs 1,000, more than a month's salary for my father. Still half-blinded, I stumbled my way home on foot. My mother was there, as she always was. I started to cry, and said, "I am so sorry, Mummy. Somebody stole my bike." She said, "*Koi baat nahin, beta*" – "It is OK, son." But I was inconsolable. How could we afford another bike for me? How would I get to school?

To this day, I do not know how our family was surviving. The math simply didn't work. Money, specifically the lack of it, was a huge thing in our lives. I felt guilty about spending anything at all.

★★★

A year and a half after our return to India, my father concocted an elaborate system for distilling hard liquor and established a bootleg operation in our rented house. Like many Rajput men, my father had to have several drinks every evening. But his salary was so low that he simply could not afford it.

To his younger brothers and nephews, my father was a demigod. They emulated him and became adept at distilling alcohol, eventually replicating the setup in Kesur; it was not unusual for two or three distilleries to be operating in different parts of the Rowla at the same time. With supply now abundant and cheap, all of them drank a lot and drank every day.

This was all illegal and reckless. My father and I never had a conversation about ethics and integrity, right and wrong. The unspoken message was "Do what you must to survive and win." Life was framed as a grim, predatory affair. A moral compass was either a luxury we could not afford or a societal nicety that we needn't bother with.

★★★

My school in Indore, St. Paul's, proved to be similar to St. Aloysius. I entered St. Paul's in ninth grade, handicapped by a middle school education that was like Swiss cheese, full of holes. I had only completed half a year of 8th grade before we moved. In a hurry to move me along, my father got the government-run school in Kesur to produce a fake report card showing that I had completed eighth grade. It showed that I had received between 35 and 40 points out of 100 in each subject (the passing grade was 33). These shameful grades were now part of my academic record.

One of my new classmates was Sangram, an affable Rajput boy who would marry my sister 14 years later. Another classmate was Sushil Shah. He lived nearby, and we soon became best friends. He was born and had lived in Kenya until he was 10, part of the large expatriate Gujarati community that controlled much of the economy there. Many had the same last name, Shah. Sushil and I shared an outsider perspective. He was extremely intelligent, but unlike me, was also savvy and street-smart. He had a quick wit and knew how to hold his own, despite not being as big as many other boys. His family were vegetarian teetotalers, the opposite of mine. I enjoyed visiting his calm and ordered home, and he enjoyed coming to our house for parties where meat and liquor were abundant. My father liked Sushil; I think he saw a little bit of himself in him: the combination of a brilliant mind with real-world shrewdness. He probably hoped that a little bit of the latter would rub off on me.

By then, I was reading and writing Hindi at about a third-grade level. In ninth grade, I confronted "Higher Hindi," a phrase that still evokes terror in me. I nearly wept when I saw what this would entail: seven textbooks, including a volume comprising a dense 300-stanza poem. Written Hindi is almost an entirely distinct language from spoken Hindi, and I was hopelessly at sea. The teacher, an ascetic white-haired gentleman named Mr. Bapat, bore my ineptitude with good humor. After I received failing grades in the first two monthly Hindi tests, he declared that if I ever did get a passing grade (a low bar of 4 out of 10), every other student's score would be increased by a full point. This united the entire class behind my Hindi-learning efforts; it was touching to see their selfless concern for my learning and growth! I finally rewarded them midway through tenth grade.

The teacher who influenced me the most was my English teacher, Mrs. Kamath. An elderly, tall, serious woman who walked with a noticeable limp, Mrs. Kamath read a piece I had written called "Food for Thought" and said, "Raj, you have a gift for writing. I hope you will keep it up." Her words were deeply affirming to me. I had always been a voracious reader but hadn't done much writing.

High school ended with a statewide exam in math, physics, chemistry, English, and Hindi — a make-or-break event that determined which college you would get into, which could set you up for life or doom you to irrelevance and poverty. Having struggled for years to catch up with my peers at school, my prospects were not good.

My savior was Sushil. He and I studied together all day, every day, for three months leading up to the exam. We both did exceedingly well; he ranked second in our class and I was fourth. His performance was not at all a surprise; mine was a stunner. I was like one of those unheralded horses in a race that emerges out of nowhere; nobody saw me coming!

A few months shy of my 16th birthday, I was ready for college. But what would I study?

Reflections

Readjusting to life in India was one of the hardest things I ever had to do in my life. Every aspect was challenging, from school to friendships to navigating the complexities of an extended family. But looking back, I am grateful I had that opportunity. Had we not moved back to India then, I would have grown up oblivious of my culture and language. I would never have developed a deep love for Indian music. I would have felt rootless and disconnected from my extended family.

This is an example of "Good thing, bad thing, who knows?" We are usually quick to label things as good or bad based on the immediate impact they have on our lives and mental state. But difficult events often result in long-term growth. Make a list of such incidents in your life. What can you say about them looking back that you could not see in the moment? How will that cause you to look differently at seeming setbacks in life that take you in an unexpected direction?

The stark realities of the caste system had a great impact on me. I came to recognize how fortunate I was, all my challenges notwithstanding. I had deep sympathy for underdogs. It awakened my social consciousness.

When was the first time you noticed the injustices and inequities around you? How did you rationalize or make sense of them?

I had been a confident and successful student in California and Canada. Rather than giving me time to adjust, my father rushed me through my middle school years in India, so that I spent only about one year combined in the sixth, seventh, and eighth grades. That shattered my confidence just as I was entering my vulnerable and challenging teenage years. I never fully recovered.

What challenges did you face as you entered adolescence? Were there holes or gaps in your development? How did you overcome them?

The nine months I spent in Jabalpur were quite traumatic. I had largely buried the memories of my encounter with the knife-wielding kid and the sexual abuse by my uncle. Both incidents certainly had a long-term impact on me.

Are there traumatic experiences buried in your past? Rather than deny or minimize them, acknowledge them and speak about them. With trauma, most people "conceal it, numb it, and relive it." Instead, try to "reveal it, feel it, and heal it." This opens the possibility of experiencing "post-traumatic growth." You can emerge from the experience stronger and more resourceful than if you had never experienced the trauma in the first place — what is now labeled "post-traumatic growth."

4

Return to Kesur

My most adventurous, carefree times in the early years after we returned to India were at our ancestral home in Kesur, where my grandfather, my father's brothers, and their families lived. Away from my father's scrutiny, I spent these breaks driving the tractor, plowing the fields, and hauling sand, gravel, bricks, and fertilizer in a clanging trolley over the unpaved rutted paths that connected our house and our land.

We also visited Kesur during religious festivals. These included the big three: Holi, Diwali, and Dussehra. We celebrated each in a grand way, but Dussehra – symbolizing the triumph of Lord Rama over the demon Ravana – was the most significant for Rajputs.

The most anticipated event of every Dussehra was a music and dance program with a "nautch girl" brought in from the big city. Everyone in Kesur referred to her as the *Randi*, which means prostitute, though her only role on these occasions was to dance and entertain.

The Rowla was open to everyone in the village on this day. At dusk, people started streaming in to take up prime viewing positions on the ground in the large square inner courtyard just past the massive entry doorway (tall enough for an elephant to get through). When the Randi and her supporting cast arrived, they were given a makeshift "green room" next to the dance area. We kids cast eager

47

glances in that direction, imagining what was going on within. Bright red rose-flavored and orange-flavored local liquor flowed freely, provided by my grandfather. Soon, the music welled up from the harmonium, the *tabla* player struck up a heart-stopping beat, and the Randi undulated out from the shadows toward the brightly lit center, her stomping feet with their jingling anklets keeping time with the pulsating music.

Nothing untoward ever happened, since the Randi danced until daylight, surrounded by hundreds of leering and increasingly drunk men. But the whole affair carried the unmistakable scent of sin. Prohibited from witnessing the spectacle directly, the women of the Rowla crowded on the inside of the large door separating the outer courtyard and public portions from the private area within. They giggled and peered over and around one another through the crevices in the door to glimpse this heroically wanton woman, singing and swaying her hips while the inebriated men uproariously egged her on. Every so often, a man stood up on wobbly feet waving a one- or five-rupee note, circled it over the Randi's bobbing head, and dropped it to the floor. Without missing a beat, the musicians swept it into the growing pile between their instruments.

In Rajput culture, Dussehra is also a time for coming-of-age rituals for young boys. This included learning how to tie a *saffa* (a turban worn by Rajputs) and beheading a goat with a sword. Both rituals took place at the local Hanuman Temple (Hanuman was the monkeygod who helped the virtuous god Ram battle the evil demon Ravana and rescue his kidnapped wife Sita). I could not master the saffa-tying technique; the unwieldy pile kept falling off my head. It did not help that my instructor was a perpetually drunk uncle from the other Rowla. The lesson invariably turned into a kind of slapstick comedy routine that had everyone in splits.

At the conclusion of the *havan* (a Vedic purification ritual involving the burning of ghee and food) came a grimmer rite of passage: the ritual goat beheading. This is a prized skill among Rajputs. One of my uncles was renowned for his ability to behead a goat of any size with a one-armed swing of his massive sword.

The scene was right out of *Indiana Jones and the Last Crusade*: drums beating, men holding flaring torches, a roaring crowd. One man crouched behind the goat, holding its hind legs. The frantic goat, its bleating drowned out in the din, hopped around on its front legs. My uncle handed me a heavy sword and told me to deliver a smooth, angled blow to the neck of the goat. If I (and the goat) were lucky, the head would come off cleanly, bouncing across the dirt, still bleating silently, the rest of the body twitching and bleeding profusely.

I jumped around trying to get a decent angle on the goat's neck and finally took a swing. The sword landed a glancing blow, injuring my pride more than the goat's neck. My uncle took the sword from my shaking hands to finish the job. The crowd started mocking me: "Try chopping onions next time!" "Put on a skirt and bangles!"

Failing to kill the goat, I instead wreaked havoc on smaller creatures using my new air gun. I had never held a gun until then, but that air gun soon became a bodily appendage. It gave me a strange kind of power which was seductive while it lasted.

I soon became a sharpshooter, firing at frogs, squirrels, birds, snakes, and lizards – without reason or mercy – simply because I could. The gun wasn't powerful enough to kill larger animals, but I could take down people's chickens and get them cooked in our kitchen.

I soon gained a reputation as a terror in Kesur – a strangely incoherent child (with my broken Hindi) intent on killing anything that moved. One day, I shot a pigeon and badly wounded it. Flapping its one functioning wing, it landed on a ledge deep inside a well behind the Rowla and staged a drawn-out death scene. This well was the principal source of drinking water for the surrounding houses, including ours. The women who were there to fetch water screamed at me, saying, "What's wrong with you, you demon-child? How can we drink this water now?"

That was the day I stopped the wanton killing. I turned into a partial pacifist, only shooting animals we ate, like wild rabbits. When I told my father, he got angry. "Why would you stop killing? What is wrong with killing?"

The Darker Side of Kesur

The first time we went to Kesur after returning from abroad, I heard a stream of profanities coming from a small corner room. It was my uncle, my father's older brother. I soon learned why he was locked up in that room.

Bhupendra, known to all as Kunwar Sahib, was born the heir apparent as the next Thakur of Kesur. In his youth, he had been an impressive and beloved figure: tall, handsome, gentle of manner. My grandfather relied on him; my father looked up to him.

A few months after his marriage, Bhupendra's demeanor started changing. It began with brief lapses into uncontrollable fury, after which he reverted to his natural gentle state. Over the next few years, the unsettling episodes became more frequent. Eventually, my grandfather had him locked up with a chain around his leg. He spent the next 25 years of his life there, until he died. Naked most of the time, Bhupendra raged and thundered day and night, yelling out foul curses and flinging himself against the wall. People in the village could hear him through the window. The terrible sounds coming from that room became an indelible part of my childhood memories, the background soundtrack to my visits to Kesur.

I gradually became desensitized to his presence in the Rowla, paying little attention to him, just as my uncles and cousins did. Decades later, I would learn the truth of what had triggered Bhupendra's descent into madness. In the meantime, I noticed things about Kesur that were jarring to my sensibilities.

A year after our return to India, a servant from the village was sent to work for us in the city, a bright-eyed, energetic boy named Bhattia. A couple of months after he started working for us, Bhattia committed some minor transgression, word of which got back to the village. My cousin Ranjeet (Bhupendra's oldest son) soon came to the city to punish him. Bhattia started crying and begged for forgiveness, to no avail. Ranjeet dragged him out to the yard. He tied one end of a rope to a tree and the other tightly around Bhattia's waist. He then took off his belt and whipped Bhattia, as passersby on the street stopped and stared.

I was shocked and paralyzed, unable to say a word. I tried to console Bhattia afterwards, but it was too late. The beating extinguished the lively spirit that had defined him. He soon returned to the village.

Eventually, I realized that this incident was not about my cousin's brutality. Ranjeet was generally genial and likable. However, as the oldest son of the oldest son, he was bred to inherit the mantle of patriarch. His pride in being a Rajput and the future Thakur of Kesur was palpable. In his mind, he was just doing his duty, harsh as that might be; tempering justice with mercy would be a sign of weakness.

The dark side of Kesur ran deep, as I soon discovered.

Ranjeet's younger brother Himmat (meaning courage) was a jovial but hot-headed kid known for his daring. I watched in awe as he retrieved dripping honeycombs from high up in trees, nonchalantly blowing cigarette smoke to temporarily blind the angry swarming bees.

Other than my father, Himmat was the only one who dared to speak back to my grandfather. He even mocked my grandfather, telling him that he knew what went on in the little cottage in one of our orchards.

I learned later that the cottage was where our grandfather had sex with women farm workers. Many of the women's husbands, brothers, and children also worked on the farm. Even if the husbands were aware of what was happening, they were powerless to do anything about it.

After a period of particularly intense clashes with his grandfather, Himmat finally snapped. He put on multiple layers of clothing and ran to the shed where my grandfather stored petrol, diesel, and kerosene in large metal drums. Using a rickety tin hand pump, he filled up a 20-liter container with kerosene and carried it to the inner courtyard.

Like many Hindu households, the Rowla had a masonry structure in the center of the inner courtyard that housed a *tulsi* (holy basil) plant. Standing next to it, Himmat shouted, "I have had enough!" His mother and others in the house ran to the courtyard. They were used to his wildness but had never seen him like this. As they watched in horror, he lifted the kerosene container and emptied it over his head, soaking his clothes and creating a large puddle on the ground. Before anyone could react, he struck a match and lit himself on fire. The layers of clothes flared into an inferno within seconds. Engulfed in flames and screaming in agony, Himmat ran out the back entrance of the Rowla and down the hill to the river. He dove into the water to douse the flames, but the damage was done; he was horribly burned over 90% of his body.

The phone rang upstairs in our landlord's home in Indore (we lived on the lower level and did not have a phone). My father immediately got into the Impala and drove the 30 miles to Kesur. It took him nearly two hours. The semiconscious Himmat was lowered onto the back seat, covered in blankets. He was softly moaning, his eyes rolling up in his head, his head resting in his sobbing mother's lap. As fast as he could, my father drove to the burn hospital in Indore.

The next day, I went to visit Himmat in the hospital. Only a small part of his face was visible through the bandages that covered most of his body. The horrible smell of burnt human flesh became seared into my memory (which I would flash back to 30 years later as another cousin lay dying in another burn hospital). Over the next few days, I fed him protein biscuits, which the doctor told us his body needed. It was no use. Himmat died a week later, the morning after telling his mother about a vision in which "God said he would take me tonight." The doctor told us that diving into the river was what killed him. If the fire had been put out by other means, he might have survived.

I was 14. It was dawning on me that there was a malevolence in Kesur that I hadn't realized. I was seeing the human consequences of my grandfather's iron-fisted loveless rule. Himmat had not been the first casualty. Nor would he be the last. His death occasioned no introspection, no questioning of what led this spirited young man to take his own life in such a gruesome manner.

I started noticing the casual cruelty of my uncles and cousins. I also saw despair and smoldering anger in the eyes of servants and farm workers. I realized how they were exploited and treated as objects.

On Saturday mornings, the workers came to the Rowla to be paid for the previous week. My uncles often refused to pay them. My youngest uncle was especially cruel. He toyed with the workers, contemptuously throwing money at them or paying them far less than they were owed. The men sat on their haunches on the ground pleading, sometimes crying. The women, their heads covered, told him in quiet deferential voices how many days they had worked. My uncle would look at his poorly maintained account book and accuse them of lying. They had no recourse. His callousness toward these hardworking people living on the edge of starvation stunned me. I knew for certain that none of us could do the work they did, their frail bodies laboring in the scorching sun for 10–12 hours a day, seven days a week, every week of the year other than religious holidays.

One day, that uncle was plowing a field on a tractor. A worker he had mistreated one time too many finally cracked. Mad with rage and resentment, he ran with an axe toward the tractor. Because of the noise of the engine, my uncle did not hear him approach. Intent on killing him, the worker swung his axe in a wide arc, the sharp edge aimed directly at my uncle's head. Fortunately, the tractor had a metal frame around the driver's seat (to which a canvas could be attached for shade). The blade of the axe struck the frame. The axe spun around and the blunt side struck my uncle on the side of his head. He was badly hurt but not killed. The worker ran away but was soon caught, viciously beaten by the police, and thrown in jail.

A deep gash remained where the blade had struck the frame – a mute reminder of the consequences of abusing the powerless without reason or remorse. From that day on, we were warned to always carry a gun with us, not to hunt or ward off animals in the forest, but for self-protection.

Trickle-Down Tyranny

The architect of this house of suffering was my grandfather Girwar. His father, Hari Singh, had been a mild-mannered and generous soul who never refused to help anyone in need. Unscrupulous workers and traders often cheated him out of what he didn't give away, and he ended up with enormous debts. Girwar was his opposite – tough as nails and incredibly driven. He worked maniacally to pay off the debts, reclaim the mortgaged ancestral land, rebuild the family's economic foundation, and construct a new Rowla. Unusually for those times, he sidelined his still living father and took control of the house and land.

A hard-core old-school patriarch, Girwar sired a large family – 13 kids, of whom only six survived. His wife was a meek, simple woman whose presence barely registered. Girwar regularly beat her. She went a little mad in her 40s and died in her 50s.

Girwar ruled over the women in the household with an iron fist and an extraordinarily profane mouth, regularly berating them for their supposed transgressions. They cowered in silence during his outbursts, heads down and faces covered past the chin (he never once saw the faces of any of his daughters-in-law, including my mother).

The men and boys fared little better. The household was devoid of love and filled with fear and abuse and a single-minded focus on hard work and money. Everyone and everything depended on the patriarch. All the income from the farm flowed to my grandfather, and he paid every expense. He kept everything of value locked up. Most of his children and grandchildren routinely stole from him: breaking into his closet to steal money, siphoning and selling petrol and diesel, selling grain from the storage bin.

My grandfather weaponized his wealth, using it as a tool to reward or punish his children and grandchildren. To hide money from his thieving kids, he buried bundles of cash in metal containers underground. We found the rusted hulks years later; worms had eaten away the now-worthless notes.

My father and grandfather engaged in frequent, prolonged clashes, shouting at each other for hours. Narayan's recurring plaintive refrain was, "Why did you bring us into this world if you insist on controlling every part of our lives?"

The only time I ever confronted my fearsome grandfather was when I was 14, after he and my father had another of their epic confrontations. My grandfather had called my father a *gunda*, which means "gangster" or "hired thug." Outraged, I demanded to know how he could say such a thing to my father, still a heroic figure in my youthful eyes. My grandfather was stunned into silence at being confronted by mild-mannered me. He later asked my cousin if I had been drinking.

Reflections

Kesur was an environment in which everyone in my family had a lot of unearned status and respect among the villagers. This can have a corrosive effect on a young psyche, unless the adults in your life guide you and put things into perspective. Unfortunately, that was not true for me. The adults around me reveled in their unearned privilege.

> *If you are reading this book, you are likely among the more fortunate ones on this planet. At what age did you recognize your own privilege? Did you take it for granted, or were you grateful for it?*

The experience at the Hanuman temple was a public humiliation and an illustration of the toxic masculinity that pervaded our culture. It left a lasting scar on my psyche until I could put it in perspective.

> *Can you recall similar episodes from your childhood? Have you been able to get over them?*

When I witnessed the horrific scene of my cousin whipping the servant, I did not speak up. I have always regretted not stepping in to prevent such cruel treatment.

Can you recall an instance when you stood silent when faced with actions that were clearly wrong? How would your reaction today be different?

My cousin Himmat killed himself, but it was really the toxic patriarchy that killed him. Many are driven to despair by the harshness, lack of respect, and absence of love that characterize such systems; some succumb to that despair by taking their own lives.

Have you ever witnessed the consequences of a toxic patriarchy in your family or at a workplace?

The chickens eventually come home to roost. The consequences of my uncles' abusive behavior were inevitable. You can only torture people for so long before they revolt.

Can you recall examples of delayed retribution by people who were treated unfairly in the past?

When a tone of abuse and oppression gets set at the top, it trickles down; everybody becomes a petty tyrant in their own way.

Can you think of families or companies where a tone of abusive behavior at the top causes others to behave the same way?

5

No Time to Dream

As I neared the end of high school and considered career options, I was confronted with the harsh economic reality of India in the mid-1970s.

In those days in India, nobody asked, "What's your dream? What's your passion?" Even asking such questions was a luxury. The only relevant question was, "How the hell are you going to get a job and survive in the world?" Unlike for my cousins, going back to the village was not an option for me. But my prospects in the outside world were not good. India had been run as a semi-socialist democracy since Independence in 1947. The country's first prime minister, Jawaharlal Nehru, deemed that the government should control the "commanding heights" of the economy, through direct ownership and heavy oversight. As a result, India had a centrally planned economy with a huge public sector; government-owned corporations dominated many sectors. Stifling government regulations bred stagnation and massive corruption.

Nehru's autocratic daughter, Indira Gandhi, became prime minister in 1966 and doubled down on state domination. She nationalized all the country's banks in 1969. The oil crisis of 1973 quadrupled the price of oil, crippling an already anemic economy. Taxes were numbingly high; the highest marginal income tax rate in 1974, the year I graduated from high school, was 97.75%![1] Per capita GDP that year was $163.[2] The economy was virtually closed to the world; non-oil, non-food imports amounted to a miniscule 3% of India's GDP in 1975. Tariff barriers were ridiculous, with import duties as high as 300%. People spoke half-jokingly of the "Hindu rate of growth" – India's per capita income growth averaged 1.3% per year from the 1950s to the 1980s, while the population grew 2.3% a year.

The heavily protected domestic industries made shoddy and expensive products. For example, there were only two car models available – an Italian Fiat model from 1953 and a British Morris model from 1955. There was a four-year waiting list to get one of them – if you could afford it. Few in the middle class could, so they bought one of two available brands of scooters (the Italian brands Vespa and Lambretta, both produced in India) and ferried around families of up to five or six on them. There was a seven-year waiting list for those! There was a vibrant "black market" for people unwilling to wait. Phone service was a government monopoly; that meant a 14-year waiting list to get a clunky, unreliable phone.

We had few career options. Our school had no career counselors; we had to figure things out on our own. Those proficient at math and science tried to get into one of the few engineering schools that existed. If you were good at biology and science, you strove to get into medicine. If you weren't in either of those two categories, God help you! You could get a Bachelor of Commerce degree and try to become a chartered accountant, or get a Bachelor of Arts and pray that you had enough connections to land a government job with petty power, miniscule pay, and the opportunity to take bribes.

I had no idea where to apply or what I should study. My father asked around and came up with two options. One was for me to join the merchant navy, the world of commercial shipping. That would

[1] https://www.business-standard.com/article/interim-budget-2019/the-70-year-journey-of-income-tax-in-india-from-a-peak-of-97-75-to-30-119013000397_1.html#:~:text=By%20FY%201973%2D74%2C%20the,limit%20of%2070%20per%20cent

[2] https://www.macrotrends.net/countries/IND/india/gdp-per-capita

mean years of quasi-militaristic training, followed by a life of mostly living on a ship. The other option was engineering school. Being good at math and science and having abandoned biology after eighth grade, my path was obvious. It certainly seemed less distressing to me than being marooned at sea for months on end. My father heard about an elite institution called the Birla Institute of Technology and Science (BITS), a philanthropic venture started by G. D. Birla, one of India's leading industrialists. Birla had been a close supporter of Mahatma Gandhi. To aid in nation-building, he established a world-class university in Pilani, his hometown in Rajasthan (the state my ancestors came from).

A big believer in the importance and power of education, my father traveled alone to Pilani – an arduous 20-hour train and bus journey each way – to explore the campus, talk to the admissions staff, and sample the food. He liked what he saw and came back with the application form, including a spare copy. Meanwhile, my friend Sushil was also trying to figure out what he should do. When I told him about BITS, he applied as well. We were both admitted to this iconic institution.

There was one problem: How would we pay for it? The fee was nominal: Rs 500 a semester for tuition and housing. The primary cost was food, which came to about Rs 200 a month – which my father could certainly not afford. He dispatched me to Kesur, saying, "You need to ask your grandfather to pay for this." After some joshing about whether engineering was a worthy career path for a Rajput, my grandfather agreed to fund my education.

With a blend of excitement and trepidation, Sushil and I set out together for Pilani, our metal trunks packed with all our worldly possessions. After an overnight train journey to Jaipur, we boarded a bus for the dusty five-hour ride to Pilani. At the bus stop, we clambered onto creaky cycle rickshaws and rolled through the Institute gate.

The campus was an impressive sight. Though surrounded by a sandy desert, it was green and vibrant. It was also relatively empty. We "freshers" were the only students on campus for the first week, along with a few unfortunates who had been forced to stay back in the brutal heat to take remedial summer courses.

The campus had 12 dorms (called hostels) for boys and one for girls. Our class had 400 boys and eight girls. The hostels were named after religious or political figures: Ram, Buddha, Krishna, Gandhi, Ashok, Rana Pratap (my ancestor), and so on. Sushil and I were allotted adjacent single rooms in Vishwakarma Bhavan for the first week. Feeling homesick, we moved both our beds into one room and our study tables and chairs into the other. That way, we could talk to each other at night to ease our anxiety. This comforting arrangement was short-lived; within a couple of days, senior students started taunting us as homosexuals. We hastily rearranged our furniture back to the way it was.

We set out to explore what would be our world for the next five years. In contrast to the chaos of much of India, the campus was an orderly oasis. The massive cream-colored main Institute building with its iconic clock tower in the middle sat at one end of a great lawn. Hostels lined the longer sides of the lawn. Just beyond the other end of the lawn and facing the Institute tower was the Saraswati Mandir, a spectacular white marble temple festooned with countless carvings (Saraswati is the Hindu goddess of knowledge, music, art, speech, wisdom, and learning). Next to that was a little shopping area known as Connaught, named after the main commercial area in New Delhi (which itself had copied the name from London), where we walked to most evenings for milkshakes, iced coffees, restaurant meals, birthday celebrations, haircuts, magazines, stationery, and other essentials.

Between each pair of hostels was a dining hall or "mess." For the first week, the freshers were housed in two hostels and ate in the same mess. Amid the clamoring of steel trays and nonstop chatter, I noticed an unusually tall, reed-thin Sikh student robotically walking behind each row of boys, making deliberate eye contact with each boy on the other side of the table. Periodically, he reached across with his long arm, glued a postage stamp on the forehead of a student, and murmured something. Finally, he came to our table and stamped Sushil and me. He bent down and whispered, "3:30 p.m., 162 Ram Bhavan.

If you don't show up, God help you. But I doubt that even God can help you, because God is a freshman this year."

Sushil and I dutifully showed up at his room at 3:30; he ordered us to sweep out his room and the corridor outside it. This was our introduction to ragging (or hazing).

Despite being outlawed by the country's Supreme Court, ragging remains a highly abusive part of college life in India. In most colleges then, ragging continued as long as you were a student. As you moved up the hierarchy, you continued to get ragged by those senior to you and got to rag those who were your juniors. Ragging was often psychologically and physically abusive. Fortunately, BITS had established a more benign tradition: it only permitted ragging for the first month, which ended with a "Freshers Welcome" feast.

But for that month it could get intense. As I had discovered in Kesur, unearned power reveals people's true natures, bringing out latent sadistic tendencies in many. Some boys were ingenious in devising ways to torment freshers, such as ordering them to sit on vertical Coke bottles. If the ragging was good-natured and fun, I went along with it. But if somebody crossed a line, I refused to comply. I said, "If you're going to rag me, rag me properly. Otherwise, I'm leaving." I had discovered a steely core of courage within me that would not allow bullies to get their way.

After orientation week, I settled into Buddha Bhavan. I soon discovered that a cultural caste system existed among the students. The westernized students who listened to rock 'n' roll music, wore jeans, and smoked pot were known as "casters." The rest of us, who preferred Indian music and had simpler tastes, were known as "maisters." The two groups rarely mixed.

Everyone at BITS had been an outstanding student in high school. The competition among students was intense, since professors graded us on a curve; only 10% got an A in any course, and about the same percentage had to fail. In my first semester, the momentum of my intense preparation for the high school exam served me well; I ended up with three As and a B.

Our life was largely contained within the campus. Occasionally, we ventured out to a dilapidated movie theater in town called Jay-shree Talkies. Sitting in the threadbare chairs with protruding springs, we noticed shuffling movements above us in the red cloth that hung under the ceiling. We could see the silhouettes of rats scurrying about. Fortunately, none ever fell on us. Our annual cultural festival called Oasis took place in October. It attracted talented actors, musicians, singers, and glamorous women from colleges all over the country. Oasis was the social highlight of the year for us; otherwise, ours was a pretty drab, all-boys, all-books existence.

Summers were long and unbearably hot, reaching 120°F. There was no air-conditioning anywhere on campus except for the room that housed an IBM 1430 mainframe computer. It hardly rained. Winters were bone-chillingly cold, dropping close to freezing at night. There was no heating, so we covered ourselves with woolen hats, heavy jackets, wraparound shawls – anything to warm ourselves. We sought the sun like flowering plants or cold-blooded reptiles.

And then there were the sandstorms. The sky suddenly darkened and the howling wind whipped the sand off the ground and swirled it around. We used wet towels to seal the crevices around our doors and windows. In the aftermath, a fine sheen of sand covered every surface and every item in our rooms. It penetrated our hair and our nostrils, even our food.

My Luck Runs Out

At the end of the first semester, I returned to a new home. My father was now the director of a wheat research station in a remote location. Ten days later, I received a telegram; the BITS student union had decided that we would be on strike to begin the next semester. At issue: whether the students or the Institute should pay the wages of the workers who made our food and served us. This was a selfish, entitled action by the students. BITS heavily subsidized our world-class education; we paid only Rs 500 a semester for tuition, rental textbooks, and housing. The foolish, self-indulgent strike lasted nearly two months before the students finally capitulated.

I was ready to return with a trunk full of new clothes, boxes of my favorite sweets that my mother had made, Rs 500 of spending money that was to last me the whole semester, my autograph collection, and my prized international money collection. Every time my father visited another country, he brought back their currency notes and coins for me. During the extended break, I had polished the coins and organized everything in an album.

On the overnight train journey to Delhi, I slept on an upper-level berth. My metal trunk was under the bottom berth two levels below. I woke up in the early dawn as the train pulled into Mathura (revered as the birthplace of the Hindu god Krishna). I slipped on my shoes and reached under the seat for my trunk. To my horror, nothing was there. I frantically searched all around in a growing panic. It was gone. I saw another BITS student I recognized and asked to borrow some money so I could get back home. He gave me what he had. I got off the train just as it was pulling away.

My heart pounding hard, I walked toward the railway police station. The constable behind the counter wordlessly pushed a form toward me to report the theft. When I filled the form out in English, the cops mocked me for not using Hindi, adding to my misery. Far from "serving and protecting," police in India often harass and intimidate the powerless. Most are corrupt and completely lack compassion.

The next train heading back to my hometown was not for another eight hours. I had no extra money to buy food or drink. I sat all day in a daze on a metal bench, berating myself and consumed with guilt. Not only had I lost the 500 rupees and my irreplaceable money collection, that trunk also contained my newly tailored clothes, which had cost my parents another 800 rupees. The scale of the loss, to my distraught mind, was insurmountable. Just as I had when somebody stole my bicycle, I blamed myself for being so careless. But nobody had warned me that I needed to secure my trunk to the frame of the seat with a chain and lock.

When the train finally arrived, it was overflowing with people, as all trains were in India. I sat down on the cold grimy floor outside the toilet and barely moved for the next 16 hours. The train finally pulled in around dawn to the station closest to our house. With no money for a rickshaw, I walked to the house, reaching just as my parents were sitting down for tea. It shocked them to see me. I had held it together for 24 hours, but now burst into tears. I told them what had happened and apologized profusely for being such a costly burden. My mom was loving and compassionate, as I expected, but my dad surprised me by being understanding as well. He did seem a bit shaken at the financial blow.

Meanwhile, my classes in Pilani had started without me. After giving me a few days to regain my equilibrium, my father told me to go to Kesur to ask my grandfather for money to buy a new trunk and to get new clothes made. Buying "ready-made" clothes was not an option then. You had to go to a cloth shop, pick out the right colors and patterns and fabrics, get them to cut the right amount, and then take it to a tailor who took your measurements and stitched your clothes in a week or so.

It all took a lot of time, and my anxiety was mounting. I finally made it back to campus two-and-a-half weeks after classes started and was immediately floundering. With a five-course load, I struggled to catch up. The semester extended long into the summer because of the strike. I managed to get one A, three Bs, and my first C. My GPA plummeted, along with my confidence.

BITS was an intensely competitive environment. It was also a land of broken – or at least diverted – dreams. All the students came there to get an engineering degree, but only half eventually did. Uniquely in India, BITS had created (in partnership with the Massachusetts Institute of Technology) an innovative, integrated five-year curriculum that included liberal arts courses. We all started with no majors. At the end of the first year, 86% of the students entered the engineering and science stream, while 14% had to pick another major, such as economics, pharmacology, or English literature.

It depended on your GPA. At the end of the second year, 50% of the 86% made it into engineering, while the other 36% had to pick a science major such as math, physics, or chemistry. At the end of the third year, you got assigned to your major within engineering: chemical, mechanical, electrical, electronics, or a combination of electrical and electronics. Again, it depended on your GPA and the relative demand for majors. It was heartbreakingly common for students to become deeply depressed and even commit suicide when they could not get their desired major in this competitive jungle.

Grim Survivor

I had an almost total collapse as I entered my second year. We had to survive some incredibly challenging courses. In thermodynamics, the average score on the first test was 16 out of 100; the top score was 34. Mine was 12. A course in modern physics introduced me to the befuddling world of quantum mechanics and Schrödinger's equation. The textbook, appropriately enough, was by H. J. Pain.

I barely understood what was going on and did not know which way to turn. I was still reeling from the shock of the previous semester: the train theft, the money I had squandered, coming back late, and getting poor grades. Now my guilt intensified. How could I waste all the money that my family was spending on me? I felt utterly helpless and worthless.

I cried alone in my room every night, suffering intensely from impostor syndrome. I thought, "I don't deserve to be here. The only reason I am here was because I did well on my high school exam, which was only because Sushil helped me." I was ashamed to ask Sushil for help again. He was getting straight As every semester; at the end of the five-year program, he would rank second out of 400, with all As and just a couple of Bs in English. He didn't even have to study very hard; he was just inherently brilliant. I felt myself drifting away from him, thinking, "Why should he waste his time with a loser?" Our friendship weakened as I sought the company of those I could relate to, those who were also struggling in this cutthroat environment.

I wrote anguished, apologetic, tear-stained letters home. My father told me to drop the semester if I needed to. But I did not know what that would mean, so I soldiered on. The semester finally ended. I had one B, three Cs, and my first D. My GPA took another precipitous drop. From 9.39 (out of 10) my first semester, I was now down in the sevens.

It became all about survival now. The fourth semester was a little better than the third; I was still flailing in deep water but my feet were now touching the ground. The drops in my GPA became less steep. I squeaked past the threshold needed to get into the engineering stream. A year later, I did just well enough to make it into the electrical and electronics engineering major. I found a few courses I enjoyed and did well in. But one nearly killed me, called "UHF and Microwaves." I still get nightmares about that course. It did not help that the professor had leprosy and was missing several fingers.

Political Awakening

During the shortened summer break after my first year (because of the strike), I was heading to my mother's village from the nearby town of Nagda in an oxcart. On a portable radio we heard the shocking news: Prime Minister Indira Gandhi had declared a state of emergency in the country. Two weeks earlier, the Allahabad High Court had declared her election void because of illegal practices. The judge ordered her to vacate her seat in Parliament (known as the Lok Sabha, or People's Assembly). Egged on by her despotic son Sanjay and suspicious of her ministers, she centralized all power in the Prime Minister's office. She refused to resign in the face of mounting protests around the country and declared a state of emergency on June 25, 1975. She cut off electric power to newspapers, suspended elections, curbed civil liberties, and rounded up and imprisoned hundreds of political opponents. She and her son issued a 25-point plan for radical "reforms," including a brutal campaign of forced sterilization of men to get the birthrate down. Over the following year, the government sterilized 8.3 million men, most against their will.

Indira Gandhi's attempts to destroy our fledgling 28-year-old democracy outraged me. Such actions could well lead to the death of democracy; I shuddered at the prospect of a despotic future for India, a swerve toward the brutal repressive politics of Pakistan. When I returned to Pilani, I joined an underground movement against the Emergency, attending secret meetings where we listened to smuggled speeches on cassette tapes by imprisoned political leaders.

The Emergency lasted 21 months. Indira Gandhi finally remembered what India stood for. Defying her son, she ended the Emergency and announced fresh elections. A frenetic political campaign ensued. Many opposition parties united into a new party called the Janata, or People's Party. The day the election results were announced, I was in Delhi. I staked out a position outside the *Indian Express* building; this was the newspaper that had shown the most courage during the Emergency. On a large board, newspaper workers periodically updated the election results. As the evening wore on, the crowd grew euphoric as the opposition neared a landslide majority. The electorate had dealt Mrs. Gandhi and her dictatorial ways a massive rebuke.

★★★

That summer, I was in Delhi for my first internship or "practice school" at the ancient Birla Cotton Spinning and Weaving Mills. I was supposed to learn how a textile factory operates. The first day I stepped into that mill, I nearly collapsed from the combination of intense heat, the almost 100% humidity that had to be maintained inside for the spinning and weaving machines to operate properly, and the unbearably loud clanging noise. Fibers of cotton floated in the air, being inhaled by the huge number of people who worked in the dilapidated structure. It was hellish.

Years later, I read Alexis de Tocqueville's description of the textile mills of Manchester in 1835 and it reminded me of that experience in Delhi: "Here humanity attains its most complete development and its most brutish, here civilization works its miracles and civilized man is turned almost into a savage."[3]

Fortunately, my friend and classmate Rajiv lived in a house on the premises, as his father was the Chief Labor Officer of the mill. For most of that summer, we sat comfortably in Rajiv's living room being served snacks and sweets and drinking tea while a succession of managers briefed us about plant operations. This was my idea of engineering!

I entered the fifth and final year of the program. It was time for Practice School 2, a semester-long experience. I ended up at the Central Bank of India in Bombay. They asked me to assess a couple of technology businesses that were seeking loans. Of course, I had no idea what I was doing. Mostly, I treated that time as a paid vacation. I indulged my writing hobby, creating, editing, and writing for a publication we called *Bombay Newsletter*, which was sent back to people in Pilani to learn about what we were up to in Bombay. I had done something similar on campus the year before, editing a publication for the electrical and electronics engineering students and faculty called *Sinusoidal Times* – engineering humor at its lamest!

I was coming to realize how much I loved writing, though I couldn't see any future in it. One incident I wrote about was when the professor in charge had to reprimand a group of students for behaving unprofessionally while at Practice School. After giving them a stern lecture, he ended with, "Remember, my friends, when you are in Rome, you must behave like Romeos."

Back in Pilani for the last semester, I geared up for campus placements. As one of India's elite engineering institutions, BITS attracted many leading companies, and I had many interviews despite being a middling student. I must have been good at interviewing, because I received half a dozen job offers. I accepted one from Larson & Toubro, a respected engineering company with Danish roots, to work in

---

[3]Alexis de Tocqueville, *Journeys to England & Ireland*.

their electric switchgear factory in a Bombay suburb, for a princely salary of Rs 800 a month – the same salary as my father when we had returned to India nine years earlier.

Bombay Bound

I headed to the big city to begin my work life. After five years in secluded, spacious, and sandy Pilani, Bombay was quite a change. I shared an apartment with a friend in a suburb called Santa Cruz. I walked to the train station around 7 a.m., squeezed my way onto a packed local train for the short ride to Andheri station, and boarded one of the waiting bright yellow-and-black L&T buses. A half hour later, I was on the sprawling hilly campus, working from 8:20 a.m. to 5:40 a.m. as a quality control engineer.

I quickly realized that my engineering degree hadn't prepared me for what I was expected to do. I buried myself in books to understand current transformers to be able to interact with vendors whose products were not performing up to par. Midmorning, a waiter wheeled a trolley around the office with a small snack and a cup of tea for each of us. At 12:30, we walked up the hill to the dining room for a sumptuous, subsidized meal – the highlight of our day. Then it was back to my desk, another snack trolley in the midafternoon, until it was time to make the reverse trek back to Santa Cruz. This was my routine six days a week – for a grand total of 29 days!

Before starting my job, I had learned that if I got a magical degree called an MBA, my salary would likely double and I would get to work in an air-conditioned office. Immersed in the heat and humidity of Bombay and the stifling atmosphere of the switchgear factory, that sounded extremely appealing to me. I had applied to the Indian Institute of Management Ahmedabad (IIMA), the leading business school in India. The competition to get in was intense, bordering on ridiculous – fewer than 1 in 300 applicants made it. IIMA had its own version of the GMAT; as an engineer with good English, I found the test quite easy. I cleared that hurdle and was asked to come for a personal interview and a "group discussion." Again, my language skills served me well. I received a letter informing me that I was 36th on the waiting list. Two weeks later came the fateful news: the waiting list had been closed after they had admitted the first 25. I was crushed.

Fortunately, I had also applied to the Jamnalal Bajaj Institute of Management Studies in Bombay, which had a similar admissions process. The entering class was only 45, and they had about 7,000 applicants that year. A few days after my IIMA dream ended, I received an admission letter from Bajaj. I was elated and immediately typed out my resignation letter. My manager wordlessly read my letter and then looked up at me over his reading glasses. "Young man, you are making the biggest mistake of your life."

I didn't care. I was on my way from being a clueless engineer to a comfort-seeking MBA. I headed home for a brief respite before school started. I put my salary in an envelope – eight crisp 100-rupee notes – and gave it to my mother, as is the custom in India. She wiped away tears, told me how proud she was of me, and blessed me.

Bajaj was located at the southern tip of Bombay island – the glamorous part of town, with the poshest hotels and the tallest skyscrapers. It was a short walk from the corporate headquarters of many of India's leading companies and across the street from the state legislative assembly. Our graduate dorm was on a short street between the Churchgate train station and Bombay's famed Marine Drive, a picturesque curved highway that ran along the Arabian Sea. Life had suddenly become a lot more interesting.

Bajaj attracted students with a variety of backgrounds from all over the country. Many of us had engineering degrees, but others came with degrees in economics, literature, and commerce. There were five girls and 40 boys. Early on, a student named Manjeev Singh Puri (who would later be India's ambassador to the European Union), with a larger-than-life personality, emerged as the unquestioned leader of our class. He came from a family of distinguished civil servants; his father was the chief secretary of the state of Punjab. His nicknames were Tito and Blonde; inexplicably, he had light brown hair and green eyes.

It was a Bajaj tradition for students to have nicknames. Tito anointed himself the official nickname giver of our class. The diminutive Sanjay Sharma became Shorty. The always worried-looking Sudhir Yadav became Hassle. A math wonk was deemed Stats. An overly Anglicized kid named Praveen Meduri was christened Wog, a mocking term the British had used for "westernized oriental gentleman." Wog embraced his new moniker with gusto; as we walked past a large lawn on our way to the Institute, he gestured toward it with his pipe and exclaimed, "Egad, the village green!"

Ashwini Malhotra's family owned Weikfield Food Products, best known for their custard powder, a staple in the pantry of every middle-class Indian household. To preempt Tito, he said, "Thanks, but I already have a nickname; everybody calls me Kitu." Tito replied, "Your choices are Custard or Pudding. Pick one." Custard it was.

With a last name like Sisodia, my fate was sealed. For the next two years, my nickname was Sis. I hated it. I had with great difficulty shed my childhood nickname Pappu, only to be saddled with this one now.

I moved into a triple room in the dorm. My roommates were two second-year students, both avid pot smokers. We made a fine trio: the law firm of Sis, Crow, and Fuzz. Every night, inhaling their second-hand smoke gave me the distinct sensation of floating above my bed, my nose inches from the ceiling.

After the rigors of Pilani and the demands of my short-lived job at L&T, Bajaj proved to be a cakewalk. This MBA stuff was easy, even fun! We took 10 courses in the first semester, but none were hard. I started informally teaching statistics and computer programming to my classmates with liberal arts backgrounds and found that it came naturally to me. The two primary choices for a major were finance and marketing. I did not like finance, which I found to be too dry and boring, so I chose marketing. It engaged my long-dormant right brain, after years of slogging through hyper-analytical engineering courses.

The two years at Bajaj were like a paid vacation. My father had recently taken a job at the University of Zambia in Africa, working for the Canadian International Development Agency. I knew he was earning a good salary in dollars; for the first time in my life, I did not agonize over money. Many kids at Bajaj came from well-to-do families. The food in our dorm was terrible, so a group of us started a nightly practice of eating out at the many excellent restaurants in that part of town.

Our strategy professor, Dr. Manesh Shrikant, was the best teacher at Bajaj. He had an MBA from Cornell and a DBA from Harvard Business School. After the first year, I interned at his company, Shrikant Consultants Private Limited. I then headed to Africa for a month to visit my family.

Zambia was a former British colony that had until recently been known as Northern Rhodesia. It bordered Zimbabwe, which had just ended its freedom struggle from the British and shed its old name of Rhodesia. True to my father's adventurous spirit, we spent most of that month traveling by car around the region, getting a genuine African experience. We visited Malawi, Tanzania, and Zimbabwe. We went on two safaris and visited the world-famous Victoria Falls. It was an easygoing and relaxed time, reminiscent of our years in the United States and Canada.

My second year at Bajaj continued the trajectory of the first. I helped organize a conference with the theme "The Business of Business Is Business" that featured a series of conversations between prominent business leaders and journalists about the social responsibility of business. I got to meet the legendary J.R.D. Tata and G. D. Birla — men who had been part of the building of modern India.

We approached our last semester and the frenzy of campus placements. I again received multiple job offers and accepted one from a prestigious consulting company called AF Ferguson, at a starting salary of Rs 2,000 a month — two-and-a-half times what I had earned as an engineer, even better than the doubling I had expected. I thought my career trajectory was set.

Back to the Future

A week after accepting that job, I came down for breakfast in our dorm on a day we didn't have any classes, still in my pajamas. A group of seven of my friends were about to leave. I asked, "Where are you guys headed?"

"The US Information Agency, to pick up GMAT applications."

"Why? We are already doing our MBA."

"We want to apply for a PhD in business in the US."

"You can get a PhD in business?! I didn't know that! Give me five minutes. I'll come with you!" I had long dreamed about returning to the United States, the site of my idyllic childhood years, but I did not know how to make that a reality. A portal had just cracked open.

Six weeks later, we took the exam. Soon, the little envelopes showed up. I had scored in the 97th percentile, transforming my dream from a mirage to a distinct possibility. I swung into high gear and applied to several schools. Dr. Shrikant wrote me a glowing recommendation that probably sealed the deal. I soon received offers of admission from Columbia University, the University of Michigan, and Cornell University – all with full scholarships, including living expenses. This was too good to be true!

When I told my father what had happened, he was stunned. He couldn't believe that on my own, I had managed to get a full scholarship to Columbia University, which had the top-ranked marketing department in the world. I was on my way to becoming a marketing professor. Two years earlier, I hadn't even known what the word "marketing" meant!

The irony is that I was the only one from that group of eight who ended up going to the United States for a PhD. Who knows how my life would have unfolded if I had come down for breakfast five minutes later or earlier that morning?

My parents were still in Africa, so I prepared to depart India on my own. I went to Kesur to say good-bye to my grandfather and uncles and cousins. It was the monsoon season; water and mud were everywhere. My cousin took me to the bus stand on the tractor. After a three-hour bus ride to Ratlam, I spent a couple of days with my mother's family. I have a picture of me with flower garlands around my neck being blessed by my maternal grandfather at the train station. The roof of the train behind me was crowded with people who

couldn't find a place inside the train. The lottery of life had handed
me an opportunity that was utterly unimaginable to them.

After a couple of days in Bombay, I headed to Santa Cruz
International Airport. I had $65 in my wallet, two suitcases in the
plane's belly, and a jumble of thoughts, emotions, and dreams
crowding my mind. I had strapped myself into a new roller coaster.
What lay ahead?

Reflections

Fear drove my decision to go to engineering school. It was all about
maximizing the prospects for getting a job. It was not about knowing
myself and following my passion.

*Think back to a time when you faced a similar decision. How did you
make that decision? How did it serve you or not serve you to make it
in that way?*

The hazing tradition revealed latent sadistic tendencies in many. It
reflected the adage that power doesn't change who you are; rather, it
reveals who you are.

*Have you observed this in yourself or in others? Once we become aware of
such tendencies, what can we do to counter them?*

The strike by the students was ill-advised and petty. It served no
purpose other than to disrupt our education.

*Have you found yourself caught up in groupthink, where a group embarks
on a course of action that is obviously flawed and cannot lead to a
good outcome?*

I experienced my first episode of deep depression in college. My
world shrank, and I felt I had no resources and no recourse. I had to
pull myself out of it and figure out how to survive.

*Can you recall an experience with depression? How did you handle it?
What would you do differently today?*

Encountering my friends who were heading to the US Information-tion Agency turned out to be one of the most significant turning points in my life. I saw a glimmer of an opportunity and immediately acted upon it.

Do you recall similar turning points in your life? Did doors open that you did not walk through? How could you think differently about such situations in the future?

6 | New York, New York

On August 25, 1981, 11 and a half years after returning to India, I landed at JFK Airport in New York City. In some ways, those years had been a departure; returning to the United States felt a bit like coming "home."

With $65 in cash and no credit card, I would have to budget every cent until I received my scholarship money from Columbia. I needed an inexpensive place to stay that first night. The lady at the visitor's desk at the airport suggested the YMCA in Times Square. The taxi ride from the airport to midtown Manhattan was exhilarating – and dispiriting. New York looked run down and a lot grungier than my golden-hued memories of America, with graffiti everywhere – on the trains, on walls, on the sides of buildings. The cab pulled up to the Y, which was next to a pornographic movie theater – something that would have been inconceivable in India. I checked in, squeezed my luggage into the impossibly tiny room, and headed outside to explore the neighborhood. Drunk and drugged people staggered around the street. Prostitutes in tight, shiny mini-skirts and impossibly high heels stood at every street corner, propositioning me as I walked by.

Stunned, I retreated to the sanctuary of my tiny room.

After a sleepless jet-lagged night, I took a cavernous yellow Checker taxi to International House, which would be my home for the next two years. Located a few blocks north of the Columbia campus, I-House accommodated 500 graduate students from over 80 countries. Reassuringly, I saw a few Indian faces, including the person who checked me in. My room was tiny and modern, not unlike the one at the Y.

With only $20 left, I headed to the university to let them know I had arrived and to ask how I could start accessing my scholarship money. The staff in the Columbia Business School doctoral office in Uris Hall welcomed me warmly. They handed me a check for the princely sum of $300 and directed me to Chemical Bank to open an account.

Before heading there, I stopped at the restroom. Scrawled on the wall in the stall were the words, "If you voted for Reagan, you can't shit here – because your asshole's in Washington." I chuckled out loud at the delightful American sense of humor – I loved the irreverence, the political awakeness! The contrast was dramatic. India had recently been led by the reed-thin Morarji Desai, a humorless puritanical man who drank his own urine for its supposed health benefits. Notwithstanding his fondness for "crotch whiskey," he lived to the age of 99, so perhaps he was onto something!

After the Mad Max vibe of Times Square, Morningside Heights was peaceful and quiet. But here, too, danger lurked. The Columbia campus was on the edge of Harlem. Crime was rampant in New York City then, with 2,100 murders and over 120,000 robberies in 1981, more than in any other year. Students routinely got mugged on the short walk between the campus and I-House.

Marketing Mecca – or Mayhem?

Two years earlier, I didn't know what marketing was; there was hardly any to speak of in India. Now I was swimming in a veritable tsunami of it. Over 50% of the world's marketing dollars were being spent in the United States, targeting 4% of the world's people. You were inundated with ads on TV, on the radio, in the newspaper, in your mailbox, on billboards, on the tops of cabs, on the sides of buses and buildings, in the subway, above urinals, everywhere! It was inescapable. In India, marketing had been a minor business function; here it was an omnipresent and oppressive fact of life.

On TV, it was a tale of two Eddies. The brash, annoying Mayor Ed Koch seemed to be everywhere, constantly accosting people on the street and demanding to know, "How'm I doing?" On every channel, the wild-eyed Crazy Eddie shilled day and night for his electronics store, waving his arms and screaming, "Our prices are *ins-a-a-a-ane!*" The Sunday *New York Times* was three inches thick, with two of those inches consumed by ads, including thousands of coupons. I wondered, "How can the same place go out of business every week? Does anyone ever buy anything that isn't on sale?"

The nonstop hype and hoopla recalled a phrase from Shakespeare: "A tale told by an idiot, full of sound and fury, signifying nothing." Had I signed on to become a future high priest of this racket – this exhausting, quintessentially American form of hucksterism?

I started feeling uneasy about my career choice. I wondered what the impact of wall-to-wall marketing was. "How much do companies spend on marketing? How well does it work? Is it efficient? Is it effective? Is it ethical? Is it good for companies? Is it good for society? Is it good for customers?" Those questions would shape my career and eventually guide my quest for a better way to do business.

Ivy League Ivory Tower

I knew little about Columbia Business School other than that it had the top-rated marketing department in the world (measured by the number of publications its faculty generated in premier journals). A boldface name in the world of academia occupied every faculty office. My first research assistantship was with the legendary Professor John Howard, who had published *The Theory of Buyer Behavior* in 1967 with Jagdish Sheth (who would become my mentor a decade later).

I soon realized that I had entered the ultimate academic ivory tower. I arrived at Columbia in 1981, early into what would come to be known and celebrated as the Decade of Greed, symbolized by Gordon Gekko in the 1987 movie *Wall Street*. Columbia Business School sat amid the grime, crime, and dysfunction of New York City and Harlem, but the work being done there had little to do with what was going on in society. There was no purpose other than to help companies make ever more profits, equip MBA students to get high-paying jobs, and produce as many publications as possible. Profit maximization and publication maximization – that was the complete value system. No one in the department could point to how his work (they were all men) had made a positive impact on the world.

Don Lehmann was the most self-aware individual in the department. He was witty and self-deprecating, saying, "I don't take myself seriously, but I take my work very seriously." Don was the only one who seemed to have given any thought to the bigger picture, occasionally bemoaning the incessant gimmickry of marketing. He would ask, "Are we just the department of Bluelight Specials and cents-off coupons?"[1]

At the first faculty and PhD student social, another faculty member, Don Morrison, made what I'm sure was his annual joke at these events: "Welcome to the PhD program. I hope you realize that a PhD student is a unique individual who willingly forgoes current income in order to forgo future income." This generated a ripple of nervous laughter, especially among the American students. "Now you tell us!" someone called out.

I soon realized that there was a key difference between the American students in the PhD program and those of us who had come from abroad, primarily from India. For American PhD students, what Don Morrison said was literally true. Most already had MBAs, which

---

[1] Bluelight Specials were a tactic used by the retailer Kmart; flashing blue sirens in the center of the store would go off announcing discounts on an item, accompanied by an announcement on the loudspeaker: "Attention Kmart shoppers!" That phrase became part of American popular culture.

was a golden ticket to a rapid ascent in corporate America. If they took a corporate job and were even moderately successful, their income would skyrocket. Those students had sacrificed the income they would have earned to enroll in a three- to four-year PhD program with a scholarship that barely covered their basic living expenses. They would then get a modestly paid academic job; their salary would rise only slowly over time and would eventually plateau. American students who entered PhD programs had to be truly motivated by love of scholarship and teaching.

The calculus was very different for most of the foreign students, and certainly for me. I did not base my decision to become a marketing scholar on purpose or passion. My opportunity cost was close to zero. My Indian MBA did not permit me to get a work visa in the United States. The PhD program for me was a means to two ends: returning to the United States and making a decent living in the future. It was certainly not my calling.

In the 1980s, there was a severe shortage of business PhD students in the United States. Demand for business education was growing rapidly, so universities needed to hire large numbers of business PhDs. There were, on average, seven open tenure-track faculty positions for every newly minted PhD in marketing. I liked those odds.

An Accidental Academic

Every discipline is a kind of priesthood. Entering a PhD program accidentally is like wandering into a monastery and becoming a priest without actually believing in God. Some priests lose their faith; I never had it to begin with. What happens when an atheist becomes a priest?

As an "accidental academic," I was more objective about what I was studying than many of my colleagues. I had not imbibed the marketing Kool-Aid, so I was in less danger of losing discernment.

I realized that marketers are in a somewhat unique position, like psychologists: they are the subjects (those performing an action) and the objects (those receiving it) of their work. They are marketers at work, and customers in their lives. I had a hard time separating the two roles, which often seemed in conflict; what was best for the marketer was usually not best for customers.

The first two years of the PhD program comprised foundational courses and doctoral seminars in which we had to write research papers. I breezed through the courses, wrote papers I didn't care about, and did well on the comprehensive exam at the end of the two years. I found most academic writing to be tedious. My professors frequently wrote on my papers, "Please make this more academic."

I didn't realize it then, but what was missing for me was a higher purpose for the research we were doing; it was all about relentlessly striving for more top publication "hits." That meant deploying heroic levels of mathematical rigor to (what seemed to me) trivial questions. The most celebrated papers were steeped in sophisticated quantitative methods and filled with unintelligible equations – the denser the better. People competed to out-quant each other.

I was becoming increasingly disillusioned with my career path; since I had stumbled upon it, I felt like my career had chosen me instead of the other way around. Marketing, I lamented to myself, is not an inherently self-justifying profession. The world needs doctors, firefighters, engineers; it even needs a few lawyers. But does it really need more marketers?

A decade into my higher education, none of it had inspired or truly engaged me: the engineering degree, the MBA, and now the PhD. I wondered: "Why am I so different from my classmates? Why can't I bring myself to really care about this stuff?"

I was a fish out of water in this environment. Hollow careerism is a weak fuel for me; if my heart is not engaged in what I'm doing, if I am not inspired, I quickly run out of energy and motivation. I was sometimes intellectually stimulated in the doctoral program but never emotionally engaged – not once.

I may have been a fish out of water, but compared to most students, I was a rich fish! The minimum wage then was $3.35. Some of my professors hired me to do statistical analysis for their consulting work, and paid me $25 an hour. I also tutored MBA students in statistics at the same rate. I off-loaded the time-intensive data entry work (done on IBM punch cards in those days) to my liberal arts friends at I-House. I paid them $5 an hour, which thrilled them, while charging the professors $25 an hour. My inner capitalist was alive and well!

Dowry Drama

I headed to India in December 1983 for my cousin Gajendra's wedding. My parents were there as well, visiting from Zambia.

At 22, my sister had reached "marriageable age," so my parents started looking for a suitable match. After graduating from college, Manju was teaching at an elementary school in Zambia. My father told us not to let anyone know that she had worked outside the home. I couldn't believe it; why was that a bad thing? Somehow, that would sully the honor of our family. He put the word out to the Rajput community back home to help "find a good boy" for her. He made it clear that he was willing to pay a large dowry. He was earning a good salary in dollars working for the Canadian International Development Agency and had been saving money for that purpose.

The eventual marriage of a daughter was the looming balloon payment every Indian father dreaded, especially a Rajput father who expected to have to pay a large dowry to secure a "good" groom. Rajput fathers routinely and unironically referred to their daughters as "liabilities," as in "I have one son and two liabilities."

His attitude outraged me. I hated the practice of dowry and was dismayed that my highly educated father had caved to these pressures. Breaking from my tendency to seek harmony, I said to him, "Why are you offering a dowry?" He angrily replied, "You understand nothing; you're naïve and idealistic. When you are part of a society, you must live according to that society's norms. I just want the best for my daughter." I said, "What kind of family and husband will she get if that is what they most care about?" He ignored my objections.[2]

After Gajendra's wedding, we stayed on in Kesur for a few days. Late in the day, we saw a cloud of dust and then a car drive up the steep incline and enter through the Rowla gate. It was Uncle Chaddha, a close family friend. The back of his car was filled with boxes of sweets wrapped in gold paper. He jumped out of the car grinning widely and said in a booming voice, "Congratulations, congratulations! The horoscopes have matched!"

The match we had been coveting for Manju was with Sangram, my high school classmate from St. Paul, who was now a doctor. Our families knew each other well. However, their astrological charts did not match. Uncle Chaddha had taken both charts to the nearby holy city of Ujjain to consult a higher order of astrologer. They found that by changing my sister's birthdate from June 18 to June 19, the charts became a perfect match!

Manju dissolved into happy tears, and we all celebrated late into the night. Two days later, we went to Indore to formalize the engagement. My father approached Manju's future father-in-law (whom everyone called *Mamosa*, meaning maternal uncle; he was the uncle of the King of Narsinghgarh) with his hands folded in a subservient gesture. "*Hokum* (my lord), how much can I offer?" The imperious Mamosa glared at him. "Who the hell do you think I am? Do you think I want money from you? Your daughter will be my daughter. Give her whatever you want. Don't talk to me about money." My father mumbled his apologies and retreated, seeming to shrink a bit at this chastisement.

Watching this unexpected response from Mamosa, I was instantly relieved and felt vindicated. I knew Manju would be treated well in this family, especially by her father-in-law. The wedding took place a

---

[2]An oft-told true story illustrates the hold that dowry had on Rajput culture. The wedding party of one of my great uncles was on its way to the bride's village when they received word that another family was willing to pay a larger dowry. The wedding bus was promptly rerouted to the new destination, while the other bride waited in vain for her future husband to show up.

few months later, and she has had a blissful marriage for 39 years and counting.

After my sister was safely married, attention turned to me. I had never discussed the issue with my parents, but I was open to either an arranged marriage or to meeting someone on my own. My parents began sending me "biodatas" of Rajput girls. After meeting a few of them, I became increasingly convinced that I would be happier with a less traditional person, someone more aligned with my own values and worldview.

Dissertation Dilemma

It was time for me to identify a dissertation topic. Given my idealistic nature, I wanted to work on something that mattered, something I could get excited about. The ideal way to do this would have been to search deep inside myself and pick an unsolved problem that I passionately cared about. But our professors discouraged us from that, saying, "the best dissertation is a completed dissertation"; they urged us to identify a small gap in the literature, collect some data, use a sophisticated method to analyze it, write it up, and get on with our academic careers.

While I was trying to come up with a topic, John Farley approached me. John was one of the most senior professors in the department. He was also on the board of a company called Greenwich Research Associates, which collected data in the financial services industry and sold reports based on the data. I had worked as a research assistant for a book on strategic planning that John had written with two other Columbia professors. He said to me, "This company has a lot of data but they haven't done much with it. I think there's a dissertation in there."

Those were the magic words; I thought I had won the lottery. I was flailing in the deep end of the pool and John had just thrown me a life preserver. My classmates, who were struggling to come up with viable dissertation topics, were envious. "You are so lucky!" Like *The Godfather*, John had made me an offer I could not refuse.

I didn't realize that I was entering into a Faustian bargain; John's offer gave me short-term relief but would lead to long-term pain. There was nothing about the project that intrigued or excited me, and nothing of value would ever emerge from it. But I was not mature enough to know what I really wanted to do, and not strong enough to say no to John.

My dissertation turned into a classic case of "cart before the horse." I already had the data; now I needed to formulate a question I could "answer" using that data. That meant coming up with a theory and developing a mathematical model. I wrote up a dissertation proposal and did some preliminary data analysis, but the flaws were glaring. The whole rickety contraption was held together with twine and duct tape. Any smart reader could see what was really going on – and academics are nothing if not smart.

Soon, it was time to go to the American Marketing Association Summer Educators Conference in Dearborn, Michigan – the big annual job placement event for marketing academics. With my Columbia pedigree and John Farley as my adviser, many leading schools were interested in me. My schedule for the three days was packed with 25 interviews, including Harvard Business School, the University of Michigan, Yale, Darden, and many other top schools. But the interviews were excruciating. When I described my dissertation, the professors saw right through it and were not shy about saying so. "This is data grubbing! You are trying to fit a model to data that already exists. Good luck with that."

I headed back to New York and waited for campus invitations to continue the interview process. I only heard from Darden and Boston University. BU made me an offer. I loved Boston and immediately accepted. I had about 10 months to finish my dissertation and prepare to teach.

During the time I was struggling with my dissertation, I impulsively and prematurely proposed marriage to someone I really liked but did not know very well. We had spent time together but hadn't really dated. But I thought I knew her well enough – far better than

I would get to know any girl I met through the arranged marriage process. Understandably, she declined. The rejection threw me into a funk, and I became quite depressed. I whiled away the days alone in my apartment, moping around and unable to work. I was unmotivated and stuck.

Six months passed in a haze. I simply did not know how to make progress on the dissertation and lacked the drive to figure it out. Columbia had guaranteed me financial support for three years, which was ending. I pleaded with the head of the doctoral program to extend my support for a semester, which he reluctantly agreed to do. I called Boston University and told the department chair that I would join a semester late. He was not happy about it, having already assigned me two courses to teach that fall, but he agreed.

I was nowhere near completing my dissertation; in fact, I was closer to the beginning than I was to the end. I was an ABD, "all but dissertation," the elephant's graveyard of many PhD students. Two out of three PhD students in some disciplines never complete their dissertations; I very much feared that fate for myself.

Escape from New York

I did not have a driver's license, so I asked two of my friends to help me move. Sushil flew across the country from California, and Ravi came up from Alabama. We rented a car and a U-Haul trailer, and headed to Boston on a frigid early January afternoon. The thought of what lay ahead filled me with trepidation.

As night fell, the highway turned treacherous. Invisible black ice blanketed large sections of I-95. Unaccustomed to driving in such conditions, Sushil pressed the brake and turned the steering wheel slightly to shift lanes. The wheels locked and the car and trailer spun around on the highway, seemingly in slow motion. We came to a stop, pointing back toward New York. Was this a harbinger of how my life would be in Boston? Invisible dangers, spinning my wheels, facing existential threats, going backwards?

We arrived in Boston late at night, driving along deserted, icy streets piled high with dirty snow until we reached the small brick apartment complex that would be my home. After my friends left the next day, I took a bus to a nearby furniture store and in one hour bought all the furniture I needed. It cost much more than I had saved. I signed up for an installment plan with an exorbitant interest rate. I then went and bought my kitchen and bathroom necessities.

At the Boston University School of Management, I met my department chair. Don Kanter was a cantankerous social psychologist and former advertising executive whose claim to fame was that he had been part of the team that created the Mr. Clean character. He assigned me a windowless office in the basement of an old brownstone on Commonwealth Avenue, close to Kenmore Square and Fenway Park. I had two weeks to prepare for my first class. I was to teach two evening MBA classes on Marketing Management.

We had not spent a single minute in my three and a half years at Columbia learning how to teach; all that mattered was that we learned how to publish (which I hadn't accomplished either). I was 26 and a half years old and had not completed my doctorate. My students were 38 years old on average with over a decade of work experience.

The dirty little secret of business education in the United States is that universities routinely entrust 26-year-olds to teach 40-year-old graduate students about something they had never themselves practiced, with no guidance on how to structure a meaningful learning experience.

I faced the prospect of a three-hour evening class – 180 minutes, 10,800 seconds, during which I would have to engage and impress 50 demanding and tired "students": experienced managers who had already put in a full day at work. They (or the companies they worked for) were paying a lot to be there; BU's tuition was higher than Harvard's.

The dreaded day of my first class arrived. In my basement office, I did voice exercises to warm up my vocal cords. I then bundled up and walked in the icy darkness on crunchy snow toward the classroom building, my breath visible in the frigid air. As I entered the wide, brightly lit classroom, I was trembling inside but tried to project an air of calm and competence. Clutching 44 pages of handwritten notes, I turned to the chalkboard and wrote in large letters: "What is marketing?"

By the end of the class, I had used only 17 pages of those notes. Somehow, the three hours had flown by. I was enormously relieved; I had enjoyed being in front of the classroom and I still had 27 pages of material I could use for the next class. Maybe I could get the hang of this professor thing, at least the teaching part.

Later that week, we had a School of Management faculty meeting. The president of BU, an imperious one-armed misanthrope named John Silber, was in attendance. A former philosophy professor at UT Austin, the caustic Silber ran the university like his personal fiefdom, eventually serving as president for 25 years and chancellor for another six. He had made himself the highest-paid university president in the country. Silber was openly contemptuous of the faculty. He was especially disdainful of female professors, referring to the English department as "a goddam matriarchy" (it had a woman as chair and six women professors out of 26). Silber reminded me of a comic-book villain. He set the leadership tone for the entire university. It permeated down to the Marketing Department, which was bitterly divided into factions of faculty who didn't speak to one another, each owing allegiance to one of two senior professors. The situation reminded me of Henry Kissinger's famous quip: "The reason that university politics is so vicious is because the stakes are so small."

After my first month at BU, I felt like I was swimming with sharks. Then I received an ominous-looking letter from the Immigration and Naturalization Service (INS). It stated that my application for a work visa had been denied, since I had not fulfilled the two-year home country residence requirement of my exchange visa. The letter was a formal deportation notice, ending with "You are herewith ordered to leave the United States within 30 days."

It was a gut punch. I had come to the United States on an exchange visa because I was told it was less likely to be denied than a traditional student visa. I could waive the two-year home country residence requirement by getting three government agencies in India to send letters to the State Department. I had requested the letters months earlier. Two letters had arrived on time; the third came one week after I had started my job. As a result, I was "out of status," no longer in the country legally.

The international office at BU advised me to hire a lawyer and file an appeal. My salary was $32,000 a year. I was already heavily in debt for the furniture. I found an immigration attorney in the Yellow Pages. He was a quintessentially Boston figure from central casting: wearing a dark three-piece pinstriped suit, heavyset, snow-white hair, pink cheeks, and very Irish. He said that he would file an appeal with the State Department citing extenuating circumstances, and assured me I could continue teaching. He told me to leave a check with his secretary for a hefty retainer.

While I was trying to get my work life sorted out, my personal life was about to get a lot more complicated.

Reflections

I quickly became disillusioned about my career choice to become a marketing professor. But in such disillusionment lies an opportunity. When you see something that most others do not, it could be your opportunity to add value, to make a difference.

Have you ever experienced discontent or strong reservations about your profession? Can you think of ways to channel that angst into productive action?

My education lacked any reference to a higher purpose, which was tragic. Education without purpose takes young people, who are more idealistic than they will ever be again in their life, and extinguishes that idealism.

Did your education feed or curb your innate idealism? If it dampened it, how were you able to keep your idealism alive? If you have children, how can you help them keep and act on their idealism?

My father's capitulation to the cultural norm around offering a dowry for my sister's wedding was disappointing and disturbing to me. I understood his rationale, but also realized for the first time how different we were in our worldviews.

Do you recall the first time that you realized that your values and those of your parents were different? How did you respond to that realization?

When John Farley offered me the opportunity to work under him on my dissertation, it seemed like a godsend. It eased my short-term pain of trying to come up with a dissertation topic, but it planted the seeds for much greater challenges in the future. It also denied me an opportunity to do research that mattered to me.

Think back to a time when you made the expedient choice rather than the "right" one. What guidance would you offer your younger self from today's vantage point about how to make such decisions?

7

Boston Blues

On one of my solitary evenings at home in Boston, I received a phone call from a Nepali friend from International House in New York. She had brought a high school friend from Kathmandu to my farewell party in New York a few months earlier. She asked me, "Do you remember my friend Shailu? Would you like to meet her again?"

I remembered her, though we had barely spoken at the party. I told my friend that I would be open to meeting again. "Can you go to East Lansing, Michigan?" she asked. "She is about to graduate from Michigan State University."

I was quite lonely in Boston, so this seemed like a godsend. It was near the end of the semester, so I had time for a trip.

I spent a pleasant few days in Michigan. Shailu and I talked late into the night. Her family was Nepali of Punjabi origin. I found her lively, intelligent, well read, and fun to talk to. She had completed a master's in communications and was about to complete a second master's in labor and industrial relations. We discovered some similarities in our backgrounds; she had spent part of her childhood in the United States, while her father was ambassador to the United Nations and then to the United States. The family had returned to Nepal when she was seven. She asked if we could drive to Kalamazoo, a couple of hours away, to meet her sister and brother-in-law, a Pakistan-born marketing professor at Western Michigan University. I found them both to be gracious and charming.

On May 15, 1985, I called my parents in Zambia to tell them I had met somebody who I might want to marry. It was early morning there. My father immediately exploded in rage. "This is outrageous and unacceptable! I will never agree to this." He poured himself a stiff drink and continued his tirade. "You will have to choose between her and us."

I had anticipated a challenging call, but nothing like this. I was shaking when I hung up the phone. My naïve belief had been that my father, a highly educated man who had lived in several countries around the world, would be somewhat open-minded about this. Several days later, a thick envelope arrived, covered in colorful Zambian stamps. Here is some of what my father wrote:

> Raj, I must say that it's most unfortunate that you are forgetting who you are and where your roots are. You are surrounded by friends who do not have a rich heritage like yours. You're too straightforward and simple a person and are being brainwashed. Unfortunately, in a faraway place you are totally deprived of sound, right counsel.
>
> I am fully confident that you will regret it if after forsaking all of us, you decide to go your own way. I think it is because of your loneliness and brainwashing that today you are prepared to sacrifice your parents, brother, sister, close and dear ones as well as your culture, way of life, and identity. Raj, think think think and analyze yourself and try to understand why suddenly you decided to throw this bombshell on us!
>
> In this, our stand is clear. You will have to make a choice between us, Kesur, Berchha, Indore, etc. and the girl you seem to be "adoring."
>
> You may call this my narrowmindedness, but it is our realistic view of the whole situation in your interest as well as in the interest of everyone else connected with it. I have made so many sacrifices for Kesur, which are very well known to you. The result is that today Kesur has come a long way and I'm proud of it. Everyone, including us, had great great hopes from you to continue adding to the name of Kesur, but it seems like a daydream after

talking to you. Under no circumstances will I let you or anyone else destroy what I have cherished and built throughout my life.

In nine out of 10 cases, I have seen such relationships flop. These should be considered as "marriages of convenience." I have many Punjabi friends, as you know, very close ones. But we always differ in matters of "values," be it social or financial. Basically, Punjabis are selfish people and will do anything for their interest. This is in complete contrast to us. It is because of this selfishness that they are quite ready to sacrifice their identity. We are not that way. From what you are suggesting, they are going to gain, and we are going to lose all the way. Look at the India Abroad *newspaper. How many matrimonial ads appear for these people? Where will they find a handsome, well-educated, settled young man like you so easily? Why should they not sacrifice their identity for that?*

Ever since you dropped this bombshell, your mom is so depressed and silent. She is a person of no words but I'm sure she is burning in fire that may destroy her one day. You know damn well what expectations she had from you.

I am starting to feel that the good days of our family are nearly over. I have never felt as helpless. It is all in your hands now. I hope wisdom will prevail and you will not decide to bury us alive.

Within a few days, two more letters arrived; my father had asked one of my uncles and a grand uncle to join in the effort to dissuade me.

Reeling from this barrage of harsh words and ultimatums, I looked deep within myself. My shock and dismay gradually gave way to anger. I refused to fall in line with a traditional system that abused so many people. My latent idealism and deeply held values came flooding out. My father's extreme response hardened my resolve and made me more determined than before to go my own way.

I compiled a 25-page letter in response. Here is some of what I wrote:

It has saddened me deeply to see the extent of unhappiness I seem to have caused you.

I want to address some points in Masosa's[1] letter. He predictably extolled the virtues of caste and community, and the "fact" that inter-caste marriages "never" work. I find such advice particularly unconvincing from a man of his background. His letter also contained a curious line: "It would have been much better had you married an American girl." Do you agree with that statement? I wonder: by what distorted sense of values am I being judged? Would the white skin of an American make up for everything else? What would your reaction be if I were to want to marry a black American girl? I dare not even speculate.

The fact is that our Rajput society is characterized by a blind, dogmatic narrowmindedness that leads to unspeakable atrocities in the name of preserving culture and tradition.

I can tell you this: the Rajput community has almost zero influence on my actions. My knowledge of caste matters is skimpy and my interest in them even less. I consider caste to be an irrelevancy; it is people who matter. I must live according to my conscience.

I beg of you not to reject me on such flimsy grounds. I deserve better as your son.

My father soon made plans to come to Boston to accomplish in person what he couldn't on the phone or through letters.

***

A few weeks after my trip to Michigan, Shailu graduated and then drove to Boston with some of her college friends. She loved Boston so much that she stayed, sharing an apartment with a classmate who had recently relocated. I was very inexperienced in relationships and enjoyed spending time with Shailu. To me, simply being able to choose whom to marry was critical.

Life began moving at startling speed. On my 27th birthday on June 28, 1985, I picked up my first car – a brand-new, dark blue

---

[1]"Masosa" refers to my great uncle, a culturally sophisticated man who had served in the British Army before India's Independence. Married to my father's mother's sister, he left his wife in the village while he lived in Jaipur with his true love, a British woman.

Honda Accord LX. Six days later, on July 4, on the banks of the Charles River, I asked Shailu to marry me. She gave a tentative yes, subject to her family's approval. They lived in Rome and were due to arrive in a few days. We drove to New York and picked them up at the airport. Later that day at their hotel, I formally asked her father for permission to marry his daughter, which he gave. I met Shailu's youngest sister and was charmed by her wit and lively spirit. The next day, Shailu and I drove to Washington to meet another sister, to whom I took an instant liking as well.

This was a great bonus of the relationship: I would marry into a large family of exuberant, progressive, highly educated, worldly people — very different from my own rather somber and formal family. Punjabis are like the Texans of India, gregarious personalities with energy to spare. I did not have a single relative in the United States; now I would have a large supportive family to call my own.

I was most drawn to Shailu's father. Ram Chandra Malhotra was my ideal of a noble father figure: strong, wise, loving, accomplished, respected, and spiritual. After a distinguished career as a Nepali civil servant and ambassador, he had joined the United Nations, first in Bangkok and then in Rome. I quickly developed a deep bond with him. Our regard was mutual; he understood and respected me in a way that my father never did.

My relationship with Shailu was moving forward like a runaway train. Though I was the one who asked her to marry me, it all seemed somehow preordained. Like many Indians, I perhaps held a subconscious belief that life unfolds the way it is fated to. Swept along in the euphoria of the moment, I ignored the many ominous signs of what lay ahead: my finances were a mess, my dissertation was going nowhere, my teaching remained a challenge, and my immigration status was up in the air. Most significant of all, the day of reckoning with my father was fast approaching.

Out of Africa

My parents flew from Lusaka to Rome, where they stopped for a few days. My father knew that my intended in-laws lived there, but he did not meet them; that would open the door to a possibility he refused to entertain. They arrived in Boston with an open-ended ticket, intent on doing whatever it took for as long as necessary to get me back in line.

My parents stayed with me in my small apartment for the next three months. The routine was the same every day. I left for work with a heavy heart and reluctantly returned home in the evening. My father drank several glasses of Scotch, soda, and water each evening, repeatedly telling me why what I was doing was wrong and completely unacceptable. "You are naïve, simple, too trusting. You don't understand how the world works. You don't know how these people are. They are very clever and cunning and disconnected from their culture and their roots. They always try to trap young boys like you." When I disagreed, he would get angry and say, "How can you be so selfish to forget about your family duty? You think only about yourself."

My mom sat silently through these tirades. She dared not oppose my father openly. Truth be told, she likely would have been more comfortable with a traditional Hindi-speaking Rajput daughter-in-law herself. But she would never put her own happiness above mine.

After six weeks, my father finally agreed to meet Shailu. He lectured her about how we were different and why this would never work. He ended with, "Go back to your people." When she tried to respond, he wouldn't let her speak. "Self-respecting girls don't advocate for themselves." Shailu bore his arrogance and insults with remarkable grace and courage. The meeting was over in 45 minutes.

Shailu taught part-time at Boston University, so I could see her during the day. On most evenings, we spoke on the phone. My father would pick up a phone in the other room to eavesdrop on our calls. One day, he couldn't restrain himself and burst out, "If you marry my son, I curse your marriage."

The atmosphere in the apartment steadily worsened. It was what I imagine living inside a pressure cooker would be like. I lost focus and found it increasingly difficult to teach or work on my dissertation.

One evening, my father drank more than usual. After repeating his standard list of criticisms of me, he added, "My mistake was that I was too lenient with you. I gave you too much freedom. I let you get away with too much." I shook my head in disbelief. He stood up, unsteadily made his way to the kitchen and said loudly, "If you marry this girl, I will kill myself." He took a large knife out of the butcher block on the counter and pierced the skin on his chest. Within seconds, blood spread on his white *kurta* in an expanding maroon circle.

I had rushed toward him when he reached for the knife. When I saw the blood on his *kurta* and some drops on the tan linoleum floor, everything turned dark; my legs crumbled under me, and I fell to the floor in tears. I had reached my physical and emotional breaking point; I couldn't take it anymore. I mumbled through my sobs, "Okay, I give up. I won't marry her."

As soon as he heard that, my father underwent a miraculous transformation. He helped me to my feet and said, "It's okay, *beta* (an affectionate term for son). We all make mistakes. Everything will be fine now."

In the past, there were many times I had seen my father use his intelligence to manipulate people into doing his bidding. He was strategic at pulling the right levers to get the outcome he wanted. I didn't realize it then, but that is what he had just done to me.

After hours of tossing and turning, not fully grasping what had just happened, I finally fell into an uneasy sleep.

The next morning, my father was quite cheerful. He had circled some listings in the real estate section of the *Boston Globe*. He said, "It makes no sense for you to be paying so much rent for this apartment. We should buy you a condo. It will be a good investment."

I just nodded and headed off to work. In time, I would recognize this maneuver. My father, like his own father, routinely used money as a weapon, as a way of demonstrating his power and conditional love. Now that I had agreed to do what he wanted, he was loosening the purse strings. The father's largess would once again be showered on the formerly wayward son. I had no interest in any of that.

I described what had happened to Shailu and explained that we had to break up. She received the news with remarkable composure and returned the ring that I had given her. A week later, mission accomplished, my parents flew back to Africa to wrap up their six-year stay in Zambia. They would soon move back to India.

For the next few weeks, I stumbled around campus in a complete daze. My recurring thought was, *"I cannot let this man dictate my life. This is my life and I get to decide. If I give in on this, I will never be able to stand up to him on anything. I will never be my own person. Even if this is a mistake, it is my mistake to make."* My father had painted me into a corner; I could see no way out of this emotional cul-de-sac.

With time and space to reflect, I slowly regained my psychological equilibrium. I reached out to Shailu and told her I would marry her if she was still willing. She said she was. Now I had to figure out how to break the news to my father.

★★★

I didn't have to wait long. A familiar-looking envelope showed up again from the INS. I ripped it open and extracted the letter with trembling hands. It said that my application to adjust my status had been approved. However, since I had been "out of status," I needed to present myself at a US consulate outside the country and apply for reentry under my new visa within 30 days.

My lawyer suggested I try to get it done in a neighboring country. I phoned US consulates in Canada, Mexico, Barbados, and several other countries. They all said the same thing: "You cannot come here; go to your home country and apply there."

It was the middle of the semester, but there was no room for delay. I asked my colleagues to cover my classes and bought a ticket to India. On the way there, I stopped in Rome for a few days (where my future in-laws lived). I went to the US consulate every day, pleading for them to stamp my passport. They refused, so I made my way to Bombay.

The lawyer had warned me that the US consulate would look for evidence that I eventually planned to return to India. If I didn't have any, they would deem me a "potential immigrant" and deny me a visa. I reached out to Dr. Srikanth, my mentor during my MBA program, who had given me a glowing recommendation for my PhD applications. I asked if he would give me a job offer at his consulting company and hold it open until I decided if I wanted to come back. He produced an impressive-looking offer letter within hours. Armed with that, I headed to Indore to collect documents showing how much ancestral property we had. I also needed to tell my father that I intended to marry Shailu.

My parents had just returned from Africa and were living in a rented house. My cousin Gajendra and some other relatives were there the evening I came. I said to my father, "Papa, what you did in Boston was wrong. You never gave Shailu a chance. You rejected her before you even met her. You wrote insulting letters to her parents and refused to meet them when you were in Rome. It is my life and my decision. I have decided that I *will* marry Shailu."

He exploded in rage, and we were soon shouting at each other. Then he went into the bedroom and emerged carrying the Remington 22-caliber rifle I knew so well. He was muttering, "I will kill the bastard. It is better that I don't have a son at all than a son like this."

Stunned by his threat, my cousin quickly jumped between him and me. He then rushed me out of the house and to my sister's place (she had gotten married a year before). I was in a daze. What had just happened?

To this day, I have no recollection of my father holding that gun. But my cousin Gajendra remembers it clearly. He told me about it a few years ago, painting a vivid picture of what had happened. I erased this episode from my memory for over three decades. I have since learned that such "dissociative amnesia" protects our psyche from reliving traumatic incidents. This survival mechanism kicked in because the scale of this trauma was too much for my sensitive nature.

Gajendra also shared how my father had spun the story to our relatives. "Raj is too simple and innocent. He has been ensnared by a wily family with shallow American values. These marriages never last. Even if he marries her, I am sure they will get divorced soon. Then I will get him married properly."

I remained at my sister's house for a couple of days. After lunch on the second day, I lay down for a nap. My mom had come over and was sitting in the verandah outside, speaking with my sister Manju. They heard a commotion on the street outside the compound. People were shouting, "Kali Devi has come!"

It was about a young boy from a poor family who lived in the vicinity. He had a severe stutter and appeared to be intellectually disabled. He would periodically become possessed, supposedly by the goddess Kali (considered a symbol of strong motherly love). When these "spells" occurred, his voice and demeanor transformed. He spoke fluently in an adult voice with a vocabulary he normally didn't possess. Having witnessed this before, my sister realized what was happening, and said, "Mummy, you have to see this." They hurried to where a crowd had gathered around the young boy. He was sitting upright on the ground with a serene expression. As my mother approached, his eyes met hers. She bent down to touch his feet to receive the goddess's blessing. He put his right hand on her head and said, "Daughter, I know you are worried about your son. Know that it will be all right. Everything is happening just as it is meant to."

My mother, a silent witness to the drama and trauma of the previous months, broke down in tears as my sister held her. Manju sent somebody to wake me up and bring me to the scene, but the spell had worn off by the time I got there. The young boy was back to being his usual self. When they told me what had happened, I was puzzled and comforted at the same time. His words had been deeply reassuring to my mother, who perhaps now felt a little more fortified to face the painful times that lay ahead. The episode also showed me that life often unfolds in mysterious ways, that there are some life experiences that are beyond our comprehension.

The next day, I said good-bye to my family (except my father) and headed to Bombay for my fateful visa interview. I submitted my application at the US consulate and waited anxiously, staring at the framed posters of American tourist attractions that lined the walls. I sat next to a picture of Faneuil Hall in Boston, a place I loved. I gazed wistfully at it. Would I be able to return to my life in Boston, or was this where my American dream would end? It was a very distinct possibility that my visa would be denied and I could not return to the US. My job, my students, my fiancée, my car, my apartment, my life were all waiting for me in Boston. Everything now hinged on the whims of a consular officer.

After several hours, a sliding window opened, and a gruff voice called out my name. A large, hostile-looking American man with a bushy red beard looked me up and down. He asked, "Do you have any other documentation that supports your claim that you plan to return to India?" My heart pounding, I put my briefcase on the counter and opened it to see what else I could give him. He reached through the window, grabbed the briefcase, and pulled it toward him. Without a word, he slid the partition shut.

I walked back on quivering legs and sat down, convinced that this was the end. The bearded man was scouring through my briefcase, searching for evidence that I had concocted the whole fiction about planning to return to India – which indeed I had. My mind was struggling to adjust to the grim new reality that seemed to be unfolding in front of my eyes. What would I do? Where would I live? How would I survive? I could barely breathe.

I have no idea how much time passed; it might have been 10 minutes, or it could have been an hour. Finally, the window at the far right slid open and someone called out my name. When I got there, an unseen person slid the briefcase out with my passport on top of it and slammed the window shut. I fumbled through the pages of the passport, desperately searching for the distinctive US visa sticker. When I finally found it, waves of relief and disbelief moved through me. The stars were on my side that muggy Mumbai night.

I flagged down a beat-up black-and-yellow taxi and headed to the airport. A few hours later, I boarded a KLM flight to Amsterdam and then back to Boston, a newly legitimized "alien" (the demeaning word the US uses for non-citizens) and very much a potential immigrant.

An Unblessed Marriage

We set the wedding date four months out, for March 29, 1986. In a semi-daze, I went through the motions of looking at menus and venues. We picked a gracious old building on the BU campus called The Castle. A professor of mathematics at Cambridge College who was also a Hindu priest would conduct the pared-down ceremony. We invited approximately 75 guests, including a handful of my friends from around the United States, Shailu's family and friends, and a few of my colleagues.

My greatest pain was that I was getting married in a distant land without my family, my beloved cousin Gajendra, and all the other relatives I was close to. On the evening of March 27, the phone rang. It was my father. With no preamble, he began, "I want you to postpone the wedding." Startled, I replied, "Does that mean that you are accepting it?" Even at this late date, I would have canceled the wedding if we could have had a traditional Indian wedding.

There was a long pause. My father replied, "I'll think about it."

Instinctually, I knew that wasn't enough. It felt like I was being manipulated again. I hung up. That was the last time we spoke for five years.

This last minute emotional "bait and switch" affected me greatly. That brief glimmer of hope shattered my already broken heart.

I felt numb on my wedding day. It was like I was at a wake instead of a wedding. I felt the absence of those I loved far more keenly than the presence of those who *were* there.

This was, of course, deeply unfair to Shailu and her family. I wish I had had the emotional wherewithal to separate my father drama from my marriage and the life I was trying to build, yet they were inextricably connected.

It was the middle of the semester, so a honeymoon was out of the question – not that I felt much like celebrating. I felt disembodied. I was disconnected from Shailu, our newlywed home felt heavy and tense, and I was barely functioning.

A couple of weeks into our marriage, we rented *Ordinary People*, a movie that had won the Oscar for Best Picture in 1981. It is a gut-wrenching story that starts with two teenage brothers getting into a boating accident in which one of them drowns. The son who died had been his mother's favorite. The surviving son had tried desperately to save his brother but couldn't. The movie depicts the unbearable grief of the family and the unspoken rebuke from the mother to the anguished, guilt-ridden surviving son: "If one of you had to die, why him? Why not you?" Drowning in pain, he unsuccessfully attempts suicide and is gradually brought back from despair by a skilled and caring therapist.

As I watched, tears were streaming down my face. My new wife glanced at me and said, "What are you doing? Why are you crying?" I replied, "This is the saddest movie I've ever seen." She replied, "I have never seen a man cry. What kind of man cries?"

My heart sank. Her words struck me as something my father might have said. A familiar feeling of shame came over me, and in that instant, I subconsciously concluded that I could not be myself in this marriage.

Marriage should be a place where you can be most authentically and vulnerably yourself. My marriage was one in which I was constantly on guard and had to adopt a persona that would make me acceptable in the eyes of my partner. I was weary from my recent battle to stand up for myself and for her. Taking on my father and the toxic patriarchy he represented had completely drained me.

That seemingly trivial incident created a deep gulf between us. Something inside me shut down. For the next two decades, I could not summon tears for anything: movies, books, personal traumas,

the deaths of loved ones, mass tragedies. Hearing those words
from her planted a seed of invalidation inside me that grew into
bitterness and resentment over the years. I began building armor
around my heart.

In hindsight, I can see how this incident could have unfolded differently. Instead of shutting down, I could have become curious about
why my wife reacted the way she did. What was it in her experience
of men and how she expected them to relate to their emotions that
caused her to say what she did? I can today imagine a different outcome, where we could have explored this topic together with curiosity and compassion and gotten to know one another better. But at the
time, I lacked the self-awareness, self-confidence, and emotional intelligence to respond in that way.

Many years later, I realized that at a subconscious level, I resented
my wife for being the reason my family had cut me off. Of course,
that was not true; I had asked Shailu to marry me and my father had
rejected the very idea of me choosing a mate outside my community.
Our marriage had simply been the catalyst to bring issues to the
surface that would have eventually found their way there. In my battle
with the toxic and abusive patriarchy represented by my father, our
marriage became collateral damage. One of my greatest regrets has
been that at the tender age of 27, I did not have the strength or
wisdom to navigate these treacherous waters in a more loving and
constructive way.

My father had repeatedly told me that most of my innate qualities –
being peace-loving, sensitive, trusting – were weaknesses. In my marriage, those same qualities became sources of conflict. My basic
essence transformed into cynicism, mistrust, and at times even explosive confrontation. To survive, I suppressed my sensitivity and became
hardened to the tears and suffering of others.

Other difficult episodes would follow, but we doggedly stayed
together for three decades, imprisoned by cultural norms and my
own determination to prove my father wrong. Giving up on the marriage would have meant admitting defeat to my father.

It did not help that my work was about to get much more challenging.

Nightmare on Commonwealth Avenue

I remained completely stuck with my dissertation. My adviser John Farley had moved to Cambridge when he was appointed the executive director of the prestigious Marketing Science Institute. I met with him regularly to advance the dissertation. I wrote a couple hundred pages about the marketing of services, the importance of relationships, and so forth. He rejected it all, saying, "This is not academic writing." I had to throw it away and start over.

Meanwhile, my department chair changed my teaching assignment. Rather than allowing me to continue teaching marketing management, which I had learned to do well, he assigned me to teach an experimental new course called "Marketing and Operations in Financial Services" simply because my dissertation had to do with financial services. I co-taught the course with an executive from a local financial services company. Somehow, I made it through the semester by leaning heavily on my co-teacher.

It got worse. Don Kanter assigned me to teach a course called "Marketing Information Systems." "You were an electrical engineer before you got into business," he said. "This should be easy for you." I had no background in information systems, a highly specialized field. The domain of "marketing information systems" barely existed at all. There was no textbook. Within a few weeks, I would have to face 40 students in BU's highly rated Master of Science in Information Systems program: a three-hour class every Monday morning for 16 weeks. What could I teach them that would justify my presence in the front of the room?

If I had more self-assurance and confidence, I would have said to Don, "No. I cannot and will not teach something that I know nothing about." But I quietly gave in.

To this day, I don't know how I made it through that semester. I became paralyzed for days ahead of my class, having nightmares about how those three hours would unfold. The reality was worse than the nightmares. The students were stunned at the lack of substance in the course and my complete ignorance of the field. I don't think any professor in the history of Boston University received worse teaching evaluations than I did for that course. It was an excruciating ordeal.

That experience – and the fact that I had not published a single article and still hadn't finished my dissertation – made it inevitable that BU would not renew my three-year contract. But when I received the termination letter, it still felt like a body blow. I would have to go back to the job market, but to be credible there, I had to finish that damn dissertation.

With a new sense of urgency, I asked a professor at MIT for methodological help; his wife was my colleague. That got me over the hump, and I was able to complete the dissertation. I went to New York for the defense and squeaked through. The nightmare was finally over. I had produced a mediocre dissertation that the rest of the world could now safely ignore.

The only good part of the dissertation was that I got to dedicate it to my beloved father-in-law. My relationship with him had grown, filling a painful void in my life. Despite my struggles, he was supportive and optimistic about my future. He inspired me to hold on to my idealism, though my father had mocked it.

To Ram Chandra Malhotra

With affection and admiration – for his uncommon integrity, clearheaded idealism, and unfailing diligence throughout a truly distinguished career. His wisdom, his great capacity for compassion, and the scope of his visionary thinking have inspired me and countless others to go beyond the narrow and the mundane that so preoccupy us. Perhaps his greatest virtue is that he has never wavered in his beliefs; in this cynical age, he has given idealism a good name and continues to give generously of himself to the truly needy of this world. May his efforts be blessed, may the world take heed, and may we all take heart from a man who stands for the best of humanity.

With my PhD finally secured, I went back on the job market, seeking a fresh start at the AMA Educators Conference in Toronto. I had 40 interviews, made eight campus visits, and received four offers. I chose George Mason University in the suburbs of Washington, DC, where one of my sisters-in-law lived. GMU had recently become known because one of its professors had been awarded the Nobel Prize in Economics. My salary would be $47,000 a year, a nearly 50% bump up from what I was making at BU.

Soon after I turned 30 in the summer of 1988, we drove to northern Virginia to look for a house. A few weeks later, we rented a truck, loaded up our belongings, and made the drive down I-95 to our new suburban life. American Dream, Take 2.

Reflections

My father's description of me as straightforward and simple had some truth to it. But he conveyed it in a way that was dismissive and disrespectful. He at once took the nuclear option, giving me a stark ultimatum that I had to conform to his demands, or he would cut me off from the family. He made the cardinal mistake of a disapproving parent; it forced my hand and left me no choice but to oppose him.

> *How would you handle such a situation if you were speaking to your son or daughter? Would you first ask yourself, "Why do I want this outcome? Is it for my selfish reasons, or is it because of what I genuinely believe is right for my child?"*

When I asked Shailu to marry me, she made her acceptance conditional on her family's approval. They were generally supportive of her aspirations, which is why she sought their input. I felt deeply controlled by my father, which is why I did not.

> *If you have adult children, consider your relationship to them. Would they seek your guidance in such matters?*

My relationship with my father-in-law was deeply healing to me because of my father wound. I experienced in him what I dreamed a father could be. He saw my essential qualities as strengths; my father dismissed them as weaknesses.

If you had a challenging relationship with one or both of your parents, have you been able to find substitute parental figures who had a similar healing impact on you?

My father's reaction illustrated starkly that his love for me was entirely conditional. It was rooted in a transactional mindset.

Did you experience conditional or unconditional love from your parents? What difference did that make in your life?

When my father threatened to kill himself, it seemed authentic in the moment. However, I later came to see it as a form of emotional blackmail, a calculated strategy to get me to do what he wanted me to do.

Have you experienced emotional manipulation to get you to act in a certain way? Were you able to withstand that pressure? Have you ever used this tactic on others?

My father's action in pointing a gun at me raised the stakes even further. This was a deeply traumatic event that my psyche buried for decades.

Are there memories that are so painful that you may have suppressed them or minimized them? Can you excavate them and process them?

The *Ordinary People* incident left a deep mark on my psyche and damaged our marriage and my ability to be vulnerable. Had I been able to respond differently, it could have led us to deeper mutual understanding.

Can you think of episodes in your life that would benefit from a reframing? Plan to have such healing conversations with the people involved, regardless of how much time has elapsed since the incidents.

8

A New Beginning

Our house was on a cul-de-sac in a "planned community" called Burke in northern Virginia, about five miles from the George Mason University campus. It was a small four-bedroom house with a one-car garage and a beautiful brick patio in the back. At $205,000, it was significantly more than we had expected to spend.

It was a relief to be in a new place after the humiliations and traumas I had experienced in Boston. George Mason was a fast-growing, ambitious state school that had benefited from the explosive growth of the northern Virginia region.

Now that my dissertation was out of the way, I needed to publish. However, I had simply not developed that part of me and idled for the first year. Instead, I had focused on my teaching, settling into the new house, and dealing with our newly discovered pregnancy.

Exactly nine months to the day after I started at George Mason, our son Alok was born. Nothing quite prepares you for the experience of having a child. The love I felt pouring out of me for this little soul was overpowering. Within days of bringing him home from the hospital, I said to Shailu, "This is incredible! Let's have another one right away!" Initially, the experience brought us closer and distracted me from the underlying tension between us and the constant overhang of my father's rejection and banishment. I was teaching a summer course every morning. Each afternoon, Shailu was able to rest as I took over and delighted in Alok progressing just as the book *What to Expect the First Year* described. Until he was two and a half, we had no inkling that he might be special needs. In fact, his verbal skills were quite precocious for his age.

Because of my bitter feelings toward my father for disowning me, I unconsciously defined good fatherhood as the opposite of his approach. But that was misguided. My father had been an exemplary father in some respects. He made sure that I went to excellent schools and had interesting experiences. He was resilient and adventurous. He instilled a sense of duty and discipline in me. But he was not communicative, never physically affectionate, and made us feel fearful rather than relaxed in his presence. My counter-script around fatherhood was to be loving and easygoing, consistent with my innate tendency to always seek harmony.

My estrangement from my father was now in its fourth year. Upon learning our story, some of our Indian friends had said, "Wait until you are expecting a child. He will definitely come around then." But I did not hear from my father when my son was born. My bitterness toward him deepened. I wrote him an angry letter condemning his heartlessness all over again and recalling that he had "cursed" my marriage. He had rendered me invisible; "canceled" me, in modern parlance. It was like phantom limb syndrome – a part of me was missing, but I still felt it keenly. Would I ever see my family again?

Then came an opening. My friend Ruby Roy Dholakia, a professor at the University of Rhode Island, was cochairing a major conference to be held in January 1991 in New Delhi with the theme "Marketing and Economic Development." She asked if I would chair a session on "Marketing and Information Technology" that would include two eminent scholars: Everett Rogers and Jag Sheth. Everett Rogers was renowned for his work on the diffusion of innovations, applying epidemiology to the study of how new products get adopted. Jag Sheth was famous for the seminal

Howard-Sheth Theory of Buyer Behavior. I had known of him ever since I did my MBA; he was one of the most prominent business academics of Indian origin in the United States. I jumped at the opportunity.

The conference attracted many top marketing scholars from the United States, including Phil Kotler, the "father" of modern marketing; we had used his textbook in my MBA program. India's finance minister and the prime minister spoke at the event. The prime minister, Chandra Shekhar, was a noted socialist. He got into a contentious debate on stage with Phil Kotler, saying that as a poor country, India did not need – nor could it afford – to waste precious resources on marketing. Phil tried to convince him that marketing could aid in economic development.

India was experiencing a serious economic crisis then; the government was close to defaulting on its obligations, and foreign exchange reserves were barely enough to cover two weeks' worth of imports. Chandra Shekhar's tenure as PM lasted only seven months. Under intense pressure from the International Monetary Fund, his successor reduced government regulation of the economy and made foreign investment far easier. A decade after China had opened its economy, India was on its way to rapid and sustained economic growth that would enable hundreds of millions to escape extreme poverty over the ensuing decades.

The session that I chaired overflowed with attendees drawn by the two well-known scholars. Jag's insights and delivery captivated me. This was the first time I met a marketing academic who inspired me. At the end of the session, Jag turned to me and said, "We should connect. Please get in touch with me after you get back to the US." I was thrilled to hear him say that.

Jag would loom large in my life from that day forward, boosting my confidence and giving me opportunities that I would never have dreamed of. He would become the second substitute father figure in my life, after my father-in-law. This happened a day before I reconnected with my father, over five years after I had last seen him.

The "Prodigal" Son Returns

After the conference, we headed to Indore like I had done countless times before. Except this time it was different. I was anxious about seeing my father, and eager to see everyone else. I can only imagine the emotions Shailu was experiencing as she was about to encounter the man who had so cruelly demeaned and rejected her.

I had made it clear to my sister and my brother-in-law Sangram that my father needed to apologize if there was to be any kind of rapprochement between us. Sangram said, "Raj, you have become too Americanized. An Indian father will never apologize to his son." I replied, "I don't care. I will not stay in his house, and I will have nothing to do with him if he does not apologize."

My father had finally built a house of his own – an imposing structure made of reddish-brown stones. He had traveled around Rajasthan sourcing materials for the house. The floors were white marble, and the custom furniture was dark mahogany.

I entered the unfamiliar space filled with familiar objects and photos from my childhood. I touched my mother's feet and embraced her for a long time as she kissed both my cheeks and cried quietly in my arms. She whispered, "I love you, Raj." The only times she ever spoke English were when she said those words to me.

I saw my father sitting in an enclosed porch on the other side of the family room, his hair as white as cotton; he had stopped dyeing it during my years of exile. He was only 54, but looked much older. I went up to him and silently bent down to touch his feet. He put his hand on my head and said, "*Jeete raho*" (live long). Shailu followed suit, and he blessed her in the same way. He tried to pick up my 18-month-old son, but Alok squirmed away.

Acting as though the previous five years had not happened, my father said, "You must be tired. Why don't you settle into your room and rest?" We went upstairs, unpacked, and laid down for a couple of hours.

I came down around 5 o'clock for tea. After taking a sip, I put my cup down and looked at him. I said, "Papa, we need to talk about the last five years. You owe me an apology for what you put me through.

You cursed my marriage and never acknowledged the birth of my son. How can a father do that to a son? You also need to apologize to Shailu and to her parents for how you treated them."

My father immediately exploded into one of his signature rages. "Who the hell do you think you are? How dare you say that to me in my own house?" He seemed to think that merely allowing us into his home was an act of great benevolence on his part. That ignited my rage and unleashed the bitterness that I had been carrying around for five years. These confrontations with my father were the only times I yelled at anybody; it would have surprised most people who know me that I was capable of such a response.

At the end of my tirade, I said, "I will not stay in this house. We will check into a hotel tomorrow."

"Do whatever the hell you want," my father growled back. I went upstairs and slammed the door to the bedroom.

My sister had invited us for dinner that evening. My father and I maintained an icy silence on the drive over and throughout dinner. When we returned, I hugged my mother goodnight and ignored him. Shailu and I retreated to our room and began packing.

In the morning, I came down in my pajamas for tea. A few relatives had come to meet us and were also staying in the house. Everybody was sitting on thin cotton mattresses on the cold marble floor of the still-unfurnished sunken living room. I joined the circle and silently poured myself a cup of tea. As I brought the cup to my lips, my father started crying.

Through his tears, he said, "We had some hopes and aspirations as a family. I did what I thought was my duty to do." I was stunned. My anger had hardened overnight. I had been heartbroken for so long, torn up over the separation from my family. After the events of the previous evening, I had steeled myself for a lifetime of estrangement and bitterness. I was flooded with overwhelming relief and gratitude as soon as I saw my father's tears.

I barely registered what he said; his tears were all that mattered. He had not uttered the words, "I am sorry," but I no longer needed him to. In an instant, all was forgiven and forgotten – or so I thought.

Much to my surprise, five years after the actual event, my father organized a wedding reception for us. Instead of gifts, guests handed Shailu and me envelopes filled with cash as we sat on high-backed chairs at one end of the tent-covered lawn. Liquor flowed freely. Harmony had once again entered my life. It felt like a fresh start for all of us. That night, I slept peacefully for the first time in over five years.

The next morning, I was jolted back into reality, receiving a hint that perhaps all was not quite healed. My father said to me, "How much cash did you receive? I need it to pay for the cost of the reception."

We stayed another 10 days. My father's true nature soon resurfaced as he started to bully my wife in subtle and not-so-subtle ways. He said, "I hear you like to cook. What do you like to make?" When she replied, "Chinese food," he announced, "Shailu will make a full Chinese dinner tomorrow night for all of us. Nobody is allowed to help her." He was intent on humiliating her. My brother Sanjay (a trained chef) ignored his order and helped her as much as he could. But the dinner was a disaster. Many ingredients were not available, so she had to improvise. The stove and cooking utensils were unsuited to Chinese cooking. When we sat down to eat, Papa criticized the shortcomings of each dish, pushing it aside after just one bite. He noisily pushed his chair back from the dining table and walked away shaking his head.

I sat at the table silently and didn't react to his boorish behavior. When we went upstairs to our room, Shailu burst out in anger and tears. "How could you let him treat me like that?" I had no good explanation. I should have spoken up about his rudeness. But the harmony-seeking part of me refused to make an issue of it. Having just concluded a five-year battle (in India, we use the term *Mahabharata* – the great war) with my father, I just didn't have the stomach to start a new fight right away. "That's just how he is," I mumbled.

We had learned over the decades that there was no changing Papa; he was who he was. My mother often sought to excuse or explain his coarse behavior by saying, "That is Papa's habit – just ignore it." I now realize how my mother's lifelong passivity enabled my father's bullying to go unchecked.

I should have responded differently to Shailu. I should have acknowledged my father's egregious behavior and empathized with how she felt. I should have told her she was an excellent cook and that it had been brave for her to attempt to prepare that meal under those conditions. I should have confronted my father and said to him, "I will not stand for this. She worked hard. I am proud of her. Don't ever speak to her like again." To my lasting regret, I did none of those things.

We had made plans to go to Nepal to visit my in-laws before we returned to the United States. We invited my parents to join us, which they agreed to do. But they backed out at the last minute, claiming poor health. I wasn't surprised. I am sure my father never intended to make the trip but said they would just to appease me. An entire decade would pass before my parents met my in-laws. It happened over lunch in Boston and lasted a couple of hours. I felt again the piercing pain of what it meant to have an unblessed marriage and an atomized family.

After that trip, I fell back into my old pattern of trying hard to impress him, to prove myself worthy of him, to get him to be proud of me. I started going to India twice a year to make up for lost time, leaving my young and growing family behind. I exhausted myself teaching executives for five full days in India to earn enough to barely cover my airfare. On each trip, there inevitably came a point at which I had an emotional outburst toward my father and all my wounds became fresh again. It turned out we hadn't really healed after all. Despite everything he had said and done and how miserable he had made our lives, how could it be that such a big part of me still craved my father's approval?

★★★

After that first trip back to India, I was a transformed human. I returned to the United States feeling lighter and nimbler, as though an invisible boulder had been lifted off my shoulders. Freed of some (not all) of the bitterness and anger that my father's actions had implanted in me, I entered a much more productive phase with my work. I finally started publishing. I also learned to recognize opportunity when I saw it.

The School of Management at George Mason was going through a strategic rethinking. On my own initiative, I wrote a detailed analysis laying out what the school's strategy should be and sent it to the dean and the entire faculty. It generated a great deal of discussion and got me noticed as a contributing junior faculty member with creative ideas.

Around this time, I read an article in the *Harvard Business Review* (HBR) by George Gilder titled "Into the Telecosm." Gilder wrote about how the coming explosion in telecommunication technologies would bring about a wholesale change in society, ushering in remote learning, remote shopping, telepresence, and other ideas that were radical at the time (this was a few years before the "World Wide Web" took off). His vision captivated me. I then read a brief article in the *Wall Street Journal* about Singapore's "Intelligent Island" project, designed to create a fully wired society in which people could accomplish many everyday tasks remotely and digitally – a real-world manifestation of Gilder's futuristic ideas. I wrote a letter to the HBR editor, commenting on Gilder's article and mentioning Singapore's plans. Instead of publishing my letter, which is all I was hoping for, the editor called me and asked, "Are you an expert on Singapore? We would love to know more about this Intelligent Island initiative." I replied, "I am not an expert, but I could become one! Do you see this as a potential HBR article?" He replied, "It could be. No promises, of course, but we would look seriously at anything you write on the subject."

That was enough for me. Getting published in HBR would be a huge career boost for me; it is widely read by senior executives and business academics. I showed the dean my correspondence with the editor and asked for funding to go to Singapore to research the topic. He gave me enough for the airfare. I then wrote to Singapore National University and asked for accommodations on campus while I did my research, which they agreed to do in return for a few lectures.

I spent nearly three weeks in Singapore, interviewing key business and government leaders. I learned that Jag Sheth had been an adviser to the government of Singapore on how a tiny country with no natural resources could position itself to thrive in the world, so I sent a draft of my article to him for his comments. The experience was highly enjoyable and reignited my passion for writing. While there, I wrote a lengthy "Singapore Diary" with my impressions of that unique society and a half dozen humorous articles about the many quirks of life there. HBR published my article in 1992 as "Singapore Invests in the Nation-Corporation," which led to me being interviewed on National Public Radio. For the first time in my life, I was tasting a degree of professional success.

A Mentor at Last

I learned from my friend Ruby Dholakia that the University of Rhode Island had invited Jag Sheth to spend a day on campus. I immediately bought an Amtrak ticket and made my way to Warwick. I spent the whole day observing Jag as he held meetings with faculty, students, and business leaders. He gave three talks, each of which I found incredibly compelling and enjoyable. The first was about the impact of changing demographics on marketing and on society, the second was about how globalization was likely to unfold, and the third was about what he called the "sacred pigs" of marketing (theories that scholars blindly accept). He joked that as an Indian, he could not use the phrase "sacred cow" since all cows are sacred! I was enthralled by how engaging, practical, insightful, and scholarly each of his talks was. Here, at last, was a worthy academic role model. Jag was enthusiastic about his work, generous with his time, and a delight to be around.

Jag told me that he had enjoyed my article on Singapore and invited me to come to Atlanta to explore shared interests. He especially appreciated my writing style. I headed to Atlanta at the earliest opportunity and spent a whole day with him. I was in shock that this eminent scholar would give so much time to an unknown, untenured academic with no track record – someone who had barely completed his dissertation. I stayed the night at his house and got to know his gracious wife, Madhu. By the end of my visit, Jag and I had identified several projects to work on. This was the beginning of a long journey of rapid personal and professional growth. Jag helped me find my voice, respect my own abilities, and dare to dream big – gifts I had never received from any of my professors or my father.

When I met Jag, I was 32 and he was 51. I was just getting started while he was at the height of his powers and global acclaim. He worked with infectious joy, curiosity, and creativity. He was in great demand as a speaker, executive educator, and corporate adviser. Once we got to know each other, Jag pulled me into his extraordinarily broad stream of activities, including the Center for Telecommunications Management he had founded at the University of Southern California, the new Center for Relationship Marketing he had just established at Emory University, and the commercial Institute for Communications Research and Education that he ran in Atlanta. We embarked on multiple writing projects, both academic and professional. I was soon flying all over the country, learning how to engage with business leaders through speeches and executive education programs. My life went from uneventful to exhilarating in a matter of weeks.

A few years into our relationship, Jag experienced a retinal detachment in his eye, and his doctor forbade him from flying for a while. Rather than cancel his speaking engagements, Jag asked me to deliver the five speeches on his schedule that week. Like a true mentor, he believed in me more than I believed in myself. The prospect terrified me, but I worked feverishly to master the material. I grew tremendously that week, surprising myself as I confidently addressed audiences of 2,000 internal auditors in Los Angeles, 500 telecommunications executives in Dallas, and several hundred marketing managers in Miami. I flew first class and was chauffeured around in luxury cars, including a ridiculous white stretch limo in Los Angeles!

My work with Jag took over my life. I flew to Atlanta at least once a month, besides all my other travel for speaking and executive education programs. We always had at least five or six projects ongoing. Jag and I wrote several seminal academic papers, as well as scores of professional papers. I wrote case studies, industry notes, future-looking analyses, and competitor profiles that we used in the many executive education programs we did together.

Being aligned with Jag gave me the courage to think big. I was watching CNBC one day in 1995 and thinking about how boring they made business feel with their incessant focus on the gyrations of the stock market. They missed the passion, heartbreak, and drama of business. Calvin Coolidge once said, "The business of America is business," but there was no meaningful business content on TV. I thought, "Why not start a new cable television network focused on all the aspects of business that people found fascinating?" Thus was born the idea for the "MBA Network." I spent nearly a year developing a comprehensive plan and trying to get the network launched. Comcast, Discovery, and PBS were all interested. At our meeting, John Hendricks, the founder of Discovery, said, "I had never thought about it before: the business of America is business, yet there is nothing on cable TV about business." We got very close, but the effort ultimately failed because of the shifting economics of the cable industry, which were upended by the upcoming launch of Fox News. Rather than receiving money from cable operators, as we expected to do, Fox *paid* $100 million to cable companies to be featured on their channel line-ups. We couldn't compete in that world. Though a disappointing end to my dream, it bolstered my confidence to think big and outside the academic bubble.

My work with Jag was financially and professionally rewarding. He saw gifts in me I did not know I had. My head was fully engaged in my work, but my heart remained disconnected. Something was still missing.

Standing Up for Myself

Jag's faith in me boosted my confidence and self-trust. I started standing up for what I believed was right and for my values, such as fairness, respect, and making a positive difference in the world. I was also learning to not settle for false harmony.

I turned on the news on the morning of August 3, 1995, and heard that Disney was planning to acquire Capital Cities, which owned ESPN and the ABC television network. Anticipating significant synergies from the merger, Disney had offered a significant premium above the Capital Cities stock price. My research on the "second-order effects of synergy seeking" showed that there is often negative synergy in "vertical" mergers, in which a company acquires its own supplier or customer. In the media industry, this meant a linkup between a content producer such as Disney and a content distributor such as ABC. If the merger went through, Disney's content would find a guaranteed home on the ABC network; however, Disney would no longer have the freedom to shop around and get the best terms for that content. Likewise, ABC would lose freedom in determining which programs it should carry, as it would now be obligated to carry Disney content. I quickly wrote a piece called "The Celebration May Be Premature" and faxed it to the *Wall Street Journal* editorial page. Around 2 p.m., the op-ed editor Max Boot called me to say that he liked the piece and would run it the next morning. We went back and forth with some edits and finalized it by 5 p.m.

The next morning, I was sitting in my office looking at the published piece. In its editorial wisdom, the *Journal* had titled it "A Goofy Deal" instead of my somber academic title. I was basking in the satisfaction that a couple of million executives would see my article (and learn my name). A loud knock on the door broke my reverie. I opened it to find my colleague Bob Buzzell standing there holding a folded copy of the *Journal*. A renowned professor at Harvard Business School for decades, Bob had recently joined GMU as a distinguished professor of business to live closer to his children and grandchildren before retiring.

Expecting kudos from this eminent colleague, I was stunned when he loudly asked, with no preamble, "What the hell are you doing?"

"What do you mean, Bob?"

"Why are you writing for the *Wall Street Journal*? You're not a journalist. That is not your job. You should be sitting here writing academic articles."

Stunned, I fumbled for the right words. "I've done some research that applies to this. I thought it was worthwhile to get it out there."

Bob shook his head and walked away. He glanced back at me and said, "By the way, you should have cited my research in this area."

Still shaken, I sat back down at my desk. The phone rang. It was my friend Vinod Singhal, a professor of operations management at Georgia Tech University.

"Congratulations on the *Wall Street Journal* piece," he said.

"Thank you, Vinod. I needed that!"

"You do realize this is academic suicide, don't you?"

Now I was angry — and a little disgusted. What kind of value system considered it a mistake for a business professor to publish an article in one of the world's leading business publications about a significant development in business? How could we academics so detach ourselves from the world of practice?

I vowed to myself that I would not succumb to such a ridiculous value system. In fact, I doubled down. Over the next few years, I published a half dozen more *Wall Street Journal* op-eds. It got to where the editor called me to ask if I wanted to write a commentary when a significant business event happened. Eventually, I started getting different phone calls from academic colleagues around the country: "Hey Raj, can you tell me how I can get published in the *Wall Street Journal*?"

★★★

The year I was up for tenure, two senior GMU faculty colleagues asked me to work with them on a consulting project with the Bureau of Land Management. I did most of the work, making trips to Wisconsin for research and to deliver the final presentation. It was a $20,000 contract. When we finished, the colleague who had initiated the project (who would soon vote on my tenure case) wrote me a personal check for $4,000. I thought that was unfair given how much of the work I had done. Rather than divide it equally, I suggested he keep $8,000 as the initiator of the project and that the other two of us get $6,000 each. He said, "Let me think about it." A few days later, he told me that he was going to stick with his original plan.

I was furious; clearly, he was leveraging his power over me because of the upcoming tenure vote. I remembered seeing the words "George Mason University" on a document he had asked me to sign. I reached out to the university's legal counsel's office, asking for help in mediating the dispute. Within minutes, I received a call from the provost's office, asking me to come in immediately for a meeting. The provost told me the university had no record of this engagement; apparently, the university's name had been illegally used to secure a government contract.

The provost launched a thorough investigation. I was advised to hire a lawyer, which I reluctantly did at considerable expense. The outcome of the investigation was that the university forced the other two professors to return the money and take unpaid one-year leaves of absence. I was told that I would not receive a pay raise that year and that a letter of reprimand would be placed in my personnel file. However, the provost would approve my tenure. I thought it was unfair, but my lawyer urged me to accept the terms; the main thing was that I was still being granted tenure – the biggest prize in academia. The provost made it up to me the following year by giving me a much larger raise than normal and removing the reprimand letter from my file.

Violations of fairness always moved me to action. This came up again in a rather bizarre development at the School of Management.

There was so much faculty infighting that a group of professors conspired with a compliant dean to split the school into two entities: a "Graduate Business Institute" (GBI), which would have its own faculty and house all the graduate programs, including the lucrative and prestigious Executive MBA program; and a shrunken School of Management whose faculty would teach only undergraduate courses.

Only two universities in the country had separate undergraduate and graduate business schools. I called professors at both; they confirmed that there were many downsides to such an arrangement and few upsides. First, it created a class system within the faculty since most prefer teaching graduate students. Second, it created inefficiency; each entity would need to hire additional faculty to cover its courses. I wrote a memo with my analysis and sent it to the faculty, the dean, the provost, and the president – to no avail.

I then learned that the dean had created a secret committee to select faculty for the GBI. I immediately called the provost's office, asking that the dean identify the committee members and use transparent criteria for selecting faculty. He quickly agreed to do so. I was invited to join the GBI faculty

The GBI experiment lasted for a couple of years before it collapsed of its own illogic. We were all one big unhappy family again.

I was becoming adept at creating what civil rights leader and Congressman John Lewis would later call "good trouble." I had become so much more capable of engaging in necessary conflict since I had faced my father and demanded an apology.

A Growing Family

All three of our children were born in the decade I was at George Mason, which took me from age 30 to 40. Our son, Alok, seemed perfectly healthy early on, but gradually started exhibiting signs of an underlying condition that we would not decipher for another 10 years. The severity of his condition increased year after year, eventually characterized by mood swings; deep interest in a few areas (which would be "raps and maps" in his case); hypersensitivity to physical touch; struggles in picking up social cues, understanding personal space, and interpreting facial expressions; and challenges with fine and gross motor control skills.

Our daughters, Priya and Maya, were also born during those years. Priya was a cherubic creature who manifested joy in her very being. She loved everything about life: music, dance, food, dressing up, movies, reading, writing, traveling. One of her many nicknames was Gulabi, which means pink (her favorite color), but also refers to the Indian sweet *gulab jamun*. She would say, "I am brown, I am round, and I am sweet, just like a *gulab jamun*!"

Maya was cerebral, intense, sensitive, empathetic, and witty from a young age. An episode when she was three illustrates what she was like. We were about to leave home to go to somebody's house for dinner when Alok said that he needed to go to the bathroom. I told him to hurry. After about 10 minutes, I knocked on the door and said, "Alok, are you almost done?" He replied, "Yes. I am wiping myself." Another five minutes went by. I knocked again. "Are you done now?" "I am still wiping myself." Losing my patience, I said, "Alok, how long does it take to wipe your stupid butt?"

Fiercely protective of her much older brother, Maya sprang up and reprimanded me, "Daddy, that is rude! You should not say 'butt.'" Then she walked to the bathroom door, knocked gently, and said, "Alok, don't worry. You don't have a stupid butt. You have a lovely bottom."

★★★

My decade at George Mason was one of intense growth. To my earlier role as teacher, I had now added speaker, author, and father. The intensity of my life in that decade took precedence over trying to transcend the rocky foundation on which our marriage had begun. Toward the end of that decade, we started couples counseling, which did not make much of a difference for me. From my perspective, it seemed something was lacking between us – independent of the circumstances that had brought us together.

Awakening My Creative Side

I had taught in George Mason's Executive MBA program since its inception. The students were seasoned executives with an average of 16 years of work experience. With my practical bent and growing experience working with companies, I was well suited to teaching in this environment. Since my research was very applied, I was able to use many of my published articles as assigned readings in my courses.

When an opening for the director of executive programs came up, I applied for it. After navigating some tricky politics, the dean offered me the position. I immediately launched an ambitious initiative to revise the curriculum. My goal was to create the most innovative and forward-looking EMBA program in the country. I emphasized services rather than manufacturing as the context, a relationship mindset, and a strong emphasis on how information technology was transforming business. I created intensive one-credit learning experiences on cutting-edge topics. I also added two new residency periods, starting with a three-day "High Performance Learning" program in which students "learned how to learn." I hired Michael Gelb, a well-known expert on creativity and integrative thinking, to design and teach the program, which included mind mapping, creative problem solving, speed reading, strategic presentation skills – and even juggling (as a metaphor for cultivating a state of relaxed concentration).

Meeting Michael changed my sense of who I was and what I could be. Until then, my self-concept was that of a left-brained, analytical engineer type. I now realized that I could be a creative individual, as evidenced by my redesign of the EMBA program. Michael and I would write *The Healing Organization* together 20 years later, which is about how business can alleviate suffering and elevate joy in the world.

Though I enjoyed the creative aspects of my role as director, I hated the administrative side: supervising staff, managing budgets, and so forth. Then, without asking me, the dean fired my experienced associate director on some flimsy pretext while I was in India. I was furious and started to think that GMU might not be a long-term home for me. The politics had become unbearable.

One day, while chatting with a colleague in his office, I picked up a magazine and saw an ad from Bentley College in the Boston area. They were recruiting for new positions called "Trustee Professor-ships." The positions were earmarked for scholars working at the intersection of a business discipline (such as marketing) and informa-tion technology. It was part of Bentley president Joe Morone's strat-egy to position Bentley as "The Business School for the Information Age." Though the application deadline had already passed, I called to see if they were still accepting applications. They said they had received 160 applications but had not filled the position and were still looking. I emailed them my CV and a cover letter.

The next day, I received an invitation for an interview with the search committee. By the time I returned home, they had invited me to return the following week for a two-day campus visit that included a presentation to the faculty and a meeting with the president. A few days after that trip, I received an offer. My salary would be 60% higher than I was making at George Mason, and my teaching load would be half, just two courses a year. I would also have a graduate assistant and a discretionary budget. It was a no-brainer for me to accept.

We headed to Boston a week later to find a house. I would be returning to a place that had left many scars on my psyche. I had left humiliated 10 years earlier; I would return as a tenured full professor in a prestigious endowed chair position. I had just turned 40 – right on schedule for a midlife crisis.

Reflections

My estrangement from my father so colored my perception of him as a father that I came to define good fathering as the opposite of everything he had done. That was misguided. Everyone has something to teach us, and he had a lot to teach me about being a father.

Have you ever been so alienated from someone that you could see none of their good qualities? What opportunities and lessons might you have missed because of such black-and-white thinking?

The more badly you want something, the lower the bar is for what you will accept. I jumped at the prospect of peace my father was throwing to me. I settled for momentary harmony rather than true healing.

When is an apology not an apology? Have you ever accepted an insincere apology simply because you wanted the conflict to end? How would you handle that differently now?

I had stood up to bullies all my life but failed to do so when my father bullied my wife. Bullies are bullies, whether or not they are in your family. Such behavior is never acceptable.

Have you experienced bullying in your life? Have you ever confronted a bully in the moment? What was the outcome?

Mentoring is one of the most powerful things that can happen in your professional career. The right mentor can dramatically speed up your growth and expand your horizons. A mentor sees potential that you don't even realize about yourself.

Have you experienced the benefit of having a great mentor in your professional life? If not, can you find one now? Have you been a mentor to younger colleagues? If not, can you start now?

I have always been a trusting soul, which is why I implicitly trusted my colleagues at George Mason University when they asked me to sign the BLM contract. I have been burned a few times, but I believe that the overall impact of my tendency to trust has been positive.

What is your default mode with trust? Do you trust others until they prove unworthy of that trust, or do you withhold trust until people have "earned" it? How has your choice served you or not until now?

Realizing that your child has a severe disability is a devastating moment in the life of a parent. Close couples handle such shocks by sharing their grief and leaning on each other. Unfortunately, my wife and I weren't able to do that. We each suffered silently and alone.

In moments of deep pain and anguish, do you have a partner or other you can turn to for mutual comfort? If not, can you make space in your life for such a partner?

9 | Back to Boston

Boston was a haunted place for me. Everywhere I looked, there were memories – many painful, some traumatic – that became fresh again: driving through the Boston University campus, the building where we got married, the classrooms where I had suffered my teaching humiliations, the undergraduate dorm in which I had been a faculty-in-residence for two years, the apartment complex where my father had put a knife to his chest, the spot by the Charles River where I had proposed.

It was time to put all that behind me and start afresh.

We rented a house in Lexington for the first year while we looked for a house to buy. Lexington played a central role in early American history. It had outstanding schools and a relatively diverse mix of residents. At least seven Nobel laureates lived in the town, the advantage of being so close to Harvard and MIT.

My new colleague and friend at Bentley College, Alan Hoffman, a professor of strategy, joked that faculty only want two things: to get paid more and teach less! I achieved those in this role. From an associate professor three years removed from getting tenure, Bentley had catapulted me to the pinnacle of the academic hierarchy: a tenured full professor with an "endowed chair."

I had a prestigious, highly visible position with all the trappings of success: a good salary, a big house in a lovely town, and a brand-new Mercedes. Yet I was quite miserable. The move had put a further strain on our marriage. Having just turned 40, I was experiencing a midlife crisis. My work with Jag had been exciting and impactful, but I was facing what felt like an uninspiring career again. My position at Bentley required me to focus heavily on information technology, a subject I no longer cared much about.

I persevered and tried to do what was expected of me. I met monthly with the president of the college. *Fortune* magazine featured us in an article touting Bentley's bold new strategy of becoming "The Business School for the Information Age" and the central role I was to play in that.

I had been teaching about technologies for various aspects of marketing such as new product development, customer relationship management, advertising copy development, media planning, and so on. Sitting in a boring faculty meeting one day, I had a vision for a "Marketing Technology Showcase" that would feature a collection of these technologies that students could experience in one place. After the meeting, I mocked up a simple brochure on my computer, listed a set of technologies we could feature, and sent it to the president. He jumped on it. The project took off; within a couple of months, the trustees allocated $1 million to renovate an existing space on campus and transform it into the newly christened "Center for Marketing Technology." It would have a large classroom with cutting-edge computers and display technologies, and four "sandboxes," each housing a different set of marketing technologies.

The problem was my rapidly waning passion for both marketing and technology. I enjoyed the creative aspects of visioning and designing the center, but had no interest in running it. We launched a search for a new director, but then the college decided not to invest the additional resources and insisted that I run the center. That was a disaster for the college and for me.

New Millennium, New Challenges

In the summer of 2000, my parents finally came to visit, 14 years after I got married and nine years after my reconciliation with my father. They had still never met my in-laws. The visit was painfully awkward. We avoided any blowups, but my parents did not connect with my wife at all; they were as uncomfortable around her as she was with them. We were all just trying to survive the ordeal of being together.

As was his lifelong habit, my father drank every evening and then unloaded all his complaints and dissatisfactions onto my mother when they went to bed. As I walked past their room, I could hear him speaking in an indistinct murmur. Later in life, as my mother grew older and required hearing aids, he would insist that she put them back in so that he could spend an hour every night filling her ears with his angry complaints.

One evening, my father became angry at my visiting sister-in-law because she hadn't made dinner before going out for the evening. That crossed a line for me. I told him they should leave earlier than planned. I realized sadly that some things are just not meant to be.

My in-laws came to visit the day before my parents left. Had the circumstances been different, the two fathers might have found much in common, given their work in international development and agriculture. But they had little to say to each other, and our mothers had even less of a connection. This was the one and only time they met.

With great relief, I dropped my parents at the airport for their flight back to India.

★★★

During this time, I continued my work with Jag Sheth. We now embarked on a long-delayed book project: *The Rule of Three*. Jag had developed a powerful theory about competitive market strategy, showing how and why most industries ended up with a "big three" dominating the market. My role was to flesh out his insights into a book-length manuscript. While I had written dozens of papers and several book-length industry reports, I had never written an actual book. I didn't think I could; how could I possibly sustain an idea and carry a coherent narrative through hundreds of pages?

Our deadline was fast approaching, and I remained paralyzed. Intuiting that I needed to be sealed off from all distractions, Jag asked me to come to Atlanta and booked me for three weeks at the Emory Inn. He suggested I think of the book as a series of 10 articles. That I could do! I wrote feverishly from early morning until late afternoon and then reviewed what I had written with Jag. I took a walk, ate dinner, and continued working late into the night. At the end of those three weeks, I had produced a draft manuscript.

In the meantime, I had become deeply interested in systems thinking, a subject I first encountered in my undergraduate engineering program. From my limited knowledge of it, I believed it was essential to understanding how to run a business as well as create a functioning society. Jay Forrester had invented the field of system dynamics at MIT decades earlier. I called John Sterman, the chair of the system dynamics group at MIT, and asked if I could sit in on his course that fall, as a professional courtesy. He immediately agreed; classes were Tuesdays and Thursdays from 10 a.m. to noon in a large, tiered classroom with about 140 graduate students.

The third class was on Tuesday, September 11, 2001. I left Lexington around 9:15 a.m. to drive to Cambridge. I heard on the radio that an airplane had struck the World Trade Center in New York. The hosts speculated that perhaps a small commuter plane had strayed off its route. When I entered the classroom at 10 a.m., we were still living in a "normal" world. When I came out at noon, that world had irrevocably changed. While John was teaching us about stocks, flows, and feedback loops, two large planes had pierced the World Trade Center towers, a third had hit the Pentagon, and a fourth had been deliberately crashed into a field in Pennsylvania by brave passengers. Students crowded around a television that someone had wheeled into the foyer. They stared at the screen in disbelief, many with their hands covering their mouths. Had this really happened? What would happen now?

On Thursday, John opened the class by saying, "Let's put aside what we were planning to do today. Let's try to understand what happened on Tuesday and how the US should respond." He did a systems analysis of the events of that day. He said, "Any event that occurs is simply the outward manifestation of an underlying system at work. On Tuesday, four groups of terrorists sacrificed their lives so that they could inflict as much damage and suffering on the United States as possible. What made them do that? What were the underlying system dynamics that gave rise to those actions?"

Over the next hour, John masterfully constructed a detailed diagram depicting all the interconnected causal factors that led up to 9/11: US policy in the Middle East toward Israel and Palestine; the tragically high levels of youth unemployment in the region, which made them easy targets for Islamic fundamentalists looking to recruit suicide bombers; the history of troubled relations between Israel and Palestine and the rest of the Arab world; the rise of Islamic fundamentalism; the role of Saudi Arabia; and several other factors. John predicted that the likely US response to this event would be to launch an all-out "war on terror," which would mean finding and killing as many terrorists as possible. He pointed out that the United States had a long history of declaring failed and usually counterproductive "wars" on many deep-rooted social problems, such as crime, poverty, and drugs.

John showed how the US needed to address the *roots* of the problem, not simply attack its branches. It needed to win hearts and minds in the Middle East and elsewhere, as much as it needed to punish terrorists and their enablers. US policy in the region needed to be revamped to help create more vibrant economies and give people a sense of hope about the future. If the US did not do so, it would catalyze the recruiting of many more terrorists to replace the ones it killed. John pointed out that terrorism and entrepreneurship are often two sides of the same coin; young men faced with bleak economic prospects are easy prey for religious fanatics.

I thought John's analysis was brilliant. Being Jewish, he was able to speak about US policy toward Israel and the Palestinians in a way that many others were reluctant to. After the class, I went to John's office to thank him for his penetrating insights. I then all but begged him to write up his analysis and publish it as an op-ed in the *New York Times* or the *Washington Post*. He immediately recoiled, saying, "That is not my job, Raj. I will probably write it up for a journal at some point."

I flashed back to the episode with Bob Buzzell a few years earlier when he told me to stick to writing academic articles and not insert myself into real-world issues. John could have had a bigger positive impact on the public discourse and on US policy on this critical subject at that pregnant moment than almost anyone else. But he chose to remain within the ivory tower, speaking only to students and other faculty. I thought to myself, "What good is our knowledge if we don't apply it in service of the largest challenges that we collectively face?"

My Winter of Discontent

The country was deeply shaken that fall and my family was struggling as well. Our son was now 12 years old, and his condition had worsened. The atmosphere at home became more tense and gloomy, affecting everyone and contributing to our marital woes. In early November 2001, after we had undergone intermittent therapy for three years, our therapist uttered the dreaded words: "I think it would be best for everyone in your family if you separate."

I did not want to hear it, but the truth of it resonated deeply. Until then, divorce had been an unthinkable concept in my mind. India has the lowest divorce rate in the world: around 1%. Of course, that doesn't mean that 99% of Indian marriages are happy. In fact, most of the marriages I had seen in India were dysfunctional and miserable. But that didn't seem to matter. Marriage in India was akin to a life sentence, a part of your destiny. It was something to be endured, a duty to be fulfilled, a means to the end of joining families together and producing children. Ending a marriage carried with it a stigma of failure, guilt, and shame. It often resulted in social ostracism.

Leaving my marriage in 2001 might have brought me peace of mind and given me a shot at happiness, but I had three children to think about: my sweet nine- and seven-year-old daughters and my loving, vulnerable, special needs son. I shuddered to think of how my leaving the marriage might devastate them.

Amid the sadness, the phone rang on Thanksgiving morning. It was Shailu's older sister. She said, "Daddy has died."

My legs gave out under me, and I sank to the floor. How could this be? A youthful 73, my father-in-law had been the picture of health and vitality. Although he had had a stress-induced mild heart attack and subsequent bypass surgery when he was 60, he had no vices (other than working too hard), a very healthy diet, and walked vigorously every day. His doctors marveled at how well his heart had recovered. Nilu filled in the details as we listened in disbelief. He and my mother-in-law had just returned from a walk near their home in Nepal. As she set up for dinner, he (literally) ran up the stairs to freshen up and say a brief prayer in the little shrine adjoining their bedroom. Moments later, she heard a gentle thud from upstairs. She called out, but he didn't respond, so she went upstairs to check on him. He was lying on his side in front of the altar, not breathing.

This was a profound loss. Ram Chandra Malhotra was everything I wished for in a father: wise and playful, strong and loving, practical and spiritual, humble and confident. In a way, he had re-fathered me for the previous 15 years. He had seen my true essence. My father had inherited nobility, while my father-in-law embodied true nobility: he was widely admired for his gentle demeanor and strength of character. My father demanded respect; my father-in-law was universally given respect. I never felt moved to dedicate a book to my father, while I dedicated my PhD thesis and a book to my father-in-law.

At this tragic time in our lives, it was unthinkable for me to leave my marriage. It was my duty and my desire to walk beside my wife and children through this dark period.

Good Thing, Bad Thing – Who Knows?

The season of failure is the best time for sowing the seeds of success.

—Paramhansa Yogananda

The Rule of Three came out soon after, but I took little joy in the publication of my first book. I felt hollow and emptied of energy and motivation. I showed up to teach my classes but did little else. I did nothing to build the Center for Marketing Technology (CMT) into something of significance. I simply did not care about marketing or technology – or about anything, really.

It was now early 2002. I was in the fourth year of my five-year term as "Trustee Professor," which meant that my appointment was up for renewal. While my teaching and publication records were fine, I had done little to justify the significant investment the college had made in the CMT. I soon received the news that I had been dreading: I would lose my chaired position the following year. I would remain a full professor with tenure, but my teaching load would double, I would lose the additional salary of $20,000 that came with the chair and my $5,000 discretionary budget, and I would no longer have a graduate assistant.

I was already depressed; this blow compounded my misery. I felt like a general whose stripes had been ripped from his uniform in front of a gathered crowd. Most people in non-academic jobs would have envied my situation as a full professor with tenure, but I took no solace in that.

As I tried to absorb the blow, I found myself in a full-blown existential crisis. I did not read Viktor Frankl's classic *Man's Search for Meaning* until a few years later, but what he wrote in that landmark book was very relevant to my situation. We can't control what happens to us in life, but we can control how we choose to respond. He called it "The last of the human freedoms: to choose one's attitude in any given set of circumstances, to choose one's own way." Frankl also wrote, "He who has a why to live can bear almost any how."

My gut reaction was to shrink and retreat in shame from this public humiliation, which would have led me to spiral downward. Instead, a hitherto dormant wiser self within me awakened and started searching for a silver lining in the situation. I gradually realized that my position had imprisoned me for four years, handcuffing me to work that I had no passion for. Bentley had given me status and some extra money, but neither of those had given me joy or fulfillment.

Could I use this moment as an opportunity to connect to the aspects of my work that I enjoyed and found meaningful? I knew I could be an excellent teacher when my heart was connected to what I was teaching. I knew I was a talented writer and could move people with my ideas when I was passionate about what I was writing. I knew I was an excellent speaker and could inspire people through my words and my presence.

I decided to commit myself to two very specific goals: first, to reconnect with my love of teaching and win Bentley's annual teaching award; and second, to do impactful research and win the "Scholar of the Year" award. These external recognitions would restore my reputation at Bentley, but more importantly would result from doing work that mattered to me and to the world.

Newly energized and filled with quiet determination, I thoroughly redesigned my courses and worked with several colleagues to create a unique new interdisciplinary course that integrated different aspects of business together in 10 team-taught sessions. I searched my own values to source ideas for research articles and focused on issues such as respect, fairness, sustainability, and well-being.

Over the next three years, I published two books and many articles. I received Bentley's Scholar of the Year award in 2007 and the "Innovation in Teaching" award in 2008. In hindsight, losing that chaired position was one of the best things that ever happened to me.

Following My Heartbreak

Few professions invite more ridicule than marketing. Even the popular *Dilbert* cartoon strip frequently made fun of it. One showed a group of engineers looking down the hall at a door with the sign "Marketing Department: Three Drink Minimum." The public perception of my chosen profession was that it was frivolous, inauthentic, wasteful, annoying, and largely unnecessary. So imagine my ambivalence when I learned that the UK-based Chartered Institute of Marketing (the largest marketing association in the world) had identified me as one of "50 Leading Marketing Thinkers" and named me to "The Guru Gallery." Talk about a mixed blessing! Was that like being named "The Most Promising Mafioso of the Year"?

That sounds harsh; I know that marketing can do good in the world. That was the premise of the Marketing and Economic Development Conference in New Delhi where I first met Jag Sheth. But the way marketing was generally practiced weighed heavily on me. Marketing includes advertising, promotions, selling, and other activities aimed at getting customers to buy products and services. The profession often preyed on young children, getting them hooked on junk food or toys. It shamelessly exploited the bodies of young women to sell products, contributing to depression and eating disorders. It targeted the elderly and other vulnerable groups through clever campaigns designed to separate them from their money.

To me, much of marketing was insidious, pervasive, inefficient, ineffective, unethical, silly, harmful to our physical and emotional well-being, or damaging to the planet. Often, it was all these things. Pointing out marketing's many ills became my passion, even my obsession.

In 2004, I did a study on the image of marketing. I surveyed 2,000 customers and business professionals and confirmed what I already believed: most people (well over 80%) had a negative view of marketing. I did a detailed analysis of how much we were spending in the United States on all forms of marketing: advertisements, sales promotions, coupons, sales, sweepstakes, direct mail, etc. It came to about \$1 trillion – which exceeded the GDP of India that year by 40%! It stunned me that 1.1 billion people were living on significantly less than what companies in the US were spending on ads, coupons, and junk mail to "serve" 300 million people. On a per capita basis, the spending came to \$3,300 per person per year, or over \$14,000 for an average family – more than the income of 85% of the world's population.

I asked a simple question: What were customers, companies, and society getting for this torrent of spending? The answer was "not much"; in fact, the negative consequences outweighed the positive. Aggressive marketing led to depression, addiction, overconsumption, obesity, diabetes, heart disease, and other conditions. Yet, marketing spending kept rising.

Something was drastically wrong with this picture. While every other business function did more with less, marketing was doing less with more – year after year, decade after decade. The whole situation reminded me of a popular book from 1993: *Stop the Insanity!*

The Shame of Marketing?

I began toying with the idea of a book a called *Marketing Malpractices* in 2002 and created a rough outline. The first chapter was to be titled "Nobody Loves a Marketer (Not Even Mom?)." As an alternative book title, I included *The Shame of Marketing*. The legendary management thinker Peter Drucker had used that term to refer to the consumer movement in America. I wrote, "Today, the marketing function as practiced by many companies has transcended shame and has become shameless."

I wanted to write about the shame of marketing, but it was really about the shame of Raj. I had long replayed the following inner dialogue in my mind: "My father got a PhD in plant science so he could help end world hunger. I got a PhD in marketing so I can help sell more potato chips." It did not help that my bemused father would say to others, "My son is a professor of 'marketing,'" holding up air quotes when he spoke the word "marketing."

Having so much disdain for your own profession is like having an autoimmune disease; it eats away at you from the inside. This book was to be my penance, the ultimate indictment of marketing, the heartfelt testimony of a reluctant and repentant marketer. Like Martin Luther, I would launch my own "protestant reformation," symbolically nailing my thesis to the door of the church of marketing.

I sent the proposal to Jag. He called me and said, "Raj, people in this country want to hear about the solution, not the problem."

"Of course!" I thought. We had spent years describing the problem but hadn't focused much on solutions. I revamped the book proposal and gave it the working title *In Search of Marketing Excellence*, a nod to the classic book *In Search of Excellence*. The premise was simple: most companies spend huge amounts of money on marketing but get poor outcomes in terms of customer satisfaction, loyalty, and trust. What could we learn from companies that spend much *less* than the industry average and have outstanding customer satisfaction, loyalty, and trust?

Jag and I subsequently changed the name to *Share of Heart,* as the next evolution in relationship marketing: from "market share" to "share of wallet" to share of heart.

Meanwhile, the American Marketing Association's annual Educators Conference was being held in Boston in August 2004. I organized a one-day symposium immediately following the conference with the provocative theme "Does Marketing Need Reform?" Jag and I invited leading scholars to present their thoughts on that question. We spent a stimulating but depressing day together. There were no dissenting voices; not one scholar sprang to the defense of "marketing as usual." Everybody agreed that much was broken in the marketing profession and in the academic discipline. Even the venerable Philip Kotler, the father of modern marketing, went so far as to say that we should abandon the word "marketing" altogether and start over from scratch. Jag and I then published a book with the same title, with 40 essays written by leading scholars.

After the conference, we turned our attention to the *Share of Heart* book and signed a contract with Wharton Publishing. Our initial research into companies that had a strong bond with their customers revealed that they had similarly strong bonds with other stakeholders. We developed a five-stakeholder model using the acronym SPICE, for Society, Partners, Investors, Customers, and Employees. As we learned more about how these companies operated, we changed the book's name one last time, to *Firms of Endearment: How World-Class Companies Profit from Passion and Purpose.*

My deep-rooted misgivings about marketing had led me to embark on a book project that would dramatically alter the course of my life, and the lives of many others around the world. It would also help launch a global movement to redefine the purpose and practice of business.

Reflections

When I started my role at Bentley College, I had it all. Yet I was miserable and felt empty. I had made an opportunistic decision to take this job, but it landed me in a position that was not aligned with my values and passion.

Have you ever had the realization that the trappings of success don't equate to genuine happiness? What should you prioritize that you don't?

My conversation with John Sterman deepened my conviction that each of us should use what we know to have a positive impact in the world. It eventually led me to transform my career, tap into my values, and find my purpose.

Think about ways in which your work and expertise can serve the greater good. Your life satisfaction will increase exponentially if you do. What support and allies do you need to make that happen?

The blow to my ego, reputation, and financial well-being from losing my chaired position was severe, even traumatic. I was able to recover and grow from it by setting concrete goals and tuning in more closely to my own heart's voice.

Most of us are too quick to label events as good or bad, based on our limited perspective. But every situation opens new possibilities; one door closes, but others often open. Have you experienced this in your past life? Could it apply to situations you are currently dealing with?

My many misgivings about "marketing as usual" fell into the category of "follow your heartbreak," in religious scholar Andrew Harvey's words. It made me angry to see abusive, exploitative, manipulative, or wasteful marketing. But simply following our heartbreak is not enough; we need to translate that into tangible action to ease the suffering that breaks our heart.

Reflect on common practices in your profession and in your surroundings. Do any of them cause you pain? What suffering leaves others indifferent, but transfixes you? Might these be signposts that can guide you toward your purpose?

10

Purpose in the Poconos

Tears of Joy

It had been 19 years since I had shed tears of any kind: the last time was when I had been moved by the sadness of the movie *Ordinary People*, to my wife's consternation. I had developed a seemingly impenetrable shell around my heart. On June 12, 2005, that shell was cracked in the most unlikely of ways.

I was sitting at one end of a rustic wooden dining table, across from David Wolfe, my coauthor on the book that would become *Firms of Endearment: How World-Class Companies Profit from Passion and Purpose*. We were in the Poconos, a hilly region in eastern Pennsylvania. David and I had just returned from a vigorous walk up and down the hills of the ski resort we had come to for a writing retreat. After a hearty breakfast of oatmeal with raisins, we sat down to work on our assigned chapters. I was reviewing a story we had selected for the book and suddenly found myself choked up. It was about a UPS employee named Christine Virelli, a ninth-grade drop-out who had been out of the workforce for 16 years. She started with UPS as a part-time package sorter after her husband was injured and could no longer work. UPS paid for her to get a general equivalency diploma (GED) and then for her to attend college. She said, "I can't leave UPS. They've done so much for me that I can't imagine not working for them. UPS helped me turn my life around, and I'm still growing." UPS gave Christine hope for the future, and it gave me hope for the future of business.

I said to David, "This is the first time I have ever experienced tears of joy connected to my work. I think my body is sending me a message. This is the story of business that I wanted to learn more about and spread in the world."

In that instance, I felt like I had discovered my purpose. Or perhaps more accurately, my purpose had found me.[1]

Elizabeth Gilbert has written, "Ideas spend eternity swirling around us, searching for available and willing human partners. When an idea thinks it has found somebody who might be able to bring it into the world, the idea will pay you a visit."[2] This happened to me that day.

Metamorphosis

Without being fully conscious of it, I had been going through a gradual transformation over the preceding years, showing small signs of awakening, tiny green shoots of hope and renewal in the otherwise barren soil of my life. I increasingly questioned prevailing corporate values and belief systems about business. Repeatedly, "experts" had told me that human considerations did not and should not factor into business decision making, other than as a way to achieve higher profits. It was never about doing the right thing for people or the planet or communities; it was always about doing the economically savvy thing for owners and shareholders. Under that logic, it was acceptable

---

[1] Today I define my purpose as "to bring heart, healing, courage, and soul to business and leadership so we can build a better world for all."
[2] https://www.irishtimes.com/life-and-style/people/elizabeth-gilbert-when-a-magical-idea-comes-knocking-you-have-three-options-1.2474157

to sell a dangerous car that would predictably kill a certain number of people if the financial consequences of doing so were less than what it would cost to redesign the car.

My business education unquestioningly advocated filtering every business decision through the lens of EVA: economic value added. If a decision was additive to EVA, it was the right decision. If not, it was the wrong decision. It was as simple and as cold-blooded as that. At first, I experienced a kind of moral injury when asked to adopt and teach this value system to my students, but gradually learned to live with it as just a fact of life – until I no longer could.

I started thinking about a word I had always hated: *boss*. It has its roots in slavery, deriving from the Dutch word *baas*, meaning "master." The question arose in my mind, "Does BOSS = SSOB?" (meaning "Super SOB"). At the next dinner party I attended, I asked some friends who were corporate executives that question. They were unequivocal: "Of course it does. That's how bosses are supposed to behave."

Adrift in this sea of cynicism, something in me resisted. The pilot light of my idealism and my belief in the fundamental goodness of human beings had sputtered over the years but was not yet extinguished. I knew there had to be a better way to think about business. I noticed that the world of business had enthusiastically embraced military principles and frameworks, routinely using military terms like strategy, tactics, operations, the front line, headquarters. Employees were like soldiers, customers were targets or territory to be captured, and competitors were enemies to be vanquished. But business is not war, and companies are not armies. Some people treated business like a machine, while others viewed it as a game. My academic colleagues mostly treated it as a math problem. I knew that it was none of those things. To me, business was about serving people and enriching their lives.

People routinely bandied about the phrase "It's not personal, it's business." I found it offensive. Business involves and impacts persons; that makes it inherently personal.

Becoming an Instrument of Evolution

Firms of Endearment was a cat with more than nine lives, an idea that simply would not die. I wrote 13 versions of the proposal before a publisher finally agreed to take it on. Something in me sensed its importance and kept fighting to keep it alive. At the end of every meeting with Jag, after we had completed all our other tasks, I would say, "Can we talk about that book idea again?"

Synchronicity was at work here. Ram Dass said, "Seek to be an instrument of the universe rather than to be a master of it." I was being called by unseen forces – the "implicate universe," in Joseph Jaworski's words – to help birth something that needed to come into being in the world, something that was part of a necessary evolutionary unfolding.

After running into several conceptual dead ends, I asked David Wolfe to join us as a third author to give the project new life. I had met David eight years earlier when I was at George Mason University. A self-educated polymath, David had endured an extremely strict Catholic upbringing with a harsh, miserly father on a farm in rural Maryland, and become a successful entrepreneur and author. By the time I met him, he was in his 70s, a respected expert on relationship marketing, developmental psychology, and the societal and business implications of an aging population. He had developed a particular expertise guiding people through midlife crises – and I met him just as I was getting ready to have my own! He soon became a cherished friend and guide. I was now attempting to write a book with two men who had both become father figures in my life.

My initial research question had been simple: Can companies become successful and be loved and trusted by their customers without spending much money on marketing? After discovering a few companies that spent virtually nothing on marketing and were loved by *all* their stakeholders (not just customers), we decided to make that our focus. We surveyed 2,000 people and asked them to identify companies they loved. From the 400 companies nominated, we picked 60 to study in more depth. In the end, 28 companies best exemplified the pattern we had discovered early in our research: they had a heroic, inspiring purpose; they sought serve and to create multiple kinds of value for all their stakeholders; their leaders were motivated by service to people and purpose rather than by power and money; and their cultures were built on trust, caring, authenticity, and joy.[3]

We did not know the financial consequences of this way of being in business. The leaders of the companies we selected never talked about maximizing profits; rather, these companies focused on living their purpose and having a positive impact on the lives of all their stakeholders.

Before doing the financial analysis, we wrote down our hypotheses. We expected that these companies did well for investors, but not exceptionally so, since that wasn't their core focus. We were prepared to argue that it was okay if their profits were lower than those of their peers because these companies paid their frontline people better, provided generous benefits such as health care, invested in the customer experience and had a positive impact on their customers' well-being, paid their suppliers well, supported their communities, and took care of the environment. The companies even paid taxes at a far higher rate than their competitors. They created a lot of value that does not show up on income statements or balance sheets.

It stunned us when our analysis revealed that the 18 public companies in our sample had collectively outperformed the S&P500 stock market index 9:1 over a 10-year period. How was this possible? My business education had taught me that there is no free lunch, that business is a "zero sum" game with unavoidable trade-offs. If these companies spent more on other stakeholders, surely their investors would suffer. But the numbers were undeniable.

We came to the life-affirming, joyful realization that companies built on purpose and love are stronger, more resilient, and more successful in the long run than companies only concerned with profits.

---

[3]These four principles would become the tenets of what we would later call "Conscious Capitalism."

I had been taught that business is about the cold-blooded pursuit of profits, that "only the paranoid survive," that it's a "dog-eat-dog" world, that emotions have no place in the numbers-driven world of business. But we had produced powerful evidence to the contrary.

This was the holy grail that I had been unconsciously seeking. It gave me faith that my idealism, my trusting nature, my belief in cooperation weren't liabilities in the rough-and-tumble world of business, contrary to what my father had told me.

Firms of Endearment started my healing. It showed me that what came naturally to me and many others was not inconsistent with achieving success and "winning" in the world. It confirmed that being caring and collaborative are strengths, not weaknesses. After the book was published in early 2007, I started hearing from people all over the world about the impact it had on their lives. Writing that book was not only the beginning of my journey toward purpose but also toward personal fulfillment and eventual healing.

Renegotiating a Relationship

Jag Sheth had become a revered father figure to me by this time. He had rescued me from obscurity and irrelevance in my career. But as with all father-son relationships, there comes a time when the son must individuate and step away from the father's shadow.

As we were getting ready to submit the final manuscript to the publisher, David said to me, "We need to discuss the order of authorship." He said it would not be fair for Jag's name to appear first, since his involvement in the project had been less than David's or mine. I had always put Jag's name first on the dozens of papers and five books we had previously written together. In most of those papers and books, his intellectual contributions had exceeded mine, even if I did all the writing. Given the academic convention of listing authors alphabetically, his name preceded mine even if our contributions were equal.

Had David not raised the issue, I would have stayed with the original order of authorship: Sheth, Sisodia, and Wolfe. I had no appetite for rocking the boat, because I avoided conflict and feared that Jag would not respond well. David said, "Don't worry about it. I will take it up with Jag. You don't need to be involved." That was a relief; I would be shielded from the unpleasantness!

David wrote to Jag, making the case that the order of authorship should be Sisodia, Wolfe, and Sheth. He did not copy me on his email. Jag immediately forwarded David's email to me, appending the question, "What are we going to do about David?"

I responded that the book idea and title had been mine, I had done the research, and David and I had split the writing. I also wrote that the project meant a great deal to me personally because it reflected my sensibilities far more than anything else Jag and I had done together. Jag became irate, and I spent several sleepless nights agonizing over the situation. I asked academic friends what I should do; the consensus was, "Don't make an issue of this. If you do, he has the power to destroy your career."

Finally, I wrote a note to Jag reiterating my case for being the first author. At the end, I left it up to him; I said I would accept whatever decision he came to. I felt that this was a way for me to stand up for what I believed to be right while also being respectful of the role he had played in my life. After a delay of several days, he wrote back, grudgingly accepting the order of authorship David had proposed.

In hindsight, this was a necessary conflict. I needed to shed my fear of confronting a father figure, to be steadfast when I believed fairness was at stake, and to stand up for my values. The experience contributed to my maturation and individuation, but it cast a shadow over my relationship with Jag that lingered for several years.

During the writing of this book, I asked Jag if we could have a conversation to reflect on what we had learned from the experience and how we saw it 15 years later. He told me that a major factor in how he had reacted was his perception that David and I had "ganged up" on him – which we had. He said, "It would have been much better if you had approached me directly to discuss the issue." I did not have the courage to do so and "hid" behind David, which resulted in a fractured relationship. The lessons for me are clear: Don't shy away from hard conversations, and speak directly *to* people rather than *about* them.

Doubling Down

A few months before *Firms of Endearment* was published, I was in New Jersey teaching an executive program for a group of Siemens executives based on my book *The Rule of Three*. Over lunch, one participant asked me what I was working on currently. I replied, "I'm really excited about a new book that I have coming out in February called *Firms of Endearment: How World-Class Companies Profit from Passion and Purpose*." Without skipping a beat, he said, "Oh, I would never read that." Surprised at his response, I asked him why. "I would be embarrassed if somebody I knew walked by while I was sitting in an airplane reading a book with that title. I bet you have a heart on the cover."

"Well, we haven't finalized the cover yet, but that may not be a bad idea!" I replied.

I made light of it, but this exchange illustrated what we were up against: the aggressive, hyper-masculine approach to business that permeates our world. We had run into that mindset at several publishers. Only after we did the financial analysis and showed that these companies outperformed the market dramatically did publishers become excited about the book. Before that, they saw it as a "touchy-feely, be nice and be kind" story. Everybody knew that "nice guys finish last" – except that we had shown that they could finish first – and by a wide margin.

Soon after that incident in New Jersey, I went to India for the 25th reunion of my MBA class. Before heading to the resort town of Lonavala where my classmates were gathering over Christmas, I went to see my former professor, Dr. Shrikant, who had been pivotal in helping me get into the PhD program at Columbia. I met him in the late afternoon and gave him a pre-publication version of *Firms of*

Endearment: "Dr. Shrikant, I would love to know what you think about this book. Everything else that I have written came from the head; this book also comes from my heart."

The next morning, he greeted me warmly. "You know, Raj, I normally go to bed at 8 p.m. because I wake up at 4 a.m. to meditate. But last night I was up until 11 reading your book."

"Thank you, Dr. Shrikant! That means a lot to me, coming from you."

"Yes, I am enjoying it. But as I read it, I realize that it is nothing new."

I was surprised. "What do you mean? This was very new to me. It was unlike anything I learned in my PhD or MBA programs."

"Everything that you have written here was written 4,000 years ago," he replied.

"What management book was that? Nobody told me about it."

He smiled at me. "It's all there in the *Gita*. So much of what we think we are discovering for the first time was actually thought about deeply by the sages of old and written about in the *Gita*."

The *Bhagavad Gita* is one of the primary texts of Hinduism. Embedded in the spiritual epic *Mahabharata*, it is a 701-verse poem about the interaction between the God Krishna and the warrior Arjuna on the battlefield of Kurukshetra. It is about knowledge, purpose, love, duty, selfless action, and many other spiritual themes. I had heard about it but hadn't read it. In fact, I was completely ignorant of the vast wisdom in the oldest spiritual tradition in the world. I resolved to educate myself right away, starting with reading the *Gita*.

Sliding Doors

After I returned to Boston, David Wolfe called. "You won't believe what happened," he told me. "I was sitting next to a woman on the plane. We got talking, and I told her about our book. She said, 'My friend John Mackey would really love that. Can you send it to me?'" David had replied, "The book hasn't been published yet. It is still a Word document." "It doesn't matter. Just send it to me." He emailed her the 300-page Word document, which she forwarded to John, the cofounder and CEO of Whole Foods Market. David had just heard from John, who was effusive about the book: "I read all the major new business books, and this is the best one I've read in a long time. I love and agree with everything you guys have written."

A few months later, John invited me to spend a day with him in Austin, Texas. When I arrived, he pointed out that he was wearing a Whole Foods cap, a Patagonia fleece, and New Balance sneakers — all firms of endearment! We toured the flagship Whole Foods store, located under the company's headquarters. It was exciting; for food lovers, visiting that store is like being in Disneyland. It had eight restaurants scattered throughout the store and a cornucopia of abundance everywhere. John had created something truly special, a sumptuous treat for the senses and nourishing for the body.

We went up to his office and talked for hours about life and business. As we stood at a window, he pointed across the street to an ad agency called GSD&M Idea City. "That is one of the best ad agencies in the country, run by my friend Roy Spence," he said.

"Is it your ad agency?" I asked.

"Oh no. We don't have an ad agency. We don't have a chief marketing officer. In fact, we barely have a marketing department. We spend 90% less on marketing than our competitors, and 90% of what we spend is at the store level, not at headquarters. Most of that has to do with community outreach."

This was music to my ears, of course. After all, *Firms of Endearment* had started out asking precisely that question: How could companies be loved by their customers without spending much on marketing? Whole Foods and the other companies in the book were living proof that if you genuinely care for all your stakeholders, including your customers, and treat them with respect and deep attention to their well-being, you don't need to waste money on marketing gimmicks. You get the benefit of the best kind of marketing there is: free marketing from loyal and delighted customers, as well as from other stakeholders.

Over bottles of Kingfisher beer at an Indian restaurant that evening, John and I shared more about our personal journeys. I then reached into my jacket pocket and pulled out a mind map of my vision for the "Institute for New Capitalism," or INC (I am a charter member of Acronyms Anonymous). I unfolded it and handed it to him. "John, this is what I want to do with the rest of my life." My vision included working with established companies to change their approach to business, with entrepreneurs starting new businesses, and with business schools to get them to research and teach this new paradigm. John looked over the mind map and handed it back to me. "That is exactly my vision, Raj. But I like the name Conscious Capitalism."

Something about the phrase instantly appealed to me. I liked the alliteration and the unexpected juxtaposition of two words that normally don't go together. I learned later that Mohammad Yunus, the micro-lending pioneer and Nobel Peace laureate, had coined the phrase years before. He had used it to describe what we now refer to as social businesses, which reinvest all their profits towards achieving their social purpose. We would use it to describe all businesses operating with higher consciousness that include society as a key stakeholder.

By the end of the dinner, John and I agreed on a plan. We would each invite about a half-dozen people who would be excited to help realize this vision to a retreat at John's ranch, about an hour outside Austin. We set a date in February 2008.

Birthing a Movement

In retrospect, the gathering at John's ranch was a historic event. An eclectic group of a dozen of us spent four life-changing days together eating organic vegan food, drinking red wine, going on long hikes, playing Frisbee golf and ping-pong, soaking in the hot tub, lounging in hammocks, and sharing our life stories, our hopes and dreams, and our vision for the future of business and capitalism. We saw ourselves as the vanguard of a movement to elevate a story of capitalism that had been over 200 years in the making. We were all passionate believers in the power and beauty of business when done right. We believed in freedom, in voluntary exchange, and most important, in bringing a higher consciousness to business and leadership.

By the end of our four days together, we had conceived of three separate entities: the Conscious Capitalism Alliance (focused on CEOs and other business leaders), the Conscious Capitalism Institute (which would work within business academia), and the Society for Conscious Capitalism (which would bring these ideas to the mainstream). We decided that our first activity would be to organize a gathering later that year, at which we would bring together thinkers and practitioners of conscious business. I left the retreat feeling exhilarated and hopeful that we were about to write a new chapter in the evolution of business and society.

The theme of the event was Catalyzing Conscious Capitalism. It was at the Crossings, a beautiful retreat center on the outskirts of Austin. Here is how we described it in our brochure:

> **This is not** a seminar, nor a conference. **It is an event.** It is like a cornerstone laying. In fact, it *is* a cornerstone laying. From Nov. 6 through Nov. 9, 2008, in Austin, TX, a gathering of business professionals will lay the foundation for turning the idea of "Conscious Capitalism" into a global movement shaped by the conscious intent of companies everywhere to make the world a better place for all.

Those were the three most exhilarating and enriching days of my life – a sentiment shared by virtually everyone who attended. It was an extraordinary gathering of visionary thinkers and leaders like education pioneer Sir Ken Robinson, strategy guru Gary Hamel, Ed Freeman (the "father" of stakeholder management), the founders of the Blue Man Group, and many CEOs.

Sadly, David Wolfe could not be with us. He had battled leukemia for years and had recently been diagnosed with lung cancer. But his spirit was very much present at the event, which he had worked hard to codesign over the preceding months. Defying medical odds, David lived for several more years and continued his passionate advocacy for this way of being in business. He was in hospice care at his home in Reston, Virginia, when I saw him for the last time. To his last breath, he spoke animatedly about the beautiful things that were possible with this way of doing business. I marveled at his excitement about the future while transitioning out of this life.

Coincidentally, that first Conscious Capitalism conference unfolded with the global financial crisis as a backdrop. Lehman Brothers had gone bankrupt a few weeks earlier, leading to one of the biggest-ever drops in the stock market. Economic devastation was all around us. Whole Foods stock had been as high as $70; it hovered around $6 when we had our conference. But through it all, John Mackey was remarkably unperturbed. I asked him how he could be so calm when his stock was down over 90%; most public company CEOs would have been in full crisis mode. "I don't know why the market is freaking out," he said. "We're still the same company we were before. Our sales are down a little, but they'll come back. I'm not worried." Sure enough, Whole Foods stock rebounded dramatically after the financial crisis, reaching $120 within a few years.

Growing the Movement

Over the next several years, the Conscious Capitalism movement took root, not only in the United States but around the world. But within academia, new ideas like Conscious Capitalism were subject to a level of skepticism bordering on cynicism, even hostility. I realized that most academics do not aspire to be thought leaders; they are content to be "practice followers." They are also deeply wedded to their theories and frameworks. Rather than trying to convince academics to embrace this new mindset, I decided we should focus on spreading it in the world of practice, with the belief and expectation that once it got established there, academics would become interested in it. If we could show that it works in practice, perhaps academics would become interested in exploring whether it could work in theory!

In March 2010, my friend Shubhro Sen and I organized a two-day Conscious Capitalism conference in Mumbai (the new name for Bombay). We believed that the consciousness part of Conscious Capitalism was deeply rooted in Indian wisdom, as Dr. Shrikant had pointed out to me a few years earlier. At the event, we had the CEOs of the most conscious businesses in India, a minister from the central government, and a prominent spiritual leader named Jaggi Vasudev, known as Sadhguru. I knew nothing about him, so I Googled him. Thinking that I had made a spelling mistake, Google asked me, "Do you mean *sad guru*?" He turned out to be anything but sad, delivering an inspiring talk on conscious leadership.

This conference launched our movement in India. *Forbes India* created a "Conscious Capitalist of the Year" award and CNBC India aired a three-part series about Conscious Capitalism. My mother was thrilled, while my father was mystified.

In 2011, John Mackey and I decided to write a book on Conscious Capitalism. John suggested I read a couple of books before we got started: *The Rational Optimist* by Matt Ridley and *In Defense of Global Capitalism* by Johan Norberg. Both were quite eye-opening for me, and I gained a deeper appreciation for how much capitalism had elevated humanity.

This set the stage for a deep learning experience while writing the book. John, introduced me to ideas I had not been exposed to before. The book that resulted from our collaboration was a synergistic blending of our perspectives and became quite impactful for many people.

The Conscious Capitalism philosophy has great appeal across the political spectrum. Conservatives love it because it is rooted in freedom and voluntary exchange and generates superior financial returns. Progressives love it because it puts people and human dignity at the center of business and treats the environment and society as important stakeholders. To me, it was a philosophical holy grail for business and capitalism.

★★★

My life in those years was intellectually challenging, purposeful, and extremely busy. I served on two public company boards. I gave 70–90 talks a year all over the world, accumulating hundreds of thousands of frequent flier miles. I helped launch dozens of Conscious Capitalism chapters around the United States and in many other countries. I was invited to meetings at the White House, the United Nations, the World Bank, and the Vatican on the future of business and capitalism.

But through it all, an emptiness remained at my core, a sense of not being firmly centered and grounded. I neglected my physical, emotional, and mental well-being. I did not feel at home anywhere except in airline lounges. I was part of a movement to bring healing to a broken system, but a lot that was still unhealed within me was now bubbling to the surface. I was learning how deep my wounds were. I had found purpose, but not peace. My next quest would be for healing.

Reflections

Significant discoveries often happen by accident. I discovered a different way of being in business because I asked a very elementary question, the answer to which touched upon much larger considerations than I was aware of. But I followed my curiosity to where it led me: to uncover and articulate the tenets of Conscious Capitalism.

How can you cultivate a "beginner's mind"? Can you ask simple questions that can help you discover fundamental truths?

In my reluctance to raise the order of authorship with Jag, I showed that I valued harmony over fairness. I thought I could avoid the conflict with Jag by "outsourcing" it to David. But that only made the conflict grow larger. Had I raised it with Jag directly, we could have resolved it quickly and with less lasting damage.

> *Ignoring a conflict you have with someone doesn't make it go away; it just gets bigger. Asking someone else to handle it for you doesn't work. Are there any "necessary conflicts" you need to engage in? How can you be clear, polite, and direct in your communication? Are you prepared to deal with the consequences?*

I was struck by the way David Wolfe transitioned from this life. To his last breath, he was channeling wisdom that would help make the world of work and business better, though he would not be around to experience it.

> *Think ahead to your own last moments in this lifetime. Will you be filled with regrets and bitterness, or will you transition with love and ease? What can you start doing today to ensure that it is the latter?*

11 | Searching for Inner Peace

As my reputation grew and my speaking invitations increased, I found myself warmly welcomed all over the world. But when the car service drew closer to home on my return trips from the airport, I found my stress level rising and my jaw clenching. I would exchange a cursory, monosyllabic greeting with my wife, check in on the kids, and flee to my refuge in the finished basement. Everything I needed was there. My large home office was on one end of a long rectangular room, while the other side was a state-of-the-art home theater, with seven speakers, a 119-inch pull-down screen, and two rows of leather couches. I had a bathroom and a guest bedroom down the hall.

Other than at the height of his manic periods, my son, Alok, had always been very loving and sweet-natured. But by 2006, while I was finishing *Firms of Endearment*, his condition had become more acute, requiring him to be hospitalized multiple times. He had cycled through several specialized programs at different schools in the Boston area. The school authorities said that they could no longer adequately meet his needs; he would need to be placed in a residential program. The only one available was the Kolburne School in the

Berkshires, 140 miles away from Boston. Keeping him at home was not an option.

Both our daughters had been doing well at school and each had a small circle of close friends. At their ages (13 and 11), they were acutely concerned about being embarrassed in front of their friends. But Alok's condition and unpredictable behavior had made it increasingly hard for them to invite their friends over to the house. We thought that the one silver lining of Alok being in a residential program would be that the girls would have a more peaceful and "normal" home environment.

A couple of weeks after Alok's 17th birthday in June 2006, we drove to western Massachusetts to drop him off. He kept asking, "Why do my sisters get to live at home but I am being sent away?" Somehow, we convinced him that this was a good thing for him, and he trustingly went along with it. We told him that both of us had left home around that age, and that this is what most people did.

"Will the girls also leave home when they turn 17?" he asked.

"Yes."

"Do you promise?"

"Yes."

Kolburne (which has since closed) turned out to be a rather grim place. Residents included special needs kids from Massachusetts and New York State, many of whom were much bigger and had more severe challenges than our son. We worried about how Alok would fare in this environment. Residents were subject to forcible holds when they acted out or became physically aggressive. Like psychiatric units in hospitals, they locked the facility from the outside at night.

We dropped Alok off, hugged him, and got back into our minivan, barely able to hold back our tears. He stood there in the twilight for as long as the car was in sight, waving at us. I felt a mixture of guilt, dread, hope, and relief. The girls were quietly crying in the back seat.

Far from thriving, the girls started having challenges of their own almost immediately after Alok was "sent away." They lost confidence and started withdrawing from their friends. They struggled with depression, anxiety, and school phobia. Over the next few years, despite our best efforts, they spiraled downwards. It was heartbreaking, almost more than I could bear as their father.

I felt additional guilt because as the Conscious Capitalism movement rapidly spread globally, my travels increasingly took me away from home. I can only imagine how challenging it was for my wife to be home alone with the kids while I was thousands of miles away. I was suffering no less for being far away. She could sublimate her anxiety and emotional pain into action; all I could do was spend sleepless nights ruminating and flagellating myself for contributing to my children's suffering.

In hindsight, I understand why the girls started struggling when Alok left. Like many siblings of special needs children, they were experiencing a kind of survivor guilt: "It is so unfair that he has all these challenges, and we don't." With Alok banished to the Berkshires, these feelings increased exponentially.

Seeking Spiritual Solace

I was hungry for relief, for some way to cope with all the suffering around me and within me. The way many people in my family and the Rajput culture I had grown up in dealt with life's painful passages was through alcohol. I had prided myself that unlike my father, I did not drink every day, usually limiting myself to a couple of drinks on weekends when I was with friends. But now I found myself reaching for comfort in the liquor cabinet with alarming frequency.

I knew I could not continue down this road. I started seeking spiritual experiences, hoping to find wisdom to make sense of my life and have some peace of mind. My spiritual yearning perplexed my wife. "Why are you always searching? What are you looking for? What are you so confused about?"

Art of Living CORE TEACHINGS

1. Maintain equanimity in all situations. Don't let your state of being swing between extremes.
2. Accept people as they are.
3. Don't worry about what others are thinking about you.
4. Don't see intention behind others' mistakes.
5. Live in the present moment.

At my sister's urging, I had taken my first Art of Living course several years earlier, when I started working on *Firms of Endearment*. A spiritual master from India, Sri Sri Ravi Shankar had started the Art of Living (AOL) Foundation in 1981. It now has a global presence, with centers in 156 countries. In the course, we were taught five simple but (to me) profound principles (see sidebar) and a powerful breathing technique called the *Sudarshan Kriya* (a Sanskrit term meaning "proper vision by purifying action"). The atmosphere in the course was suffused with love, gentleness, acceptance, and peace – the very characteristics I naturally showed as a child, but which had largely disappeared from my life.

The teacher told us a story about Sri Sri that struck me. He was teaching in California during the O. J. Simpson trial in 1995. After one of his talks, somebody asked him, "Guruji, what do you think about this murder trial?" He replied, without hesitation, "I am responsible." People asked, "What do you mean?" He said, "When somebody does something like that, it means that they don't know how to manage their own emotions. We know how to help people regulate their emotions and their anger. If I had worked harder, we could have reached more people. If we had reached him in time, he would not have done this terrible thing, and those two people would still be alive. Therefore, I am responsible."

I took the course 14 years after my father and I had ended our estrangement. Things had remained intermittently tense between us. I could not fully release the resentment, bitterness, and anger that I had carried toward him. Every time I visited India, some stray comment would set me off and I would be right back in the frame of mind that I thought I had left behind.

Before taking the Art of Living course, I read the book *Tuesdays with Morrie* and saw the movie based on it. It is about a troubled journalist who learns that his beloved professor is dying and starts flying to Boston on Tuesdays to spend time with him and learn from him. One part stood out vividly for me. Near the end of the movie, author Mitch Albom asks Morrie, "What is the one thing you know today that you wish you had known when you were younger? What would you do differently?" Without hesitating, Morrie replied, "If I could live my life over again, I would forgive everyone for everything." Holding on to hatred (especially for his father) had served no purpose other than to embitter Morrie's life. I resolved to find it in my heart to forgive my father.

Michael Fischman, my AOL teacher, said that we should accept people for who they are and what they do. I asked, "Is that the same as forgiving them?" He replied, "No. Forgiving someone implies that you are right and they are wrong, that you are above them. Acceptance simply means that you accept that this person acted a certain way for reasons you don't understand. Countless factors affect our behavior, which we don't fully understand: our innate nature, our upbringing, the values that were instilled in us, our circumstances, and many other things outside our control. People do what they do, and they don't do what they don't do. They are on their own journeys learning their own lessons. The best thing to do is to accept it and move on."

This insight helped me move toward accepting my father and his actions surrounding my marriage. I came to understand that he was a creature of his upbringing; certain ways of being and responding were hardwired in him and he lacked the self-awareness to be able to change them.

I was enthralled with what I learned in the course and how it made me feel, and immediately signed up for an advanced course the following week in Atlantic City. It would span five days, including three days of silence, and would be led by Sri Sri Ravi Shankar himself.

When I called to tell my sister how much I had loved the course and that I was going to take the advanced course, she said, "Please ask Guruji about Alok. I'm sure he can help heal his condition." My rational mind told me that such things are not possible, but as a father, I couldn't help but hope for a miracle. When I got my few minutes with Sri Sri the following week, I asked for his blessing and his advice about my son's condition. He looked into my eyes and said, "*Uski seva karo*," which means "serve him." "*Seva*" is a facet of yoga that means selfless service as an expression of compassion for others, expecting nothing in return.

That was not what I was hoping to hear, but his message stayed with me. My son cannot serve himself in most normal ways. I know it is my duty to provide for him financially. But I was now being guided to think that it was my *privilege* to serve him. That was not an easy mindset to adopt, certainly not an easy one to sustain. I still struggle with it every day.

After the second Art of Living course, I was on a "spiritual high." I called several friends on the ride home to share what I had experienced. It was around midnight and lightly drizzling when my friends dropped me off at my house. As I walked toward the front door, I noticed something strange: my precious *tablas* were lying on the grass, completely drenched.

Tablas are Indian percussion instruments, paired small drums you play with your hands. Since childhood, I had loved the sound and had been taking lessons to learn how to play them. Why were they out on the grass in the rain in the middle of the night? Had the kids done this?

It turned out that my wife was upset that I had gone to the spiritual course. Some friends at a dinner party had asked where I was. When she told them I had taken back-to-back Art of Living courses, one of them said, "It sounds like he is joining a cult." That was the source of her anger, which she expressed by throwing out something that meant a lot to me. We got into an argument, and I came crashing down from my spiritual high.

The chasm between us grew.

For the first time in my marriage, I contemplated moving out. One evening, I searched for apartments online. But with my children's ongoing challenges, it felt selfish to focus on me. I thought, "I cannot do this now." Unfortunately, I didn't close the browser window with the Apartments.com website, and my 14-year-old daughter, Priya, later saw it. She didn't mention it to me but went to her mother in tears.

This incident planted a seed of deep insecurity in her. For the next several years, until I finally did move out, Priya lived with the daily fear that she would wake up and find me gone. She became hypervigilant, expecting the worst. She stood on the other side of the door when my wife and I talked. She checked my wife's email to see what she was writing to her sisters. She took the burden of the entire family upon her young shoulders. She worried about our marriage, her brother, her sister. In all this worry, my poor daughter lost focus on her own growth and happiness.

This is one of my great regrets: that my carelessness caused so much uncertainty and anguish in her young life.

I have learned that sacrificing one's own happiness and well-being for the sake of others (even those we love) rarely works. In my family, each of us was sacrificing our happiness, but to no higher end; nobody in the family was thriving. I was deeply unhappy and desperately wanted to leave, but felt that I could not. Priya was sacrificing herself by worrying about everybody else. Maya internalized the pain around her and became depressed. Our son bravely endured the loneliness and harshness of his residential school.

We were wounded, unhappy people unable to help ourselves or each other. We needed to break the cycle and start healing. But we didn't know how.

Could I Be Happy?

With all the pain and tumult around and inside me, I doubled down on my spiritual explorations. After Dr. Shrikant's wake-up call about the wisdom in the *Bhagavad Gita*, I started to explore Indian wisdom. I read a translation of the Gita and immediately understood why

Dr. Shrikant had seen parallels between it and the principles of Conscious Capitalism.

I also dipped into the Vedanta, which literally means the "end of knowledge." It is a distillation of the purest wisdom in the Upanishads. I learned from deep thinkers on the subject and helped organize a conference at the Indian Institute of Management in Kozhikode, Kerala, on what the ancient wisdom of India offered modern business and leadership.

These experiences gave me new insights into life and a modicum of inner peace. I was at peace while attending the programs but couldn't sustain that when I dropped back into my daily life. I still could not say that I was happy.

Like most people, I had always been driven by external goals, milestones, and recognitions. First, it was about getting a job after college. Then it was about finishing my PhD. After that, it became all about attaining tenure, the ultimate prize for academics. I used to have fantasies about my serene and relaxed post-tenure life. I imagined I would take up golf, not be so frenzied about my work, lose my anxiety about finances, and live happily ever after. None of that happened, of course. My struggle in my marriage and having a special needs child had a lot to do with that.

I looked at my friends with happy marriages and thriving kids and wondered what that felt like. I became convinced that happiness was simply not an option for me – not in this lifetime. This lifetime was a harsh sentence to be endured, duties to be fulfilled, sacrifices to be made. The best I could hope for was not to give in to despair.

Still, I kept reaching for that next milestone, that next accomplishment that would make me content. Would it be when I became a full professor? No. Getting an endowed chair position? Nope. What about when I published my first book? Not then either. Then I got it in my mind that if I published five books, I would finally have arrived. What if I got my net worth up to a certain number? None of it mattered.

There is no shortage of books on happiness. I read my fair share, but none of them made a dent. Then I was invited to an event in Aspen.

One participant arrived late and apologized: "One of my kids was having a crisis and I couldn't leave. You know how it is: You're only as happy as your least happy child."

The parents around the table (including me) nodded, readily identifying with that sentiment. But later I thought about the implications, not only for parents but also siblings. If each person in a family system only allows himself or herself to be as happy as the least happy person in that system, then everybody will always get driven down to the lowest level of happiness. From that place, how can any of us lift another up?

After returning home, I read Gay Hendricks's book *The Big Leap*. He writes of the "upper limit problem," about the constraints many of us place on how happy and successful we feel we deserve to be. It is not about what we are capable of; it is about what we feel we *deserve*. The upper limit could be set by our parents, our siblings, the culture, or other factors. Gay cites his own example. When he published his first book, he joyfully brought a copy to give to his mother. She said, "That's nice," and put it down on the table. Gay was deflated. His mother did that because she didn't want Gay's brother (who was also in the room) to feel bad. She had placed an upper limit on how happy or how successful Gay could feel.

I certainly had an upper limit problem, probably several of them. My father had called me selfish and self-centered so often that I deemed myself unworthy of being happy, and felt guilty about doing anything for myself. Gay wrote that the siblings of special needs kids are especially susceptible to this. I was sitting next to Priya while I was reading this. I asked her, "Priya, do you think you have the right to be happy?" Without hesitation, she replied, "No." Startled, I asked, "Why not?" She said, "Not everyone deserves to be happy." She couldn't explain it beyond that. My heart was crushed.

The experience of having a special needs child had been so overwhelming that I hadn't thought enough about the impact on our other children. When Alok was first diagnosed, the girls attended a single hour-long class for siblings of special needs kids. After that, we focused our energy and attention on dealing with Alok's

challenges. Concerned about hurting Alok's feelings, we told the
girls to hide any significant milestones or achievements – anything
worth celebrating – from him. For example, if they were learning
how to drive, had done well in school, or were going on a trip, they
were not to mention it in front of Alok, because "your brother will
feel bad." While well intentioned, this culture of secrecy made the
girls feel even more guilty than they already did about anything
good in their lives.

Soon after that exchange, I went to John Mackey's ranch for a
Conscious Capitalism board retreat. John had met Priya and had
bought courtside seats for us at a Boston Celtics basketball game
because I told him she loved sports. I told him what she had said. He
said, "I want you to give her a message about happiness from me."
I had him record it on my iPad. Here is the gist of what he said:[1]

*Hi Priya, I wanted to talk to you about happiness, about depression and
things that I've learned in life that hopefully will be useful to you. But
that's for you to say.*

*One thing I know is common in life is that we have a certain amount
of guilt for our own well-being because others, perhaps family members or
friends, do not have it so good sometimes. . . So it's not uncommon for
people to basically damper down or not allow themselves to be happy and
joyful in life.*

*What I've learned is that this is a mistake, that ultimately, happiness
is a choice that we make. It's a way that we see ourselves and how we see
the world. If we damper back our own happiness, not only do we make
ourselves miserable, we also make other people around us unhappy. What
I've learned is that we have an ethical responsibility and obligation to be
happy. Because when we are happy, we help others to be happy. We give
them permission to be happy, we role model it, we show that it is okay.*

*The opposite is also true; if we're unwilling to be happy, then we make
others around us unhappy. By really opening up to the joy and beauty in
the universe and letting it flow through us, we are giving one of the great*

---

[1]You can listen to an audio recording of this message at https://www.youtube.
com/watch?v=iAkGXrQEmus&t=1s

gifts that we can give to others. We are giving them the opportunity, the permission, and the role modeling they need to live a happy, joyful life.

John's message was for Priya, but it applied to me as well. I had heard about the idea that everyone deserves to be happy. I also knew that we can choose to be happy. But the idea that we have an ethical and moral duty to be happy was revelatory to me. I used to feel a twinge of guilt when I experienced moments of joy, which usually had to do with the impact my work was having on people and what those people said to me. My thought was, "What right do I have to be experiencing joy and receiving accolades when my children are suffering?"

John's message was a plea to elevate my gaze from the very real difficulties and challenges that brought me down, and look at the larger reality. Instead of focusing on what was lacking, I could will myself to put things in perspective and look at all that was beautiful and right in the world and in my life.

I learned to look beyond the short-term struggles my children were going through. I came to realize that each one of my children's souls was a gift that I would continue to unwrap for the rest of my life. They were my teachers as much as I was theirs. Every exchange with each of these beautiful souls was an opportunity for each of us to learn and grow.

Growing . . . and Sinking

My work remained a source of meaning and fulfillment, more so with each passing year. I developed a deeper understanding of the pillars of Conscious Capitalism and could convey the message in ways that caused genuine shifts in people around the world. I wrote several more books that explored deeper dimensions of Conscious Capitalism. It seemed like every time I went to India, I had a new book that I could present to my parents. My father would look somewhat stunned and set the book aside, while my mother beamed with pride, even though she couldn't read the books. On one of those trips, my father paid me a rare compliment: "It is amazing that you're able to do all of this despite all your challenges in your personal life."

My spiritual insights and personal growth were helping me show up with greater equanimity and impact in the world, but my marriage was still sinking. After 28 years of being deeply unhappy, I just couldn't do it anymore. In late 2014, I made the wrenching decision to leave my marriage. I found an apartment in the same building where a close friend lived, bought furniture, and made plans to move in mid-January, after a trip to India. But a deep sense of unease grew in me, becoming markedly worse while I was in India. I had a constant pit in my stomach and an intense, visceral feeling of guilt. Being around my father didn't help. I imagined how he would react to the news. On the one hand, he would be triumphant as that had been his prediction and hope all along. But he would also be witheringly critical of me for taking such a drastic step, mostly because of what the "community" would think. He would hold it up as another example of my selfishness.

My misgivings grew. Had I done everything I could to save the marriage before taking this drastic step? We had intermittently been to couples counseling for many years with different therapists, to no avail. But my wife had recently spoken of a therapist who did online counseling and supposedly worked miracles. I had declined to try it. Now I thought to myself, "Maybe we should try that before I give up." So after I returned to Boston, I canceled the lease on the apartment, returned what furniture I could and put the rest in storage. I told my wife about my decision and asked her to set up the online counseling. I also asked if she would read a book that I had recently read called *Leadership and Self-Deception*, which had introduced me to the idea of "putting people in a box": prejudging them without giving them a chance or being open to their potential transformation.[2] I thought that we might have fallen into that pattern with each other.

---

[2] The Arbinger Institute, *Leadership and Self-Deception: Getting Out of the Box* (Berrett-Koehler, 2000).

Over the next few months, I waited for my wife to do those two things, but she did neither. Slowly, I started shifting mentally from *whether* to *how*: what would be the least painful way for us to separate? In early 2016, I told my wife that I would move out later that year. I suggested we work with a family therapist to prepare for this big change in all our lives. I wanted our daughters to express what they were feeling, rather than keeping their emotions bottled up. We decided not to include our son, which, in hindsight, was probably a mistake. Still, the therapy was helpful. The therapist met with all four of us on multiple occasions, sometimes with one of us and the kids, sometimes just the two of us, and sometimes just the kids. With the therapist's approval, I asked my daughters to help me choose an apartment that would be comfortable for them.

I moved into my new place on September 1, 2016, 30 years and six months after getting married. I was dreading the first night, anticipating the return of that pit in my stomach and the accompanying feelings of guilt, regret, and shame. But, to my surprise, I slept peacefully. I believed I had done everything I could before taking this major step.

For the first time in decades, I started looking forward to coming home to my cozy apartment overlooking the Charles River. There was no tension and conflict awaiting me, and I had the freedom to do what I wanted.

With space and distance, I continued working on myself to be a more positive, peaceful, and happier person. But I soon realized most of what I was doing was to trick myself into feeling and behaving differently. I was still ignoring some underlying realities; there remained many blind spots and buried landmines in my psyche. Most of all, I had traumas I had never adequately acknowledged or dealt with. Reckoning with those would be the next step of my journey.

Reflections

Perhaps because of my nomadic childhood, or because of my discomfort around my father, I have never felt fully at home anywhere. I am now trying to create a feeling of "being home" wherever I am, as well as co-creating a physical space that truly feels like home.

What comes to mind when you think of "coming home"? Is there a place you can truly relax into being yourself? What would it take to create that?

Many of us implicitly believe that if we sacrifice our own well-being, others will benefit. But that is usually not the case. Many of us also believe that it is selfish to prioritize our self-care over that of people close to us, including our children and spouses. But that too is a false belief. The most important thing we can do is to work on our own healing and growth. That equips us to help others in much more effective ways.

Have you made yourself into a martyr so that others may flourish? In which areas – physical, mental, emotional, spiritual, social – have you been neglecting your self-care?

Most of us also believe that we will be happy when we achieve some external milestone. Happiness becomes an ever-receding goal, always out of reach, just over the horizon. Many have now realized that success does not lead to happiness; rather, learning how to reside in a state of happiness fuels our ability to succeed. This requires us to cultivate gratitude, mindfulness, and service to others.

What is your relationship to happiness? Are you always delaying gratification to some future date when you will "deserve" it? How can you make your default a state of contentment and happiness?

Gay Hendricks's concept of the "upper limit problem" had a profound impact on me. After realizing this universal tendency, I consciously strive to eliminate this artificial "glass ceiling" on my well-being.

Do you have an upper limit problem? Can you trace where it comes from? How will you remove it?

12 | Conscious Awakening

In early 2018, I told my friend Betsy, an author and leadership expert, that I was planning to write a book called *The Healing Organization*. It would be about healing in business: the idea that businesses can be places of healing for those who work there, sources of healing for those they serve – their customers and communities – and a force for healing in society. I defined healing as alleviating suffering, elevating joy, and promoting healthy growth The book had nothing to do with me or my need for healing – or so I thought.

Betsy suggested I come with her to experience a "plant journey," which she had found to be very healing. I had no idea what she was talking about; I thought we would eat potted plants with medicinal properties. I trusted my friend and made plans to join her for a journey in March 2018.

Around 3 p.m., my Lyft entered the locked gate of a sprawling estate in Westchester County outside New York City. We drove down a long curving driveway toward a large house set next to a lake. I had no idea that I was about to have a transcendent experience that would illuminate aspects of my psyche that I had never examined and connect dots in my story that I had never connected before.

I met an eclectic group of people inside, from fashion models and opera singers to hedge fund managers. Those who were there for the first time looked nervous, while the rest were filled with joyful anticipation for what lay ahead.

Our host and guide, Laura, had apprenticed with a Peruvian shaman to learn how to use a variety of psychoactive plants to help humans heal traumas. She had made this work her life's calling after these plants had helped her recover from extreme trauma in her own life. She told us that the experience was intended to return us to our core selves, to connect us to the natural state of innocence and wholeness we all exist in before life takes ahold of us. Many of us predictably experience certain traumas before we turn seven: feeling inadequate, being rejected, being deprived. As our traumas accumulate and compound over time, we develop coping mechanisms to protect ourselves. We betray our true selves to maintain harmony or gain the approval of others. This prevents us from accepting and loving ourselves and connecting authentically with others.

After understanding our individual histories and the challenges we were facing, Laura intuited which plant was the right one for each of us. For those new to the experience, she usually picks a plant that functions as a "heart opener."

Around 5 p.m., we all went downstairs to a large room where a dozen single mattresses had been arrayed on the floor. Each had a blanket, a pillow, and an eye shade. The room was dimly lit with several large candles. Mystical music was playing, and an electric apparatus created the illusion of moving stars and other astral objects on the ceiling. Laura called us up individually to the altar at the front of the room. She reached into an ornate metal chest and picked out a capsule containing the plant medicine she had selected for us. After we had each received our medicine, we swallowed the capsules, lay down, and waited for the medicine to take effect.[1]

I soon found myself transported back in time and across the world to Kesur, to a time when I was about a year old. It was like watching a movie, with a narrator explaining what I was seeing. I saw my mother sitting on the earthen floor in the kitchen next to a smoky cooking fire fueled with wooden logs and cow dung patties. She was rapidly making *chapatis* (Indian flatbread) with a rolling pin and cooking them on the griddle, periodically stirring a pot of curry on another fire nearby. Outside the kitchen, I lay motionless in a gently swaying bassinet, covered in a blanket. When she saw me start to stir, my aunt (my father's older brother's wife) slipped a pea-sized pod of opium into my mouth. The drug soon knocked me out and I grew quiet again. In my vision, I could see tears streaming down my mom's face as she watched my aunt do this.

In the next scene, I saw my formidable grandfather standing in the doorway that led to the exterior part of the house. It was dark; the dim, flickering light of a sooty kerosene lamp behind him framed his silhouette. Several women sat in front of him on the ground in the inner courtyard, their faces covered with their saris. My grandfather stood there for a long time, shouting abuses at the women, calling them whores and witches. The women cowered in silence, my mother and grandmother included.

In all the darkness, I was shown three points of light, little islands of innocence – my mother, me as a baby, and my cousin Gajendra, a

---

[1] Psychedelic-assisted psychotherapy is a fast-growing but still evolving practice. The recent upsurge in the popularity of psychedelics as a healing modality has a lot to do with a best-selling book published in 2018 by Michael Pollan called *How to Change Your Mind: What the New Science of Psychedelics Teaches Us About Consciousness, Dying, Addiction, Depression, and Transcendence* (Penguin).

Plant journeys appear to give us access to a universal consciousness that connects all human beings, perhaps all beings. Pollan writes, "We all assume that consciousness is generated by our brain. But it is important to understand that this is just a hypothesis. There are those who believe that consciousness is a property of the universe, like electromagnetic radiation or gravity."

year and a half older than I. I saw how the cunning and predatory ones in the family used and abused the innocents.

The visions lasted for a few hours. As the effects of the plant wore off, I stood up on unsteady legs, made my way upstairs, and sat down at the kitchen table. I took out my journal and started writing:

> *My life journey now makes sense. It fits together like a puzzle, though it is not yet complete.*
>
> *I was forged in the fire of extreme patriarchy: a father who was absent and uncaring, a grandfather who evoked fear, workers being exploited and mistreated, rampant sexual abuse, intemperate lifestyles, alcoholism. I was able to survive with my innocent essence intact, but it became deeply buried.*
>
> *I realize now that I needed to experience the worst kind of toxic masculine energy so that I could write a book decades later about elevating the sacred feminine.[2]*
>
> *Scenes that I witnessed as a child became indelibly imprinted on me. There was misery, abuse, and tragedy all around, but islands of innocence survived in a sea of venality, like lotus flowers blooming in a swamp. They are the beacons of resilient goodness. They show us what we can and must return to.*
>
> *I need to reclaim my innocence, but fortify it with courage and confidence and resilience. I need to find the innocence on the other side of wholeness.*

The next day, I saw my life through a different lens. I thought about the people I've known. I could readily identify the corrupt, the cynical, and the cunning. I realized that I instinctively resonated with those who had held on to their fundamental innocence. I saw ways in which I had allowed myself to become corrupted, and how I could reclaim my innocence.

The Wise Women

A couple of months later, I did a second plant journey. Before the journey, Laura asked me, "Raj, why do you seem so unsure of yourself? You have accomplished a lot, but you are so diffident."

---

[2]Nilima Bhat and Raj Sisodia, *Shakti Leadership: Embracing Feminine and Masculine Power in Business* (Berrett-Koehler, 2016).

I didn't have an answer, but I understood what she was talking about. I felt it keenly – the absence of a solid core to my being. My sense of self was a fragile thing, easily bruised by doubting and mocking voices from within as well as from outside. It didn't matter how many accolades I received for my work, how many people told me that their lives had been transformed after they read one of my books, how large and mainstream the Conscious Capitalism movement was becoming. Living inside me still was a frightened guilt-ridden little boy who thought of himself as unworthy and deeply defective. How had I fooled so many people for so long?

Before I left the next day, Laura pulled me aside. "Raj, you need to slow down. Please take time to go inward and be with yourself. I suggest you take the summer off to do that." I was speechless. "I can't do that, Laura! I have a book deadline on October 5. I have planned my entire summer as a series of writing retreats. I will be working day and night." Laura replied, "I'm sure you can delay your book. This is important. You can't write about healing until you work on your own healing."

Soon after that conversation, I interviewed Lynne Twist, author of *The Soul of Money,* for *The Healing Organization.* The next day, she called me. "Raj, you were in my dream last night. I got the message that you need to come with us on the next Founders Journey to the rainforest in Ecuador. You are going to learn more about healing in those 10 days than you could learn in years of research."

How could I say no to that? Lynne and her husband, Bill, had started the Pachamama Alliance 25 years earlier, along with John Perkins, an international development expert turned author and shaman.

Wisely choosing to listen to the women who were urging me to slow down and go inward, I delayed my book by five months. I said yes to additional experiences that I had previously declined: a silent retreat in upstate New York and a Shakti Leadership spiritual journey into the high Himalayas (led by Nilima Bhat, my coauthor on that book). I celebrated my 60th birthday in Ladakh, the seat of profound Buddhist wisdom close to the border between India and Tibet.

The Founders Journey was a 10-day trip in August 2018 into the rainforest of Ecuador where we immersed ourselves in the wisdom of ancient Indigenous cultures (the Achuar and the Zapara), connected to nature, and experienced a variety of healing modalities with shamans. I realized that we are as much a part of nature as a tree or a bee, but we have used our intellect to separate ourselves, causing great suffering to ourselves, to others, and to the planet.

The centerpiece of the trip – an optional ayahuasca journey – was on a warm, sunny Saturday. The ayahuasca brew is prepared by boiling the leaves of the *Psychotria viridis* shrub and the stalks of the *Banisteriopsis caapi* vine for a few days. The shamans of the region call the brew "grandmother ayahuasca"; "a mother spirit of nature who provides guidance and healing to those who work with her."[3] Many also call it the "vine of the soul."

Guided by our tiny, ancient shaman, we hiked for several hours through the dense, muddy rainforest, past trees with giant mushrooms growing out of them and surrounded by birds and insects. We arrived at a sacred waterfall, where we stripped down for a cleansing ceremony that involved inhaling water in which tobacco leaves had been soaked. I waded through the curtain of cascading water and sat on a natural ledge behind the waterfall to contemplate and release what no longer served me.

We resumed our hike. It took several more hours to reach the shaman's hut, which was in a tiny settlement on the banks of a large river. The hut had a thatched roof and no walls. Drenched in sweat, we bathed in the swiftly flowing river and changed into clean clothes. We approached the shaman's hut just as the sun was setting. In the twilight, we sat in a semicircle around him as he ladled the thick dark brew into small wooden bowls. For several minutes, he blew into the bowls and chanted and whistled. I nervously drank from my bowl. The taste was unpleasant but not unbearable. I lay down on banana leaves that had been spread on the ground next to the shaman's hut, a small lumpy pillow under my head and a threadbare sheet covering me.

---

[3] https://www.simonandschuster.com/books/Grandmother-Ayahuasca/Christian-Funder/9781644112359

That night, it was a lunar eclipse. I could see five planets lined up from horizon to horizon and countless stars dotting the sky. In his elaborate feathered headgear, the shaman stood over me and swished a leafy branch above my head, his silhouette framed against the twinkling sky. He swayed slowly and continued whistling and chanting and blowing. It was a surreal scene, and I slowly drifted into an altered state.

Hearing a baby cry in the distance, I too started crying. I felt that I was a little boy again, lying in my mother's lap. I had been emotionally blocked for 32 years, unable to cry for any reason whatsoever. My whole body was now convulsed with sobs; I cried as I had never cried before, without shame or self-consciousness, as I remembered all the sadness in my life, in my family, and in the world. Two attendants assisting in the ceremony took turns holding me as I sobbed.

I cried for the sadness and suffering that had afflicted so many in my family. I cried for my grandfather, whom life had hardened and robbed of humanity. I cried for my father, a brilliant and idealistic young man who had to abandon his dreams and became angry and cynical. I cried for my mother, for all the suffering she had endured and for losing her own mother when she was a little girl. I cried for my children, for the many struggles they had endured. I cried for my wife and our marriage, for the loneliness and sadness that we had each lived with for decades. And I cried for myself – for the traumas that I had experienced as a young child and as a young man.

Crying is healing but so many of us, especially men, are unable to access its healing power. I am reminded of part of a poem by Charles Mackay:

> O ye tears! O ye tears! I am thankful
> that ye run;
> Though ye trickle in the darkness, ye shall
> glisten in the sun.
> The rainbow cannot shine, if the drops
> refuse to fall,
> And the eyes that cannot weep, are the
> saddest eyes of all.

My tears finally subsided, and I lay back down, drained and cleansed. I then began to experience a series of visions, each with a clear and beautiful message.

The first one was simple. I heard a gentle voice whisper, "Love that is not expressed is like a check that is never cashed. It doesn't do any good for anybody." I realized I had been guilty of withholding my love and resolved that my love would never again be silent or concealed.

In the next vision, I was shown a long line of hundreds of people, standing for hours in the scorching sun, waiting for a hug from a tiny woman at the end of the line. I recognized her as Amma, the "hugging saint" from India, who travels the world hugging strangers. After being held tightly by Amma, people walked away in tears, overcome at having experienced unconditional love, perhaps for the first time in their lives. The message I was given was that all those people standing in line could be hugging each other; they didn't need to wait for a hug from Amma. The wise voice whispered, "We humans are the cause of most unnecessary suffering. We are also the source of healing for that suffering."

The highlight of the night was a vision in which four words floated behind my eyelids, shimmying around before arraying themselves into a single row: *love, innocence, simplicity,* and *truth*. Even in my altered state, I couldn't help notice that they formed a handy little acronym: LIST. This was the list. An audible gasp escaped my lips, "Oh my God!" I had come on this trip to learn about healing, for business, for the world, and for myself. A voice whispered, "This is what we all need to do to heal. We have gotten far away from all these things. This is what we need to return to."

Each word in turn then came into sharp relief, starting with *love*. The message was clear: we must always be rooted in love and always act from love. Even the hardest and harshest things that life sometimes demands of us should be done with love. Too often, we operate from fear, anger, greed, and other base emotions. We must be love, and we must express our love.

Then came *innocence*, which had been the centerpiece of my first plant journey five months before. We are all born innocent, and then we become corrupted by the ways of the world as we grow. We use our intelligence to trick each other and climb over each other rather than care for each other. We lie and cheat to get what we want. The voice whispered, "We must return to innocence – not the innocence of a helpless child, but the chosen innocence of a strong, mature, aware adult."

As the ancient Chinese divination text *I Ching* teaches, "All good comes when we are innocent. In the very center of each of us there dwells an innocent and divine spirit. If we allow ourselves to be guided by it in every situation, we can never go wrong."[4]

Next was *simplicity*. We humans make life too complicated and hide behind that complexity. The most important things in life are profoundly simple. We must seek the true simplicity that comes with mastery, and not settle for the simplistic. I was reminded of one of my favorite quotes from Oliver Wendell Holmes Jr.: "I would not give a fig for the simplicity on this side of complexity, but I would give my life for the simplicity on the other side of complexity."

And, finally, *truth*. Truth is the highest value. Sadly, most of us have lost our commitment to the truth – in business, in politics, and in our personal lives. As Gandhi (who titled his autobiography *My Experiments with Truth*) said, "The way of peace is the way of truth." The truth matters even more than peace because without truth, there can be no real peace. That is why post-apartheid South Africa needed to go through the "*Truth* and Reconciliation" process to start to heal from centuries of oppression.

The visions continued through the night. I eventually drifted into a trancelike sleep. I woke at dawn, grabbed my journal, and wrote down what I had been shown. The wisdom that came to me and through me that night would transform my life and set me on the path to healing. I believe that wisdom wasn't just intended for me; it is meant for all of us.

---

[4]http://www.harrisonbarr.ca/?p=164

Twin Bombshells

Seven months later (in March 2019), I went to India for my niece's wedding. I went straight from the airport to the hospital. A week earlier, my father had fallen in the bathroom and severely fractured his right hip and wrist. He came home from the hospital a few days later. This was the last time I saw my father alive. He died 17 days after I left; my mother died four months after that.

I went to spend a night at my cousin Gajendra's house. The next morning, we went for a walk. We started talking about my father. Gajendra had always had a difficult relationship with him as well, and I can see why, since Gajendra's mild-mannered and innocent nature is similar to mine.

I asked him how he had experienced the day in 1985 when I came to Indore to tell my father that I was going to marry Shailu after all. He said, "I remember that day vividly. He went into the other room and brought out a gun and said he would rather kill you than let you do this."

I was shocked. "What are you talking about?" I exclaimed. My mind had completely erased all memories of this traumatic incident, probably as a matter of survival. What could be more traumatizing than your father, the person who created you, threatening to kill you? I had read about dissociative amnesia, but it weas shocking to realize that I had experienced it.

We walked in silence for a while as I digested what he had just revealed to me. I had something else on my mind as well. "Do you know anything about the curse that Papa often talks about? He says that there were two souls in our family that never attained peace. He also says that is why there has been so much suffering in our family."

"Yes, I've known about that for years. It has to do with Kunwar Saheb."

Kunwar Saheb was Bhupendra, Gajendra's father, the oldest son of my grandfather. He was the one who had gone mad in his early 20s and had been locked up in a room in the corner of the Rowla for the rest of his life.

"Our grandfather had 13 children in all. Six died in their infancy or as young children and six survived. They are the ones we all know about. But there was one more. We had another *Bhua* [father's sister], who became pregnant as a teenager. People say that it was the priest who got her pregnant. He probably raped her. I don't know those details.

"When Daata [our grandfather] found out, he was furious. This would bring shame and dishonor upon the family and destroy the prestige he had worked so hard for. He summoned Bhupendra and said to him, 'As the oldest son, it is your duty to take care of this problem.'"

The implication was clear. Taking care of the problem meant getting rid of it, one way or another.

Bhupendra was a gentle soul, barely 20 years old. He had gotten married a couple of months prior. His sister's belly had started to show at his wedding; she looked distinctly pregnant, setting many tongues wagging.

Gajendra was close to tears. "So Kunwar Saheb went to her bed while she was sleeping and strangled her with his bare hands. She pleaded for her life and her baby's life, but he was in a frenzied state. She and her baby both died. Those are the two souls. That is the curse. Soon after that, he started to go insane."

I later heard other versions of the story, including this: that our aunt was forced to ingest herbs in the middle of the night that caused her to abort her nearly full-term baby, who started crying loudly. Kunwar Saheb quickly stuffed ashes into the crying baby's mouth to silence it. The baby died; our aunt died soon after from massive bleeding, shock, heartbreak, or a combination of those things. Kunwar Saheb and some trusted servants rushed in the darkness to cremate her body by the river's edge before the sun came up. In his haste, he badly burned his hands throwing smoldering logs into the river so no one would know that a body had been cremated. When he came home, his wife woke up and saw his burned hands. He broke down and told her what had happened.

It is impossible to know the full truth of what really happened that night. But this much is certain: two people died, and my uncle was so consumed with guilt over it that it seemingly led him to a psychotic break.[5]

I became dizzy; everything around me was spinning. Not only had Bhupendra been forced by his father to commit this act, but many others in the house had known about it. Gajendra's mother, my father, his sister, my grandmother – all of them had to live through this awful atrocity and bury this memory. From that day forward, they had to pretend that my aunt never existed, that what had been done to her and her baby had been for the best.

The immense amount of suffering our family had endured made sense now. This incident represented the ultimate loss of collective innocence: the brutal murder of a young girl and her child. I could not imagine a darker stain on a family. How could someone *not* go mad after doing something like that? How could all the other souls who were complicit in this heinous act not be tainted and wounded forever?

As far as we know, the priest suffered no consequences, nor were there legal consequences for anyone. But the spiritual consequences would cascade through the generations, casting a dark shadow over our family. We could escape the Rowla, as I had and my father had before me, but we could not outrun this curse. My father carried this secret with him to his grave. How much damage had it done to his psyche, his soul, all those years? How could our family heal from it?

No More Denial

That walk with Gajendra was a turning point for me. Within one hour, he had shaken me to my core. He told me about a successful

---

[5] Over the years, the "cover story" about Kunwar Saheb was that he developed schizophrenia in this 20s, and that there was no inciting incident. While this story is plausible, I don't think it is probable; there is no longer any dispute that the honor killing did take place, and that he was centrally involved.

honor killing and a threatened one. My father's action in picking up that gun also demonstrated a willingness to kill to protect a distorted sense of family honor.

I could no longer minimize the existence or extent of my own traumas. There was no more pretending they didn't matter, that other people had it far worse. I had experienced direct trauma from my father's actions, and indirect trauma because of the honor killing. I later learned that through epigenetics,[6] the accumulated traumas of my ancestors, near and distant, impact me as surely as the traumas I directly experienced.

All my life, I had shied away from conflict and averted my eyes from ugliness. I could not bear to look at the disfigured beggars and wounded animals on the street in India. But now I had to confront my own demons. I had to find some deeper meaning in all of it, to mine the suffering for nuggets of wisdom I could use to heal myself and share with others to help prevent such atrocities and suffering in the future.

My journey from settling for false harmony to realizing true healing was finally underway.

Reflections

We don't know what we don't know. I have always been open to new modalities of healing and self-awareness. When people I trust suggest that I try something new, I almost always say, "Yes." This has enabled me to have some profound experiences that have had a lasting impact on me.

Do you reflexively reject anything that is not "proven" or known to you? Do you believe that science can explain everything in the world, or do you think that what we don't know probably far exceeds what we know? What can you say "yes" to today that offers the promise of significant personal growth?

---

[6] R. Yehuda and A. Lehrner, 2018, "Intergenerational Transmission of Trauma Effects: Putative Role of Epigenetic Mechanisms," *World Psychiatry* 17, 3: 243–257.

When four wise women I trust and respect told me the same thing ("Delay the book and work on your own healing"), I had the good sense to listen to them. That changed my life. I believe we don't sufficiently value feminine wisdom in our lives. I now pay especially close attention when the advice is coming from that source.

Are people you trust and respect telling you something that you are rejecting? Pay particular attention to what you are being told by the women in your life.

I had been emotionally blocked for two decades before my ayahuasca journey. That experience opened me up, and I have remained that way.

Are you able to express emotions? Are you able to cry when you are sad? Are you embarrassed to cry in front of others? Crying and laughing are uniquely human behaviors; we reject or minimize each at our peril.

My vision of the LIST − *love, innocence, simplicity*, and *truth* − had a profound impact on me. I see it as a gift from universal consciousness. I strive to manifest LIST as much as possible in my life.

Does LIST resonate with you? How can you manifest each of these in your life, your work, your parenting, and your leadership?

13 | Healing the Father Wound

A few years ago, I called my parents' home in India. As usual, my father picked up.

"Happy Father's Day, Papa."

"You have become too Americanized, Raj. In India, every day is Father's Day."

I wasn't surprised. He jokingly said the same thing every year, but there was always an edge to it. In India, especially in Rajput culture, every day is indeed Father's Day.

The Father Wound

At my nephew Krishna's wedding in India, the husband of one of my cousins confided in me that his adult daughter had recently told him how bad she felt because he had never hugged her. He choked up as he told me the story. I replied, "I hope you gave her a big hug after that conversation." He seemed embarrassed and looked away. "How could I? A Rajput father can't do that."

My heart ached for my cousin's daughter – and for her father. She had practically begged him to show her some affection, but he couldn't and wouldn't. I understood her pain. I have no memory of my father picking me up as a child or hugging me or communicating his love for me physically or verbally. That along with his absence while he was getting his education, the control and oppressive domination, and his withholding of blessings for my marriage and family made me a textbook case of a *father wound*. It predictably led to emotional pain, poor self-esteem, and a profound lack of self-acceptance.[1]

According to Philip Moffit, "A trauma involving the mother or father is sometimes referred to as a 'wound' because it damages the body–mind, needs proper healing, and often leaves a scar or weakness in your body or emotional makeup."[2] The father wound is often passed on through generations. My father's own unhealed father wound meant he could not show up for his children in a genuinely loving way. He received only conditional love from his father and that became all he was capable of giving.

My Arc with My Father

From my first memory of my father when I was seven, I was in awe of him. That gradually morphed into a kind of fearful anxiety. Through my teenage years, I was never comfortable in his presence. After I left home at 16, we were largely disconnected. That continued until the events surrounding my marriage that led him to disown me. My feelings toward him from then on progressed in the following way:

> *Anger and Bitterness*: For over five years after he cut me off, I could not think about my father without feeling angry and bitter. My heart would start racing, my jaw would clench, and my breathing became jagged whenever I thought of him. I viscerally felt the unfairness of it; what had I done to deserve this? By any objective measure, I had been a model son. I did what I was expected to do: I worked hard at school, never got in trouble,

---

[1] https://www.focusonthefamily.ca/content/understanding-and-healing-the-father-wound
[2] https://dharmawisdom.org/healing-your-mother-or-father-wound/

helped at home, and contributed on the farm during school breaks.

Forgiveness and Acceptance: I eventually came to forgive my father after reading *Tuesdays with Morrie*. In my first Art of Living course, I realized I needed to go beyond forgiveness to acceptance. He was who he was, and he did what he did for many reasons that I did not fully comprehend.

In *The Way of the Superior Man*, David Deida advises adult men to "live as if your father were dead." Not that we should wish our fathers dead. Far from it; we should love our fathers. But to be free men, we need to insulate ourselves from our father's expectations and criticisms. Deida asks, "How would you have lived your life differently if you had never tried to please your father? If you never tried to show your father that you were worthy? If you never felt burdened by your father's critical eye?"[3]

Deida's words were liberating for me. I gradually unhooked from my father's energy in a way that allowed me some detachment and peace. I was no longer as triggered by his words and actions, even when they seemed designed to wound (as when he once said to me, "I love your brother more than I love you").

Understanding: Over time, I moved beyond acceptance to understanding. My father had long bounced between the pulls of self-determination and duty to family: the fierce centrifugal inner drive that enabled him to escape the village and travel across the globe in pursuit of higher education and a meaningful career; and the powerful centripetal force inexorably drawing him back into the constricted orbit around his father and his village. I tried to put myself into his shoes, to feel what he had felt. He had gone a long way from his roots in that tiny village with its medieval values and customs. But his core beliefs and values had been hardwired into him at a young age by a

---

[3]https://theintegratedmanblog.net/the-way-of-the-superior-man-part-1/

domineering father and a seductive culture. He was able to escape and transcend that for a while, but ultimately, he could not fight the programming that was implanted deep in his DNA.
Empathy and Compassion: Narayan's dream had been to become a doctor, but his father would allow him to go to college only if he studied agriculture. He wanted to marry someone other than my mother. He gave up those dreams. Other abandoned dreams would follow.

I think now about the rich promise that defined my father in his 20s and 30s. His professors expected great things to come from his fertile mind and incredible work ethic. After we returned to India, he wrote an article about his life purpose for the November 1971 issue of *SPAN* magazine, a publication of the US Embassy in Delhi. It was about the dream he had returned to India to fulfill: to spread awareness and adoption of triticale, a wheat-rye hybrid that was created at the University of Manitoba (his alma mater) in the 1950s. Compared to wheat, triticale had higher yields, required less water, was more resistant to bugs, and was richer in protein. It seemed like a godsend, a miraculous solution to India's then-chronic food shortages and widespread malnutrition. Unfortunately, triticale never caught on: the reddish color and slight wrinkle of the grain and the somewhat different taste and texture of *chapatis* made from it proved to be barriers too big to overcome in a country where people had eaten a particular kind of wheat for millennia. The failure was an enormous blow to my father. His dream died young. He never found a worthy second act. His work just became a job rather than a calling, and his career gradually faded into obscurity. Life became a matter of survival and duty. His was a tragic story of unfulfilled potential.

Oliver Wendell Holmes Sr. said, "Many people die with their music still in them." Sadly, my father was one of them.

Seeing the Whole Picture

I can now see my father's gifts more clearly. There were many. He was brilliant and ambitious. He was resilient and fearless. He was diligent and hardworking. He was imaginative and daring. He had a large and loud appetite for life. He transcended the circumstances of his birth to imagine and author a very different life for himself and for his family – for a while.

But along the way, he lost his innocence and shed his idealism. He allowed himself to become harsh and corrupted. He voluntarily checked himself back into the box that he had, with great difficulty, managed to escape. He shut down his critical thinking and became once again a prisoner to dogma and outdated traditions.

My father was highly educated but never acquired real wisdom; he had no spiritual education and no mentors to steer him in that direction. His overflowing intelligence and scientific bent made him stubbornly resistant to spiritual perspectives. As he grew older, he became increasingly narrow-minded, exclusionary, and suspicious. His life (and his family's) could have turned out very differently if he had the guidance, awareness, and tools to deal with the many traumas in his past.

His mother was neither strong nor loving, so he had no feminine influence to speak of. His natural, healthy masculine energy became unhealthy and toxic over time, as it was unbalanced with feminine energy. He married a woman who was docile and accepting, who did not push back against him when he went too far, enabling his bullying ways.

There were glimmers along the way of my father searching for grace, of him trying to fight his own nature. After I repeatedly and angrily confronted him about having "cursed" my marriage (which he insisted he hadn't done), he asked a priest what he could do to atone for it. The prescription was that he had to stop drinking alcohol and eating meat for a full month; this was not an easy challenge for him. He was also told to donate an amount of wheat equal to his body weight and have a special *havan* in the house. He did all this without telling me; I found out later and was quite touched by his gesture.

Innocence Lost – and Reclaimed

I realize now that my father carried within him a deeply wounded inner child who had experienced severe trauma that was never processed. Like the rest of the family, he had been a passive witness to atrocity. His acquiescence and participation in the conspiracy of silence rendered him guilty by association of the horrendous act that lay at the root of the curse, leading to the abuse and suffering that have defined our family for generations.

As the decades wore on, Narayan could clearly see the horrific toll of suffering that the honor killing had inflicted on the family. It sent his beloved brother careening into madness and led that brother's son to kill himself.

We do what we need to do and believe what we need to believe so we can live with ourselves. Narayan changed his name from Mahendra to Narayan, symbolically disconnecting from the brotherly pattern of names: Bhupendra, Mahendra, Hirendra. He perhaps rationalized what had happened as being in the service of some greater good. Since my grandfather had sacrificed Narayan's innocence at the altar of family honor, my father eventually came to exalt the preservation of family honor above everything else. As he wrote to me in 1985 after my "bombshell" about wanting to marry a person of my own choosing, "I have made so many sacrifices for Kesur. The result is that today Kesur has come a long way and I'm proud of it. . . Under no circumstances will I let you or anyone else destroy what I have cherished and built throughout my life."

This realization unlocked another piece of the puzzle for me. For as long as I can remember, my father showed a disdain bordering on contempt for people whose defining quality was innocence, who related to others without guile, who radiated love and simplicity – his wife, me, my cousin Gajendra. Perhaps this is how his subconscious processed this: "My innocence was taken away from me. Why do they get to be innocent?" He tried hard to erase that innocence in me, to make me as cynical and ruthless as he had become.

It didn't have to be this way. Narayan could have taken a stand, done everything in his power to prevent the honor killing, pleaded with his brother to refuse to go along, searched for a better way. But he did not. Over the years, he became trapped in a prison of his own making. He had no way to heal from the trauma because he could not and would not reveal a truth that in his mind would irretrievably tarnish the family's honor. He sentenced himself to relive the trauma repeatedly. He buried the secret deep within himself and numbed himself nightly with copious amounts of alcohol, followed by sleeping pills to snatch a few hours of relief.

Grief or Relief?

The full measure of our lives, the final verdict, is revealed at the end. Will those closest to us deeply mourn when we pass? Will they celebrate our life or simply commemorate our death? *Will they feel grief or relief at our passing?*

Regardless of where it starts, a life trajectory that points upward as it nears the end is a rare and precious thing. It comes from a combination of living for a higher purpose, working hard, cultivating personal power, and manifesting unconditional love. The absence of one of these is damaging; the lack of two or more of them is debilitating.

My grandfather's life started in hardship, followed by hard-won triumphs. It then went into a long decline and culminated in a lonely and bitter end. Girwar created a certain grandeur around himself for a while. He had a strong but uncompromising sense of duty, unleavened with love, compassion, or mercy. He was self-righteous and egotistical, with little self-awareness and no spiritual dimension. He brutally exercised power *over* others. He was more feared than respected. He was certainly not loved. He kept his children dependent and powerless. His ethical compass was deeply compromised. He committed or sanctioned atrocities in the name of family honor.

Girwar's passing was momentous, marking the end of an era. But there was no grief – just a palpable sense of relief, of a relentless pressure finally eased. Some in the family had been waiting for years for him to die so they could inherit property and move up in the feudal hierarchy. His legacy was a crumbling empire; 30 years after his death, the dilapidated Rowla still stands today as a mute symbol of decline, frozen in time, a grim daily reminder of an abusive past.

My father's trajectory looks somewhat similar: early challenges, hard-won triumphs, worldly acclaim, and then a long decline and sad end. He had a brilliant mind, an incredible work ethic, a strong sense of self, and an indomitable will. Hounded by his unrelenting father, he sacrificed a promising career at the altar of family and duty, only to regret it later. His youthful idealism curdled into cynicism and bitterness. Like his father, he had a strong sense of duty that was unleavened with compassion or mercy. Also like his father, he was feared, but not loved. He had no spiritual dimension and little self-awareness. As he got older, he was increasingly filled with anger, regrets, and bitterness.

As with my grandfather, my father's passing evinced little grief, just a sense of relief for most. He had been a domineering and formidable presence in all our lives, a person to be reckoned with. But in the end, his story was one of unrealized potential and needless suffering for himself and many whose lives he directly affected.

A Two-Time Destroyer of Families?

Responding to my "bombshell" news in 1985 about the woman I wanted to marry, my father said three things that became seared into my psyche: "You are destroying this family." "You are selfish and only think about yourself." "You are bringing shame and dishonor to this family."

Thirty-one years later, I finally mustered the courage to leave my marriage. It had a profound impact on my son. In the subsequent few months, he made statements that eerily paralleled what my father had said decades earlier: "Trump is tearing this country apart, and Dad is tearing this family apart." "Dad only cares about his own happiness. He doesn't care about the family's happiness." "When will we tell our relatives about the shame of our family?"

His words stung me deeply. Self-doubting questions played in a loop in my mind: Am I a monstrous, selfish human being? Do I truly care only about my own happiness? Had I in one lifetime managed to destroy not one but two families – my family of origin and the one that I had created? Do I deserve to suffer a lifetime of regret and recrimination?

With time has come clarity and a degree of grace for myself. I had to defy my father's self-serving strictures about whom to marry to be true to myself. I needed to take the incredibly painful step of ending my marriage to give myself – and my children and wife – a chance at happiness.

Healing My Son's Father Wound

Deep down, I believe most fathers dream of having sons who are "mini-mes," unblemished miniatures they can mold into ideal versions of themselves. Neither my father nor I got a mini-me. Alok is as different from me as I am from my father – a pattern that goes back at least five generations in my family.

In trying to understand and heal from my father wound, I eventually came to the sobering realization that my son has a father wound of his own – because of my relationship with him. When he was small, our interactions were playful and joyful. But as his condition manifested and steadily worsened, I found myself resenting him, spending less time with him and frequently losing my patience. His psychiatrist told us, "Alok views himself as damaged goods." I was deeply disappointed (mostly on my own behalf) that my son would never attain the conventional markers of a successful life: a college degree, an impactful career, marriage, children of his own. I saw him as a burden, an albatross holding me back. I felt trapped and constrained by him. I saw him as curtailing my freedom: I couldn't move to another city or country, I couldn't accept visiting professorships, I couldn't do many things most people take for granted.

I was ashamed of these thoughts and couldn't say them out loud, even to therapists. My wife and I never grieved together over the "life sentence" his condition had imposed on him and on us.

Just as I had experienced my father's love to be conditional, my son must have felt the same way. In the middle of one of his manic episodes, he said to me, "You never loved me." I was frustrated and angry with him in the moment and did not reassure him otherwise. At other times, after he accomplished (in my mind) something trivial and mundane, like completing a video game or a long virtual drive on Google Maps, he would plaintively ask me, "Are you proud of me?" I would mumble, "Yes" in a half-hearted way. Many times, I denied him even that level of affirmation, saying that what he had done wasn't that big a deal, certainly nothing to be proud of.

My experience in the Amazon rainforest transformed my relationship with my son. My partner Neha Sangwan helped me realize that Alok *is* LIST (love, innocence, simplicity, and truth), a living embodiment of the vision I received during my ayahuasca journey. He is incredibly loving, has the innocence of a young child, derives joy from simple pleasures, and is incapable of telling a lie. I am learning to love and embrace him exactly as he is, in his "stuckness" and his repetitiveness. I see him now as a complete human being, not a broken one. He has become a heroic, inspirational figure to me. I now realize that he is here to teach me compassion and patience, as much as I am here to teach him what I have learned about life.

I now spend more time with him and try to be fully present when he is with me. I celebrate his small successes. I hug him and tell him unprompted that I am proud of him because he's sweet, loving, funny, and always truthful. He tells me he's proud of me because "you are a kind and loving father, because you call me *beta* (an affectionate term for "son" in Hindi), and because you buy me expensive electronics!"

I am applying the same lessons to my relationship with my daughters. I hug them and tell them I love them and I am proud of them. I tell them I am here to witness their journeys and support their dreams; I do not expect them to fulfill mine.

Last Words

On an episode of the iconic television show *This Is Us*, a father on his deathbed spoke his last words to his son. Decades earlier, believing that the child's mother had died, the father had reluctantly given his newborn son up for adoption. After being diagnosed with stage IV cancer late in his life, he reconnected with his now grown son. William held his son's hand and said, "You deserve the beautiful life you've made. You deserve everything, Randall. My beautiful boy. My son."

William left Randall a priceless gift – words of acceptance and validation to live and heal by. I watched the scene in tears, thinking, "If only my father would say something like that to me."

My last conversation with my father was in 2019, a week after he fell and badly fractured his leg and wrist. He had come home from the hospital a few days before I was to return to the United States. Two weeks later he was readmitted to the hospital and never returned home, dying there of an infection.

Seeing how frail he looked, I realized this was probably the last time I would see him alive. I sat down next to his bed, held his hand, and said, "Papa, I want to thank you and let you know that I love you. I know your life wasn't easy. You worked very hard to provide for us. You took us all over the world and gave me a very interesting childhood."

I wanted to say those words to him to release him from any heaviness that he might have been carrying as he neared the end of his life. I didn't know if he had any regrets or guilt about belittling me, cursing my marriage, and disowning me. He listened to me quietly, looking into my eyes with a half-smile. Then he said, "Raj, you are your own boss."

What did he mean by that? It could have been "I am proud of you. You are your own man. You followed your heart and made your own path, even when it was difficult." Or he could have meant "You never listened to me. You just did what you wanted. You are selfish and care only about yourself." I would like to believe it was the former.

"I am not sure what you mean by that," I replied. "I think everyone should be their own boss." He didn't say a word, just kept looking at me with that half-smile. I stood up and leaned down for a last awkward hug, feeling his heart beating faintly through his thin *kurta*. I walked through the front door and left for the airport. We never spoke again.

Reflections

The story of my cousin's daughter craving a hug from her father made me think about "cultural casualties." Some unspoken cultural norms have benefits but many cause significant suffering. Violating cultural norms can be very dangerous in many societies, leading to ostracism and worse. We should examine these norms for their underlying rationale and question whether they still serve us.

> *What cultural norms imprison you and constrain your behavior in ways that have negative consequences for you and those you care about? What will you do differently with this awareness?*

Whether someone's death elicits grief or relief is the clearest evidence of the impact they had on the lives of others. Iron-fisted patriarchs who adhere to a rigid sense of duty and social order but never demonstrate unconditional love are rarely mourned.

> *Picture the scene at your funeral many years from now. How much grief is evident and how much relief? How do you need to change so that there is only grief and gratitude, rather than relief or apathy?*

Without conscious awareness and a resolve to break the cycle of victimhood, father wounds perpetuate through generations of stubborn, uncommunicative men. Once I became aware of my father wound, I realized my children may have a similar wound with me. That sobering realization led to a dramatic shift in my relationship with them, especially with my son.

> *Do you have a father wound with your father? Do your children have one with you? How can you heal them?*

As far as I know, my father did nothing to prevent the honor killing. Inaction has consequences. Idealism that stands mute in the face of injustice or cruelty curdles into a malevolent force that eats away at your soul. Silent shame morphs into shamelessness.

Are there times when you have remained silent in the face of obvious wrongdoing? How did that impact your sense of self over time?

14

Honoring My Mother and Becoming Whole

I started working with a life coach for the first time after turning 60 in 2018. At our first session, I told her my life story. I described my challenges with my father and the trajectory of my work. By the end, I was in tears. Suzanne asked if it was OK for her to hug me to comfort me. After the hug, she leaned back, closed her eyes, and was silent for a few minutes. She then looked at me and said, "Do you realize that you have been honoring your mother with your work for the last 15 years?"

Now it was my turn to be silent. Her insight startled me. A chill went through my body.

"What do you mean?" I asked.

"You spent 45 years trying to impress your father, trying to make him proud of you and accept you for who you are," she replied. "All that did was make you feel miserable, inadequate, and unfulfilled. But then you found your true path, which was to bring your mother's loving energy to the world of business. That is when your work began to have an impact on the world."

Her words struck me with the force and illumination of a thunderbolt. I felt the truth of what she had said in my bones. I had inherited many of my mother's qualities, and she had nurtured me as a single mother for my first seven years. My spirit had always been much more in harmony with her spirit than with my father's. I was born a calm, sensitive, and affectionate child. My innate nature, my *swabhav*, was to be trusting, peace-loving, and idealistic. After my father started telling me that all those qualities were weaknesses, I tried hard to suppress them. I tried to show my toughness by becoming a hunter and getting into unnecessary fights. In my work, I became a market warrior pursuing money, power, and accolades. In the process I made myself miserable and had minimal impact on the world.

But then unseen hands guided me onto a path that was more resonant with my essence and my mother's being: manifesting love, compassion, empathy, forgiveness, inclusion; above all, a refusal to cause unnecessary suffering in the world. My mother had imparted these gifts to me, through her genes, her nurturing, and her example. But I had been oblivious to them. Like most people on the planet, I took my mother for granted and chased after the worldly markers of success that my father valued.

I turned to Suzanne. "Thank you for that insight. I think you are right."

"Does your mother know that?"

"Well, I didn't know it until five minutes ago, so how would she know it?"

"I would like you to call her and tell her."

"Oh, that would be awkward. We never talk about such things in my family. You know how it is; we talk about the weather and about how her knees are feeling and other neutral subjects."

"This is important, Raj. You need to call her."

"The problem is that my father always answers the phone and puts it on speaker. He will think, 'Why is he talking like this? What is wrong with him?'"

"It doesn't matter. Call her."

"Suzanne, I just remembered that I'm going to India in three weeks. I can tell her in person."

"Your mom is 81. Anything can happen in three weeks. You need to call her."

That evening, I had dinner with my friends Dipinder and Meera. DP and I were in business school together in Bombay and have been friends for 39 years. When I told him about my exchange with my coach, he said, "You must call your mom."

"Okay, I will."

The next morning, I sat down to compose my thoughts about what to say to my mother. I wrote them down in English, and then translated them into Hindi, with help from Google Translate; my Hindi vocabulary never fully recovered from my years abroad as a child.

The phone rang. It was DP. "Have you called your mom?"

"I am about to, DP!"

I pressed the familiar digits of my parents' home phone. To my surprise, my mother picked up; my father was in the shower. After a few preliminaries, I said, "Mummy, I called to tell you how much you have meant to me in my life. Everything that I have done in the world that has mattered, everything that has touched people and impacted their lives, is because of you. It is because of what I learned from you. You live your life with so much love and gentleness. You have taken such loving care of us for our entire lives. I feel so blessed and am so grateful to have you as my mother."

Mummy started crying. She said, between sobs, "I am nothing, Raj. I am nothing." This brought on my own tears. I am crying now as I write this.

"No, Mummy, please don't say that. That is just not true. You are everything."

Ever since she became a wife and mother, my mother thought of herself as "less than"; her father had only educated her until the eighth grade and she didn't speak English, while my father was a gold medal–winning scientist with a PhD.

"I am just a simple uneducated woman. I am blessed to have a son like you. I am so proud of you. Every mother should have a son like you," she told me.

"Mummy, most of what is good in me comes from you. What the world needs is what you've taught us and shown us. You have such an enormous heart, and you never knowingly hurt anyone. I don't remember a single time you got angry or said anything harsh to me, or to anyone else. If you hadn't loved us the way you did, I don't know if I could have survived in the world."

It was by far the most healing conversation of my life, and I believe for her as well. I think it gave her some satisfaction that her life had not been without meaning, that her legacy was substantial and would live on in her children. It is not a coincidence that all three of her children have been called to do healing work in their own ways: I am dedicated to bringing healing to the world of business, my brother is working to heal our ancestral land, and my sister helps heal individuals and families through her work with the Art of Living Foundation.

Until that morning, I had never attempted to express the depth of my feelings toward my mother and everything she meant to me. My love for her was so deep that it seemed to transcend language. Being able to express it was deeply cathartic, vividly illustrating one of my cherished realizations from my ayahuasca journey: "Love that is not expressed is like a check that is never cashed. It doesn't do any good for anybody."

Who Was Usha?

Like my father, Usha also came from a feudal Rajput family. She grew up in a village less than 70 miles from Kesur. But the two families were completely different; the same soil had produced two very different gardens.

Usha's father was Jaswant Singh, the fifth Thakur of Berchha. An only child, Jaswant's father died young, and he inherited the title and estate when he was only eight. His father had appointed a regent to manage the fiefdom until Jaswant came of age. Jaswant was sent to a boarding school that educated children of Rajput aristocrats. He was accompanied there by a full-time, live-in attendant who never let him out of his sight. The manservant washed, ironed, and laid out Jaswant's clothes; polished his shoes; tied his turban on festive occasions; and tasted all the food before my grandfather ate it — not to check for freshness or flavor, but to guard against poisoning. It was not uncommon for scheming uncles to kill underage heirs to usurp their property and title.

When he turned 18, Jaswant was formally installed as the Thakur. He was not a typical feudal overlord. He enjoyed his large estate and lived a life of leisure — quite a contrast from my fanatically hard-charging and hard-working paternal grandfather. In his youth, Jaswant befriended British colonial officers and missionaries. After India's independence in 1947, he invited young American Peace Corps volunteers to visit him in Berchha. An easygoing soul with highbrow tastes, he delighted in Western culture and food. He subscribed to *Reader's Digest,* loved to bake, and distilled fine liquors with exotic flavors like fennel, blackberry, saffron, and deer musk — considered Royal Heritage spirits. He buried scores of bottles of the precious elixirs in the ground, excavating them on special occasions.

Jaswant was a renowned hunter and marksman; he once shot a bird circling above by tracking its shadow on the ground. The most iconic story was of a black panther that once terrorized the region around Berchha, killing and eating many goats and calves. One day, a frantic villager interrupted Jaswant during his lunch with the news that the panther had carried off a child from the village. This was the last straw; when a predator became a man-eater, it had to be eradicated. Jaswant grabbed his shotgun and a rope, jumped on his horse, and rode off alone into the jungle. He returned a couple of hours later, the panther's lifeless body dragging behind the horse. He sat down and asked his wife to have his lunch reheated.

The tiny village was once ravaged by the plague, which made its way slowly across India, killing 10 million people by 1940. During the outbreak, the dusty cobbled streets of the village were strewn with dead rats. The family left the Rowla and lived in the forest for months until the disease subsided.

Jaswant married Laxmi Kunwar Rathore of Badgara when he was 18. Usha, their first child, was born in 1937, when he was 20. A second daughter followed a couple of years later. But tragedy soon struck the young family. My grandmother contracted tuberculosis in 1942, when she was 23. My mom was just five.

One of the deadliest diseases in the world, tuberculosis killed millions every year in those days. There was no vaccine or effective treatment until 1944 – two years too late to save my grandmother. When she realized she was dying, my grandmother decided to remove herself from every photograph that she was in – from her childhood, her wedding, and with her husband and daughters. She sat down with a pair of scissors to carry out the grim project, telling her heartbroken husband, "I don't want my girls to cry about me their whole lives after I'm gone. It is better that they forget me completely." Usha was bewildered at what her mother was doing. Treating it like a game, my three-year-old aunt scampered around the house looking for more precious photos for her mother to destroy. Little Usha cried as she helplessly watched the growing pile of mutilated memories. When she finished, my grandmother transferred the pile to a small metal drum and dropped a lighted match into it. The highly flammable photos were reduced to ashes in seconds, spreading a pungent smell through the house.

My grandmother died a few months later, but not before handpicking a woman for her husband to marry next. She said, "You must marry a woman who's going to be kind to my girls."

Watching her mother die when she was just five took Usha's legs out from under her. A couple of years later, her father sent the gentle little girl to a boarding school in faraway Banasthali in Rajasthan. Her memory of her mother slowly faded, but never fully disappeared. Usha returned home after eighth grade at age 15 and became a surrogate mom to a growing brood of half siblings. There would be five of them – four boys and a girl – by the time Usha turned 20 and got married.

Usha learned to endure at a young age. Her mother had been strong and loving; her stepmother was also loving but could be harsh. Even more than before, Usha became a people-pleaser. All her life, she adored and worshipped her father, a benign, loving, smiling patriarch – her model for how men should be.

Nothing in Usha's upbringing prepared her for the cauldron of Kesur, the toxic stew she was abruptly dropped into. The version of the patriarchy that prevailed in Kesur muted and extinguished the spirit of pliant women like Usha. Her brutal father-in-law mocked her, her shrewd sister-in-law bullied her, her absent husband left her unprotected and alone.

Portrait of a Marriage

Late in her life, a sad expression would cloud my mother's face when someone said, "Happy anniversary." On her 80th birthday, she confided to her daughter-in-law that she had experienced little joy in her life. She didn't say so, but the reason was clear: the domineering and demeaning marriage she had endured.

Like most Rajput women in her circumstances, Usha was bound by duty – her *dharma* – and resigned to her destiny. Day after day, night after night, year after year, she did what a "good" wife and mother was supposed to do. Her life was more about what she couldn't do than what she could. She couldn't make a single decision – even about what to cook for the next meal – without asking her husband first. Her confidence, her autonomy, her interests – her very personality – were all sacrificed on the pyre of her marriage. She retained her inherent innocence and goodness, but her sense of self gradually vanished.

She couldn't write letters to me, her banished son, for five long years because her husband forbade it. (Nonetheless, she periodically smuggled a letter to me through my sister.) She couldn't go to a restaurant for lunch with her younger son (who lived in the same house) because "Papa won't like it if I go." When they did go out for lunch once, my father – ever vigilant for signs of uprisings and budding conspiracies against him – demanded a minute-by-minute recap of everything she and my brother had talked about.

Late in life, her heart weakened by age, she hobbled around the house all day long on her two artificial knees to fulfill her husband's incessant demands – for hot water, for milk, for tea, for his medicines, and a hundred other things. The household had plenty of domestic help, but he insisted she do many things that younger, paid hands and legs could do far more easily. At day's end, he theatrically pointed to her exhaustion in a never-ending attempt to shame his adult son and daughter-in-law into further acceding to his dominion over their lives. "Look at your poor mother. At her age, she shouldn't have to do all these things; her daughter-in-law should be doing them."

All her life, my mother bathed her children in unconditional love, but she lacked personal power. Her ability to absorb toxic words and tolerate egregious behavior from my father was heroic and heart-breaking at the same time. It made her a passive witness to abuse and thus an unwitting enabler of it. Her only sins were of omission rather than commission.

Even her bottomless patience had its limits. On rare occasions, she would snap at my father, causing him to back off immediately. It never failed. It showed that she had enormous latent power; everybody knew it except her. Her anger was more powerful for its rarity. But her fuse was so long that it rarely reached its limit. She became a protective shield for my father. Despite how he insulted and alienated people, most stayed connected to our family because of her. My brother moved away but came back to live in the house because of her. She was the pole of the magnet that continually drew us back home, while my father was the pole that pushed us away.

Passages

My father died on March 30, 2019. My mother died four months later. Both died of hospital-acquired infections, taking their last breaths in the same intensive care unit.

Soon after my father died, my mother started experiencing severe dizzy spells. It was as though she lost her bearing and couldn't support her own weight after leaning on my father for so long. Once she recovered, her true self slowly emerged, like the sun breaking through the clouds. Everybody in the extended family craved more time in her loving, healing presence and pleaded with her to visit them. Freed of her husband's constant scrutiny and prodding, she developed a more loving and easygoing relationship with her daughter-in-law. She started regularly checking in on family members, offering her love and encouragement. We all delighted in hearing her laugh, seeing her smile, experiencing her real personality. We looked forward to getting to know this delightful new Usha.

Sadly, it was not to be. She suddenly started experiencing intense abdominal pain, had emergency gallbladder surgery, and died within a week. She had absorbed too much poison over her lifetime for her body to endure.

Both my parents were 82 when they died suddenly and unexpectedly. The responses to the two passings could not have been more different.

My father's passing evoked little sorrow; my brother, my sister, our cousins, and I – none of us shed a tear. We were just numb. My mother cried, of course, for the end of the only life she had known for 62 years.

When my mother died, it broke my heart and the hearts of countless others. She *was* my heart. I didn't know I was capable of such grief. I have never cried so much. I had lost the one person on this planet who loved me unconditionally and saw me and understood me.

A few days after the funeral, we gathered to share what she had meant to us. We were all bereft. People tearfully spoke of her loving nature, her gentleness, how she was soothing, self-sacrificing, patient, utterly selfless. Usha was a pure embodiment of the mother archetype: life-giving, unconditionally loving, kind, inclusive, compassionate, and forgiving.

Three weeks after my mother passed, I returned to Laura's for another plant journey. I wanted to connect with my mother's spirit and ask her for guidance. She came vividly to me that night as a *devi*, a goddess resplendent in her power and beauty. She was in her full power, completely at ease with herself. It reminded me of the end of a Broadway play, when the actors return to the stage as who they really are, no longer playing a role. Usha had dutifully played her roles for 82 years: obedient daughter, loving sister, supportive wife, devoted mother, doting grandmother. Come what may, she had done her duty and never wavered from the path of love. Her message to me that night was simple: Never deliberately cause pain in anyone's heart; and know that you will always be loved.

Bringing My Mother to My Father

As Suzanne had discerned, I had been unconsciously honoring my mother with my work for 15 years. Now that I understood that, I thought: What would it mean to do so *consciously*? Should I double down, make explicit what had thus far been implicit?

I also recognized the danger in going too far toward the feminine, of becoming unbalanced and neglecting the vital masculine side. I realized I can best honor my mother by empowering her unconditional love with strength, courage, and resolve, by making active what had largely been passive.

Having understood my parents in a deeper way, I am now able to integrate what is most valuable from each of their journeys. Neither of my parents embodied the healthy aspects of the other. My father had no healthy feminine energy, and my mother completely lacked healthy masculine energy. Therein lies my lesson: blend the healthy and positive aspects of each of my parents into a harmonious whole. I have learned that the combination of empowered mother energy with open and loving father energy is what I need – and what the world needs – to heal and become whole.

Reflections

Most of us have unresolved issues with our parents, typically about memories from childhood that remain stubbornly stuck in our psyche. Many of them result from misunderstandings. It is important that we strive to become "complete" with our parents by having hard conversations with them before they pass. If we don't have those conversations and our parents pass away, those issues don't disappear; they remain permanently embedded within us but become impossible to resolve.

What are your most painful memories of your childhood that involve your parents? Have you discussed these with them? If not, do so as soon as possible. Have the conversation from a place of curiosity rather than anger, hurt, or blame.

Many of us don't express deeply appreciative and loving feelings toward our parents until it is too late. Once they're gone, that too is a tragic loss.

As I did with my mother, tell your parents what they have meant to you, what they did right, and what you will never forget about them. It will probably be the most healing and meaningful conversation of your life. Make sure you record it!

One of my regrets is that I didn't talk enough with my mother about her childhood and young adulthood. She experienced severe trauma at the loss of her mother. She lived through catastrophic events like the plague and momentous events like India's independence from colonial rule. All those priceless details of her life and times are lost forever.

Ask your parents about their childhood experiences and influences. If you have children, have them interview their grandparents about what their lives were like when they were young.

Marriage for most women of my mother's generation was a matter of fate, a life sentence to be served without the possibility of parole. She expected little, and she received even less in her marriage.

List five things that would make for an ideal marriage. What can you do to make those a reality?

My mother had power in her relationship with my father, but rarely exercised it. This is true for all human beings; we have innate power, but most of us don't exercise it.

In what ways do you give away your power in your relationships at work and at home? How can you exercise that power in a healthy and life-affirming way? What would you lose by not claiming that power?

The combination of personal power and unconditional love can change the world. They are rarely in the same person. My mother loved unconditionally, but lacked personal power. My father had a lot of personal power, but his love was entirely conditional.

*How can you cultivate personal power **and** be a source of unconditional love in your life in all aspects of your life? That is the holy grail.*

15 | Discoveries

My life is an unfinished canvas, a work in progress. I wrote this book to look back on what I have experienced and learned so I can illuminate the path forward with greater clarity for myself and, I hope, for my readers. I have sought answers to timeless questions that are relevant to all humans: How can we stay true to ourselves? How can we live in alignment with what we're meant to bring into the world? How can we manifest love and strength in equal and full measure?

Our lives are amalgams of countless forces and influences, some subtle and others obvious, propelling us forward and sideways and sometimes backwards in seemingly inexplicable ways. But ultimately, each of our lives is a journey toward purpose, coherence, inner peace, wholeness, and healing. I navigated the journey in my own way. You may find other pathways. But our goals are the same: to find and live our purpose, become whole human beings, and heal the traumas that lie buried within ourselves.

This book was the easiest and the hardest to write of all my books. It was easy because at one level it was a straightforward process of excavating my memories from a crowded and eventful life. But it was also the hardest thing I've ever done because it was painful, even traumatic, to relive difficult memories, come to painful realizations, and confront harsh truths.

In the end, this is neither an exercise in self-flagellation nor self-absolution. It is about learning to live from the inside out, rooted in your authentic self. It is about stepping into your personal power so you can use that power to serve, comfort, and heal.

Following are my greatest lessons from this journey.

Stay True to Yourself

I lived most of my life in separate airtight compartments. I was a different person at work and at home. A small part of me remained rooted in the conservative feudal culture that I came from, and a larger part of me was of the modern world. My thoughts, words, and actions didn't always align. I was *acting* much of the time, pretending to be someone other than I am. I lacked personal power in many parts of my life.

The goal for each of us should be full alignment between who we are, what we say, and what we do. This means showing up as the same integrated being in every situation, operating with consistency from an unshakable core.

How can we stay true to ourselves? I have learned that there are three keys: knowing yourself, loving yourself, and being yourself.

Know Yourself

Before I can tell my life what I want to do with it, I must listen to my life telling me who I am. I must listen for the truths and values at the heart of my own identity, not the standards by which I must live but the standards by which I cannot help but live if I am living my own life.

—Parker Palmer

We spend decades learning about the ways of the external world, but most of us know very little about our inner world. Yet it is impossible to lead an impactful, fulfilling life if you don't know who you are. Ask yourself: "Who am I? What is my essence, my true nature? What qualities defined me as a young child? What matters to me? What am I passionate about?"

For much of my life, I didn't know who I was. Was I a proud Rajput, scion of a feudal warrior family? Was I Pappu, the simple innocent one? Was I Raj, the worldly ambitious one? Was I Indian? Was I American? Was I an engineer? Was I a marketing professor? Was I a writer? Was I a journalist?

We are all born with certain qualities. When I was a very young child, I was innocent, idealistic, trusting, simple, peaceful, empathetic, gentle, and cooperative. As I grew, I discovered I was articulate, intelligent, loving, humorous, humble, ambitious, creative, nonconformist, and resolute.

I also recognize my challenges. For example, my desire to seek peace led me to become too averse to conflict. Craving harmony, I was frequently not assertive enough and silenced my truth. Such awarenesses have given me a roadmap for my self-development.

Ask yourself: What are my natural gifts and talents? What are my well-developed skills? What are my core values?

Love Yourself

You yourself, as much as anybody in the entire universe,
deserve your love and affection.

—Buddha

Our primary relationship in life is with ourselves. If that relationship is dysfunctional, it pollutes everything else. We must make sure it is a loving relationship. It is impossible to be happy or peaceful if you don't love yourself. This includes loving our body, mind, heart, and soul. As Francis Meehan said, "Men are at war with each other because every man is at war with himself."[1]

Many people are never able to make the leap from knowing themselves to loving themselves. It took me decades to see my qualities as strengths rather than weaknesses. To the extent that I knew myself, I despised myself, primarily because my father saw most of my

---

[1] https://proverbicals.com/war-proverbs

innate qualities as weaknesses and tried to root them out of me. I came to view myself as defective, and was convinced that I needed to be the opposite of who I really was. I suppressed my idealism. I became cynical and suspicious. I became unnecessarily confrontational. No wonder I was deeply unhappy for decades.

Loving yourself, having compassion and grace for yourself, is the first step to being able to evolve yourself. As Carl Rogers said, "The curious paradox is that when I accept myself just as I am, then I can change."[2]

> *Affirm to yourself: "I am a unique being who is here to contribute to the world in ways nobody else can. I accept, embrace, and am deeply grateful for all my innate qualities. These are gifts I have received. Even though I may have undeveloped and unhealed parts, I still accept those aspects even as I strive to grow and heal. I am grateful for my body—every part of it."*

Be Yourself

> To be yourself in a world that is constantly trying to make
> you something else is the greatest accomplishment.
>   —Ralph Waldo Emerson

There is no right path or wrong path; there is only *your* path. All of us are embedded in systems that pressure us to conform to prevailing norms: for me, to be a "true" Rajput, to be a certain kind of man, to be a "typical" professor.

Refuse to be a typical anything! Embrace Polonius's advice to his son in Shakespeare's *Hamlet*: "To thine own self be true." Strive to be the purest, fullest, most evolved version of yourself, your highest self.

Most of us spend too much of our time and energy acting, taking on various personas in our professional and personal lives. Let yourself be directed from within. Revel in your uniqueness. What do you see that no one else sees? What do you say that no one else says? What

---

[2] Carl Rogers, *On Becoming a Person: A Therapist's View of Psychotherapy* (Houghton Mifflin, 1961).

do you know that no one else knows? Cultivate a healthy level of awe for yourself!

Unfortunately, most people never discover their uniqueness. For many years, I was one of them. I tried on different identities – an engineer, a marketing professor who was an expert in financial services and then in technology, a strategy expert, etc. I eventually realized that I need to trust myself and express my truth, rather than allow the voices of others to steer me. I resolved to live my life to fully express myself rather than to please my father and other authority figures. I started to become who I was meant to be.

Be Open to New Adventures

Every human life has infinite creative potential. Life gifts us a sprawling canvas and a dizzying array of colors to create with.

Live your life in a creative rather than reactive space. Be a sailboat with a rudder, not driftwood in the ocean that goes whichever way the waves and wind take it. Harness the wind and currents to chart a course toward fulfilling your singular purpose and destiny.

Life continually presents us with choices between growth and safety. If we always choose safety, we will never grow. When we stop growing, we start dying. Make sure you blend in a healthy amount of risk-taking into your life, even as you make some decisions motivated by safety and prudence.

Be alert for calls to adventure. Say "yes" to possibilities outside your comfort zone, those that offer the potential for you to grow. Don't cling to stability and security. Embrace the unexpected.

It is impossible to have a master plan for every aspect of your life. The possible paths forward are revealed in glimpses; remain vigilant and nimble. Be ready to walk through doors that suddenly slide open. When I came down for breakfast in Mumbai during my MBA program and found my friends dressed up to go to the US Information Agency, it was an invitation for me to dramatically alter the trajectory of my life. I seized the opportunity rather than letting it pass me by.

Trust your body's wisdom. When I encounter an idea that resonates with my soul's purpose, I get chills, shaky legs, or other strong bodily sensations. In such moments, I recognize that my body is telling me something important and I need to pay attention. I get similarly strong signals from my body when an idea feels "off," when it is misaligned with my higher self. It could be a pit in the stomach or sudden shortness of breath.

Be Your Own Best Friend and Coach

When my father said, "Raj, you are your own boss," in our last conversation, he was likely acknowledging that I had done what he couldn't. I had resisted pressures to conform in my personal and professional lives and chosen to live according to my own dictates. As a result, I gained personal power and greater relevance in the world as I grew older, while my father came back into his father's orbit at age 34, gave up on his dreams, and faded into irrelevance.

My father's last words are a worthy mantra for all of us to live by – with one caveat. No human deserves to be "bossed." We should each be the captains of our own ships. We should never give up the controls of our lives to others, never acknowledge another as our "boss." Instead of being our own boss, we should strive to be our own parent, coach, and best friend.

Challenge Orthodoxies

I have simultaneously been an outsider and an insider in the worlds I have inhabited: as an Indian child in the West, as a westernized child back in India, in the Rajput culture, in academia, in business. All along, I refused to blindly follow the traditional way of doing things. I reject the phrase "This is how we've always done it." I strive to do things my own way.

As a teenager, I rebelled against the Rajput orthodoxy I experienced in the feudal culture of my village. Early in my career, I disavowed academic orthodoxy, refusing to adhere to norms of what faculty members are supposed to do and not do. I challenged "business and marketing as usual," which led me to discover my purpose and launch the Conscious Capitalism movement. I rejected damaging notions of masculinity and the use of gendered and militarized language and mindsets.

I urge you to challenge any conventional wisdom that runs counter to your values and your essence. Cultivate detachment and discernment so that you do not get caught up in groupthink. Notice when something inside you doesn't resonate with what other people are asking of you. If you ignore that inner voice, you are certain to make decisions that betray your true self.

Choose Your Life

> It is important to take every experience, including the
> negative ones, as merely steps on the path, and to proceed.
> Everything in your life is there as a vehicle for your transfor-
> mation. Use it!
>
> —Ram Dass

At a silent retreat at Peace Village in upstate New York in the summer of 2018, we were served at mealtimes by volunteers. They did not ask us what we wanted; they simply put a little bit of everything on our plates. The thought came to me: "Life is not a buffet. Nor can you order off a menu. You're given a tray full of stuff – the right things in exactly the right amounts. Some may be bitter and unappetizing, but you need it all."

I spent too many years lamenting the many difficult things in my life: the harshly feudal family I was born into; my father's absence for the first seven years of my life; my always uncomfortable, frequently painful relationship with him; my traumatic reentry to India; multiple setbacks in my career; my father's cruel reaction to my marriage; my unhappy marriage; having a special needs son; and many more. But I now realize that even painful experiences, things I wouldn't wish on my worst enemy, shaped me in important ways. For example, I needed to experience the worst aspects of the patriarchy to be able to write a book about the need to elevate the feminine decades later.

I cannot go back in time and change the challenging aspects of my life, but I *can* consciously choose them. By doing so, I make it possible to alchemize those painful experiences and extract something positive from them. If I do not choose those parts of my life, I forever remain a victim to them.

Affirm to yourself: "I choose and embrace my past. I choose all the people in my life, past and present. I choose my parents, my grandparents, my siblings, my uncles and aunts, my cousins, my marriage, my children, my friends, my colleagues, my leaders, my teachers, my supposed enemies, and everyone else who came into my life. I choose all the experiences I have enjoyed or endured, positive or negative. I release all bitterness, anger, and regrets about my life. I am grateful for it all and I choose it all."

Embrace Seeming Opposites

In a world of competing ideas, the answer is often not "*or*" but "*and*." My life, my work, the Conscious Capitalism movement – all are built on this understanding.

Integrating seeming opposites has been a major theme in all aspects of my life. The biggest "polarity" that I needed to integrate in my life was masculine and feminine. Others include modern and traditional, idealism and pragmatism, harmony and conflict, self-care and selfless service.

Polarities are ideas that seem like opposites but are actually interdependent pairs. They need each other to exist. Each pole offers something of value, something essential. If you reject the "other" pole, you inevitably end up with the excesses of the "chosen" pole. This applies to ideas such as progressivism and conservatism, profit and purpose, justice and mercy, and countless other facets of life.

In our extremely polarized world, too many people pick a "side" and become deeply wedded to it. They don't realize that it is possible to get the best of each pole while avoiding the downside of each.

What are the seemingly opposite poles that are tugging at you in your life? Use Barry Johnson's Polarity Mapping to learn how to gain the upside of each without suffering the downside of either.[3]

Acknowledge and Heal Your Traumas

We are all wounded beings. Life is hard, and trauma is an inescapable part of it. Every human being suffers from some degree of "post-traumatic stress injury." But we cannot heal our traumas if we don't acknowledge them. And we cannot live full, healthy, joyful lives unless we heal our traumas. Once we do heal them, our wounds can gift us with unexpected power and the ability to help others dealing with similar wounds. It is what the Japanese call Kintsugi – the art of precious scars. When a piece of pottery breaks, they put it back together using a mixture of glue and gold powder. The result: a work of art that is beautiful and stronger than it was before it broke.

If we have unhealed traumas, we are not in control of our thoughts and actions; they arise from subconscious impulses that we don't understand. As Carl Jung wrote, "When an inner situation is not made conscious, it happens outside, as fate."[4] This is often paraphrased as "Until you make the unconscious conscious, it will direct your life and you will call it fate."

Avoidance and silence allow trauma to continue. Trauma that is not transmuted is transmitted; traumatized people inflict trauma on others. The only way to break this "victims of victims" cycle is to face the trauma and do what is necessary to heal from it. Those who do this heal their own lives and can help others do the same.

For a long time, I didn't realize that I had any traumas. Later, I deemed them insignificant in comparison with people who had "real" trauma. In fact, I had plenty: a near-death experience, sexual abuse, a profound father wound, the trauma of the generations before me in Kesur, and more.

---

[3] https://www.polaritypartnerships.com/
[4] Carl Jung, *Collected Words 9ii*, "Christ, A Symbol of the Self," Paragraph 126.

Trauma occurs not only in individuals but also in families and in cultures. Many, if not most, traumas result from inhumane systems. Ultimately, it was the feudal patriarchal Rajput system that killed my aunt and unborn cousin. It caused my uncle to go insane. It drove my cousin Himmat to take his own life. This doesn't absolve individuals of personal responsibility. But we must acknowledge that the system created a deeply distorted sense of right and wrong. It blurred ethical boundaries to the point of rendering them invisible.

It is imperative, therefore, that we work on healing our systems as well as working on healing ourselves. That requires taking a clear-eyed look at the past and confronting the wounds that sit there. That is what the United States needs to do with its history of slavery, and it is what I needed to do with my family's past. My ancestral village Kesur has long been a symbol of decay, abuse, and suffering. If we can heal the collective trauma that exists there, Kesur could stand for something beautiful and life-enhancing.

I realized while writing this book that the *dharma,* the divine duty and nature, of Rajputs is to be protectors. Over its long history, India has been invaded over 200 times, far more than any other country. The vast majority of the invaders came from the northwest, which is where the Rajput kingdoms were located. My ancestors fought ferociously and with great courage to defend the country, absorbing massive trauma. The men repeatedly went to war and many died in battle against enemies with overwhelming power. Women and children committed mass suicide by burning themselves rather than risk enslavement. That is a huge amount of unhealed trauma that sits in my lineage — and in my own DNA (as the field of epigenetics is revealing to us).

Many (perhaps most) people on the planet can trace their ancestry back to either the perpetrators or victims of brutal aggression, including slavery, genocides, and ethnic cleansing. There can be no true healing without acknowledging and atoning for this history. Each of us needs to undergo our own "truth and reconciliation" process for true healing to occur.

Think back over your life. Identify the most significant traumas you have personally experienced. Identify traumatic events that happened in your family of origin. What kinds of ancestral traumas might you be carrying in your DNA? How have you been psychologically impacted by the pandemic, climate change, and other kinds of collective trauma?[5]

Be a Peaceful Warrior for Truth and Love

You have no enemies, you say? Alas, my friend, the boast is poor. He who has mingled in the fray of duty that the brave endure, must have made foes! If you have none, small is the work that you have done. You've hit no traitor on the hip, you've dashed no cup from perjured lip. You've never turned the wrong to right. You've been a coward in the fight.

—Charles Mackay

For much of my life, I was enveloped in so much discord that I craved harmony above all else. Like my mother, I often overlooked egregious behaviors for the sake of keeping the peace.

I was born into the warrior caste, an identity I rejected for most of my life. But I eventually came to realize that I *do* need to be a warrior — for the values and ideals I hold dear. I need to be a *peaceful* warrior for truth, love, idealism, and innocence.

A peaceful warrior is rooted in high ideals and in innocence. We all are born innocent, and then gradually lose our innocence, just as we lose our baby teeth. We get corrupted and adopt the coarse and devious ways of the world. We use our intelligence to trick each other and climb over each other rather than care for each other. We lie and cheat to get what we want.

We need to return to innocence — not the innocence of a helpless child, but the chosen, powerful innocence on the other side of

---

[5] If you do uncover significant traumas that you were previously unaware of, I strongly recommend that you seek professional help. Many modalities are now available to help process, release, and heal from trauma.

wholeness: the inviolable, resilient innocence of a strong, loving, aware adult. That means never knowingly inflicting suffering on another. If we don't choose innocence, it means we are choosing corruption.

Strive to become a peaceful warrior on behalf of the ideals you hold dear. Ask yourself: Have I fought the good fight? Am I creating enough "good trouble"? Do I lean into necessary conflict?

Stay Awake!

What does it mean to "awaken"? To me, it means that your life makes sense; you know who you are and why you are here. Awakening means letting go of judgment and bitterness and choosing to live in gratitude. It means doing what's right, not what's comfortable. Awakening allows us to experience deep connection and joy by realizing that life is ultimately about giving and receiving love. It means losing your fear of dying.

It is one thing to awaken; it is another to stay awake. Use this book to recognize patterns that have shown up repeatedly in your life, to uncover hidden truths, and to chart a more conscious path forward. I hope it serves as a starting point for you to undertake your own journey toward purpose, wholeness, and healing.

We are given life, but we must choose how we are to live. When we commit to healing our traumas and living by the LIST – Love, Innocence, Simplicity, and Truth – we can in fact help heal the world, and leave behind a legacy of love and healing for future generations.

Epilogue: Healing the Patriarchy

Why was my soul born in a place like Kesur to a father and a mother like mine? To a casual observer, my deeply feudal origins are completely at odds with the person I have become: a modern multicultural global citizen who embraces the need for feminine and masculine energy in business and in family. It just doesn't add up, which means there is probably a deeper purpose to it.

The way I have come to make sense of it is this: I left India to make a life in the United States of America, to thrive in the "land of the free." But wherever you go, there you are. I carried inside me the DNA of Kesur as well as the traumatic history of the Rajputs. My journey of healing and the reason I helped launch Conscious Capitalism is that through the lens of business, my real work has been to try to heal the patriarchy. Unconscious capitalism was clearly the product of patriarchal traditions. Conscious Capitalism has been a stepping-stone to my greater purpose, which is to challenge patriarchal mindsets across all sectors of society. I believe I was destined to connect these worlds and do this kind of healing work.

The Need to Heal Kesur

For much of my life, I thought of Kesur as a place of darkness and decay, of abuse and tyranny. I assumed that it had always been that way, with some exceptions like my great-grandfather Hari Singh, who was renowned and loved for his kind, generous, and forgiving nature. He reflected the benign paternal side of the patriarchy.

People sometimes took advantage of Hari Singh because he offered help to anyone who needed it. If he discovered that someone had cut down a tree from his lands and stolen it, his response was, "He must really need it." Later, he would say to the person, "Why didn't you ask me if you needed something?" When Girwar caught people stealing, he punished them harshly and publicly, often beating them with a stick.

***

Many in my family have bought into the idea that "we must not let anything sully the name of Kesur." Now more than ever, Kesur has become an integral part of the identity of members of my extended family. Most don't use Sisodia as their last name anymore; they use Kesur. Late in his life, even my father started calling himself Narayan Singh Kesur. The license plate of my car in the US has been KESUR for over 20 years. I don't know what caused me to do that, other than thinking it would be easy to remember. But every time I looked at it, I cringed a bit. The word Kesur had come to stand for cruelty, misogyny, and selfishness in my mind.

Only after writing most of this book did it occur to me that Kesur itself may have a soul or a spirit that is yearning to be healed. If healing can happen there, it can happen everywhere.

Looking for guidance, I turned to Mesina, a healer I have come to trust. I asked her to tell me what came to her when I said the word "Kesur."

After closing her eyes for several seconds, Mesina replied, "When you mentioned Kesur, I felt a hugely masculine vibration. But the energy is very pure, not negative or malicious in any way. It is a forgiving and giving energy, a powerful vibration that seeks to preserve and protect the family and the community. This energy doesn't want to create chaos; it wants to absorb and remove chaos. It is not a warlike energy; it is the energy of a peaceful warrior, a protector, a preserver. A desire for peace reigns over this vibration."

This was a pleasant surprise to me. Could it be true that I came from a place of light rather than darkness? Could it be that Hari Singh was closer to the founding energy of Kesur than my grandfather Girwar was? How could I help reconnect Kesur to that light?

Kesur is a microcosm of the wounded toxic patriarchy in India and across the world. I realized that healing my personal story was incomplete if I didn't also help heal Kesur's story.

What would a healed Kesur look like? What could it stand for? What could it become a symbol of?

My Duty and Destiny

By June 2022, I had been on a personal healing path for over four years. That had strengthened me to the point that I was able to take on the challenge of trying to heal my extended family and the soul of Kesur.

Independently, two friends spoke to me about the role they saw for me. "Not everyone has your child essence; it's not everyone's archetype, but it is yours," said my friend Nilima. "It takes an innocent to bring the truth to light. . . Your psyche has taken on all the challengers and has survived. You're now the immune innocent, the resilient innocent. No one can make a fool out of you. You have become the wise fool: you have wisdom, but you still lead from your innocence. Only the truly innocent can be trusted with power, to not get corrupted by it."

In other words, someone needed to be Frodo from the *Lord of the Rings,* the innocent who takes the ring to the volcano to burn it, saying, "We've carried this curse long enough." I didn't choose that responsibility; it chose me.

Not long after that, Mesina said something similar. "Raj, this is your soul's journey: to break this cycle for your family, as hard as that is to do. You represent a new class of energy that has come into this family. That's why it's often difficult. They're edgy with you at times. What you have done and the way you have educated yourself are so different to them. You see the world in a more balanced way. You're here to set a new precedent and a new vibration for the younger generations. You and your energy have already healed many of these patterns of behavior. That's what makes you a cycle breaker. This will also further your children's healing because the healing filters to all the family members. It's a part of their history too."

★★★

Could Kesur become a place of pure, loving energy? It couldn't happen unless we first acknowledged and atoned for what had happened to my aunt and her baby.

My aunt and her baby were erased. I believed that restoring her identity and honoring her memory would help heal the women in the family. I also wanted to inspire the men of the next generation to look at women differently and question their male desire for dominance and control. I wanted them to see women as equal partners whose emotional and spiritual needs matter as much as their own.

Ten days before I was scheduled to go to India, I called my sister, Manju, and brother-in-law, Sangram, to tell them that I would be arriving in Indore on June 27, 2022. Manju said, "Oh, wonderful! That is a day before your birthday! How would you like to celebrate?"

"I would like to gather our entire extended family so that we can go through a healing experience together. Sangram, I am counting on you to help orchestrate this experience in your wise and loving way," I told them. "I will start by sharing why I asked them to come. I will then invite each person to reflect on how we can honor the memory of the souls that were extinguished and seek forgiveness on behalf of the whole family. I especially want the younger generation to play an active role. I want this to be a powerful and loving healing experience that will transform the Kesur family for generations to come."

A Healing Circle

As the extended Kesur family sat around me in the sunken living room of my late father's house, I looked around with anticipation and some trepidation. How would they react to hearing the details of the incident from 72 years ago? Would they be angry, shocked, or dismissive? Would we be able to navigate the turbulent emotional waters to get to a place of hope and healing by the end of the evening?

I gathered myself and started reading the Hindi text I had prepared:

Thank you all for coming and being part of this important gathering of our extended family. I believe that we will look back on this day as a very significant one in our family's history.

I think all of you will agree that our family has experienced an incredible amount of suffering over the last three generations. For example, I was stunned to learn that my father had six siblings who died in childhood. We can only imagine the suffering the family must have experienced at the loss of each of those precious lives.

Other tragic things that our family has experienced include Kunwar Saheb's mental illness and its impact on his wife and children; his son's suicide; a worker trying to kill Mohan Kakosa; Mohan's son's death; Baby's murder by her husband; Channu's cancer; and so much more.

I've asked us all to gather here today because of something that Papa used to talk about. He said, "I have heard that there is a curse on our family because two souls died unnaturally and never found peace." But he never revealed the truth of it, even though he was aware of it. Three years ago, Gajju Bhaya told me what he had heard about it. Since then, I have tried to find out additional details about that episode. The details are fuzzy, but I have pieced together the story as best as I could. As we all know, memory is tricky, especially after so much time has passed.

I described what I had learned about the events of that night. My cousin Ranjit then spoke:

I do believe there is a curse. It is a natural human response to bless others when they do good to you and curse them when they harm you. This was the ultimate harm, so the curse is equally powerful.

The fact is that there were many such cases in the old days. Daughters and daughters-in-law were killed and cremated right within the Rowla compound. Such actions have an impact on future generations, who pay the price in suffering. Kunwar Saheb paid a price for his actions: going mad and being locked up for the last 24 years of his life. As his children, we paid a price by growing up without a father.

My brother-in-law Sangram spoke next:

It is true that such incidents were quite common back then. But that doesn't mean they didn't have a huge impact on the family. We should not minimize or hide this. We must accept that this happened and ask: Now what?

If somebody dies in an unnatural and untimely manner after great suffering, it casts a long shadow on the family. If they are not properly grieved at the time, that too affects what happens to their souls and the lives of those left behind.

None of us gathered here today were alive when this happened. But we still have a collective duty to heal from it.

One thing we must do is a Narayan Bali, a special pooja *(a worshipful ritual) to honor and bring peace to our ancestors, including the mother and baby who were killed. That will happen tomorrow.*

The greatest healing must happen within each of us — starting with a deeply heartfelt acknowledgment that this was wrong. We must beg forgiveness on behalf of our forefathers. We must pray to a higher power to guide us and release us from the shadow of this act and give our family the strength and wisdom to move ahead.

I responded:

Many families in India try to neutralize painful histories simply by having a pooja. *But that is not enough. We cannot heal and experience peace without first acknowledging the truth of what happened 72 years ago. Let us meditate on what we need to learn from this, and how we can honor the memory of those two souls. Let us collectively seek forgiveness and find ways to atone for what happened.*

This is part of our DNA; the trauma that our ancestors experienced still impacts us today. It will remain in our bodies until we find a way to release it.

My hope is that our gathering today and the pooja *we will have tomorrow will prove to be a loving and life-altering experience for all of us. I believe that this process can transform the destiny of the Kesur Family. It will help us reconnect to our true Dharma* (our divine duty) *and the Dharma of all Rajputs, which is to be the protectors and defenders of people.*

I asked everyone to sit in silence for a few minutes to reflect on what had been said. I then invited other voices into the room, starting with the women. My sister, Manju, spoke up, then Gajendra's wife, Mohini. Both thanked me for taking on this difficult challenge.

Ranjit's wife then told us about a mysterious incident that happened after my nephew Chandraveer died of cancer a few years earlier. Four women – my mother, Ranjit's wife, Gajendra's wife, and my cousin Beena – all had the same experience in their own homes the night before the family gathered to mourn. Around 4:00 a.m., each of them heard a baby crying, hungry for milk. They each believed that they had heard the voice of the baby who had been killed in the middle of the night 72 years earlier.

After we absorbed that information, I asked the gathering, "Let's talk about the future, where we go from here. We have all been born to privilege and status. How should we commit to living in the future? What do we need to change?"

One by one, my family members replied. Their resounding answer? We must help others. We must abandon harm. Our duty is to leave all that we own better than it was given to us.

My cousin Gajendra said, "Our village and community should benefit from our resources, our success, and our achievements in the world. But we are so disconnected from people's lives in Kesur. What can we do for the people who live there, especially the young people? I would like Raj and my daughter Rohini to come and speak at the village school to inspire the kids. More than money, they want our time and our involvement. They want to know that we care about them. This is how we will win the hearts and minds of people in the village."

Tearing up, Gajendra continued, "I don't feel that there is much love between family members in Kesur. For example, we have been fighting for years over tiny amounts of land. How do we awaken love amongst each other so that we become a truly united family? If any one of us is suffering or needs help, we should all be there for each other."

I could see transformation beginning. I caught a glimpse of how Kesur could once again become symbolic of something positive and beautiful, rather than a suffocating and decaying place that elicits sadness and grief. It could become a place of atonement, humility, and healthy pride. The experience we had shared could open new horizons for our family members. It could cohere our fragmented family and enable us to become a single powerful unit. It could herald the rebirth of Kesur as a place of healing and renewal, the effects rippling out to the Rajput community and beyond.

The Path Ahead

My family's story may be extreme in some ways, but its contours are familiar and all too commonplace. Just like there is a "Me Too" movement, I hope my story gives others the courage to say "We Too" as they realize, "My family also has a troubled history. We have dark secrets too."

I concluded our family gathering with a simple thought: Just as I needed to blend my mother's love with my father's strength, the Kesur family needs to blend Hari Singh's heart with Girwar Singh's toughness.

Over the last several years, I have worked on healing myself, my relationship with my mentor, and my relationship with my children. I have started the process of healing the soul of Kesur, and continue to work on healing the world of business. In coming years, I hope to be able to come to a place of healing with my failed marriage.

What are you ready to face and heal? Remember, with every wound and trauma, we must reveal it, feel it, and grieve it in order to heal it. The singer Juliana Hatfield reminds us, "A heart that hurts is a heart that works." A heart that hurts is also a heart that loves. The only way to heal is through love. We all need to be healers now, starting with ourselves.

Acknowledgments

This book would not exist were it not for the sage advice given to me by four extraordinary women in 2018 while I was in the process of writing *The Healing Organization*: Nilima Bhat (my wise coauthor on *Shakti Leadership*), the luminous and inspirational Lynne Twist (author of *Living a Committed Life* and *The Soul of Money* and cofounder of The Pachamama Alliance), Suzanne Vaughan (my brilliant and insightful coach) and Louisa Bohm, who helped me connect to my true nature and understand myself at a deeper level. Each of them told me to slow down, spend time with myself, and work on my own healing – a process in which each of them played an important role. I will be forever grateful for the many gifts they have brought to my life and to the world.

I am deeply grateful to Betty Sue Flowers for her wisdom and her generosity in taking the time to listen to my life story and assuring me that it was a story worth telling. She was the first reader of the first draft of the book and gave me invaluable feedback on what the book needed to be.

Joseph Jaworksi is a towering figure in the world of leadership development and one of my heroes. His book *Synchronicity* stands alongside Viktor Frankl's *Man's Search for Meaning* among the books that have had the greatest influence on my life. I am blessed to be able to call Joseph a friend and a guide. Thank you, Joseph, for writing the Foreword to this book, and for introducing me to Betty Sue Flowers.

Jag Sheth has been so many things to me: a mentor, a teacher, and a father figure. I shudder to think how my life might have turned out if I had not had the great good fortune to connect with Jag when I was just 32 — half the age I am now. Thank you, Jag, for recognizing something in me that I was unable to see.

The late David Wolfe was another father figure in my life from whom I learned a great deal as we were writing *Firms of Endearment*. I miss his sage, loving presence in my life.

I would like to thank the organizers and participants of the "Call of the Times" silent retreat at Peace Village. During those four days in the company of 35 seekers and sages, I received countless downloads from my higher self, compiling 45 pages of handwritten notes. This is where the seven steps on "the path" came to me: Know Yourself, Love Yourself, Be Yourself, Express Yourself, Choose Your Life, Become Whole, and Heal Yourself. In particular, I want to thank Peter Senge, David Cooperrider, Lawrence Ford, Patricia Klauer, and Rama Mani for enriching that experience for me.

Early in the process of writing, I decided to invite a group of people who know me and my journey well to listen to me read chapters of this book as I was writing them. They gave me very useful feedback and reflected on the relevance of what I had written to their own life stories. This "Sunday Book Club" also forced me to produce a new chapter every week, so that by the end of 15 weeks, I had a first draft of the book. The book club included Amy Powell, Bethany Hilton, Carlos Bremer, Carolina Leñero, Catarina Soares, Christina Dyer, CV Sudhir, Rosie Ward, Elaine Dinos, Hitesh Shah, Hugo Bethlem, Jeff Cherry, Kiran Gulrajani, Meera Singh, Steve Lishansky, Susan Leger Ferraro, Shubhro Sen, Thomas Eckschmidt, Vijay Bhat, Vinay Gupta, and Vinit Taneja.

I particularly want to thank Indu Sangwan and Haley Rushing for their deeply insightful suggestions. Above all, I want to thank my partner, Neha Sangwan, for her countless contributions to the book. She detected patterns and connected dots that were invisible to me. Writing the book was often emotionally and psychologically painful;

she helped me navigate those challenges and find deeper meaning in them.

I would like to thank my dear cousin Gajendra, who has been a soul brother to me since we were babies in the village. He is the very embodiment of pure love. I would also like to thank my sister, Manju, and her husband, Sangram. They have long been my spiritual lighthouses and helped me organize the healing experience we created for my extended family.

I would like to acknowledge the editorial assistance of the exceptionally talented Andrea Martin.

Finally, I would like to thank the team at Wiley, including Angela Morrison, Donna J. Weinson, Jozette Moses, and Michelle Hacker. I especially want to thank Jeanenne Ray. I am glad I finally got a chance to work with Jeanenne after years of trying. I appreciate her patient stewarding of a project that took several twists and turns along the way.

About the Author

Described as an "Intellectual Shaman" in a book with that title, Raj Sisodia has been on a mission to bring purpose, caring and healing to business and capitalism since the 2007 publication of his groundbreaking book *Firms of Endearment: How World Class Companies Profit from Passion and Purpose,* which was named a top business book of 2007 by Amazon.com. Raj is a preeminent thought leader in the rapidly growing movement to redefine the purpose and role of business in society. He is cofounder and Chairman Emeritus of Conscious Capitalism Inc. and President of Awaken Inc.

Born in India, Raj spent parts of his childhood in Barbados, California, and Canada. He was educated as an electrical engineer from the Birla Institute of Technology and Science. He received an MBA in Marketing from the Jamnalal Bajaj Institute of Management Studies in Mumbai and a PhD in Business from Columbia University.

Raj has published over 100 academic articles and 15 books including *Conscious Capitalism: Liberating the Heroic Spirit of Business, Everybody Matters: The Extraordinary Power of Caring for Your People Like Family, Shakti Leadership: Embracing Feminine and Masculine Power in Business, Conscious Capitalism Field Guide: Tools for Transforming Your Organization,* and *The Healing Organization: Awakening the Conscience of Business to Help Save the World.* His work has been featured in the *Wall Street Journal,* the *New York Times, Fortune, Financial Times,* the

Washington Post, CNBC, and other media outlets. He cohosted a show on business for National Public Radio.

Raj is FEMSA Distinguished University Professor of Conscious Enterprise and Chairman of the Conscious Enterprise Center at Tecnologico de Monterrey in Mexico. He previously taught at Boston University, George Mason University, Bentley University, and Babson College. He has received numerous awards and recognitions, including an honorary doctorate from Johnson & Wales University and the Business Luminary Award from Halcyon in 2021.

Raj has consulted with companies around the world, including AT&T, Verizon, LG, DPDHL, POSCO, Kraft, Whole Foods Market, Tata, Siemens, Sprint, Volvo, IBM, Walmart, and McDonald's. He served on the board of directors at The Container Store and Mastek. He lives in Boston, close to his beloved children: Alok, Priya, and Maya.

Index

241